D0909511

AMERICAN EDUCATION

Its Men

Ideas

and

Institutions

Advisory Editor

Lawrence A. Cremin
Frederick A. P. Barnard Professor of Education
Teachers College, Columbia University

Early Quaker Education in Pennsylvania

Thomas Woody

76337
74909

ARNO PRESS & THE NEW YORK TIMES

New York ∗ *1969*

LA
355
W66
1969

Reprint edition 1969 by Arno Press, Inc.

*

Library of Congress Catalog Card No. 72-89255

*

Reprinted from a copy in
The New York State Library

*

Manufactured in the United States of America

Editorial Note

AMERICAN EDUCATION: *Its Men, Institutions and Ideas* presents selected works of thought and scholarship that have long been out of print or otherwise unavailable. Inevitably, such works will include particular ideas and doctrines that have been outmoded or superseded by more recent research. Nevertheless, all retain their place in the literature, having influenced educational thought and practice in their own time and having provided the basis for subsequent scholarship.

Lawrence A. Cremin
Teachers College

229474

Early Quaker Education
in Pennsylvania

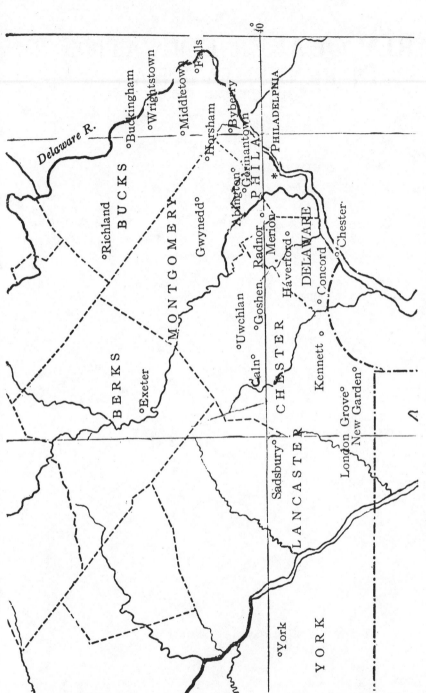

MAP OF SOUTHEASTERN PENNSYLVANIA SHOWING LOCATION OF PRINCIPAL MEETINGS

EARLY QUAKER EDUCATION IN PENNSYLVANIA

By
THOMAS WOODY, Ph.D.
ASSISTANT PROFESSOR OF EDUCATION
UNIVERSITY OF PENNSYLVANIA

TEACHERS COLLEGE, COLUMBIA UNIVERSITY
CONTRIBUTIONS TO EDUCATION, No. 105

Published by
Teachers College, Columbia University
NEW YORK CITY
1920

Copyright, 1920, by THOMAS WOODY

PREFACE

The purpose of this monograph is to present to the students of education, especially to those interested in the historical phase of it, some materials relating to education among the Quakers in Pennsylvania previous to 1800. Since the greater part of the source material on the subject is almost inaccessible, it has been thought desirable to incorporate in this work many reports on schools, such as may be convenient references for others who are interested in the early educational history of Pennsylvania.

The manuscript records which furnish the most direct light on this study are found in various depositories in southeastern Pennsylvania. Those that have been preserved and made accessible to the writer have been examined by him in person. With the exception of a few cases, the minutes of the preparative meetings have not been well kept; hence, that source of information is very limited.

If this work possesses merit, it is by reason of the coöperation of many men and women. I am obligated to the members of the Society of Friends who, as custodians of records, have been instrumental in forwarding the investigation. It is also a great pleasure to acknowledge the friendly encouragement and assistance given by Albert Cook Myers, of The Historical Society of Pennsylvania. I wish also to thank Professor Paul Monroe for the initial encouragement and continued interest, during the progress of the investigation.

T. W.

Teachers College, New York
July 11, 1917

CONTENTS

I   Origin of the Quakers 1–13

II   Meeting Organization: Its Connection with Education 14–25

III   Educational Ideals of the Quakers . 26–40

IV   Education in Philadelphia . . . 41–84

V   Schools of Bucks County . . . 85–104

VI   Schools of Montgomery County . 105–121

VII   Schools of Chester County . . . 122–146

VIII   Schools of Delaware County . . 147–166

IX   School Support, Organization, and Curriculum 167–203

X   Masters and Mistresses . . . 204–227

XI   Education of Negroes and Indians . . 228–267

XII   Conclusion 268–271

   Bibliography 272–282

   Abbreviations 283

   Index 285–287

EARLY QUAKER EDUCATION IN PENNSYLVANIA

CHAPTER I

ORIGIN OF THE QUAKERS

Reforms, discoveries and inventions are, at the outset, conceived by individual minds; seldom, if ever, are they the simultaneous product of several. The original connection is seen and made by an individual, and afterwards may be accepted by his fellows, who may appropriate the new idea to themselves and make its applications manifold. The novel idea or relationship, once seen, thoroughly comprehended and expressed becomes either the common property of many, extending far afield from its original source, or is rejected because it fails to prove attractive to human interests or necessary for the satisfaction of human needs. By this means changes are wrought in a group or society of individuals, and the belief or the contribution of one individual becomes the faith or the possession of a nation. The meaning of the above statement is at once made clear by mere mention of a few names, such as Luther, Bacon, Pestalozzi, Confucius, Whitefield, Gœthe and Fox. It is with the ideas and the formally stated doctrines of the last mentioned that we are in this connection chiefly concerned. *An essential in leaders*

In a study of education among the Quakers it is desirable, if not absolutely imperative, to go back to the origin of the society and note, at least in part, the tenets of the society and the reasons for its foundation. For this purpose the best materials are to be found in the life and works of George Fox, the founder of the Society of Quakers. It would, perhaps, be unnecessary at present to make any considerable study of beliefs or tenets, if it were not for the fact that, in times past, some of the expressions of their belief have been misconstrued. For instance, reference may be made here to the so-called doctrine of *inner light* which was promulgated *Brief study of Quaker beliefs necessary*

by George Fox at the very beginning of his work in 1647.[1]
It will be of advantage to first sketch briefly the early life of
this exponent of Quakerism.

George Fox was born July, 1624 (old style), at Drayton-in-
the-clay,[2] in Leicestershire, England. His father, Christopher Fox, otherwise known as "Righteous Christer," was a
weaver by trade and "an honest man." His mother, he says,
was of the stock of martyrs.[3]

Fox's youth
and early
education

His earliest life was spent in the home of his parents, under
whose tutelage he received a careful religious training. He
says of himself that he was unusually grave for a youth of his
age and that his thought constantly turned to subjects of
religious nature. This characteristic religious disposition,
noticed by his mother, was the cause of a more indulgent
attitude toward him than was granted the other children in
the family, especially in regard to their religious instruction.
Of his school education we have but a meagre account;
according to Sewell, his only education was received in the
home and consisted of the bare necessaries such as reading
and writing.[4] The essence of his religious education seems
to be adequately summarized in his own words as follows:

> The Lord taught me to be faithful in all things, and to act faithfully
> two ways, *viz.*, inwardly to God, and outwardly to man; and to keep
> to yea and nay in all things.[5]

As he advanced in years some of his people, being aware
of his religious tendencies, would gladly have had him enter
the priesthood, but others dissenting, he was placed with a
man who was a shoemaker, grazier and dealer in wool.[6] In
this employment he seems to have given much satisfaction to
his employer, and, as for himself, he too enjoyed the work of
shepherd, affording, as it did, ample opportunity for close
communion with nature and limiting his connections with
the corrupt society of mankind, from which he sought to free
himself.[7]

---

[1]Fox, *Journal*, I, 53.
[2]Now called Fenny Drayton (see *Friends Library*, I, 28).
[3]Fox, *Journal*, I, 49.
[4]Sewell, *Hist.*, I, 11.
[5]Fox, *Journal*, I, 49.
[6]*Ibid.*, 50.   [7]Sewell, *Hist.*, I, 12.

About the age of nineteen, his dissatisfaction with the world and the people about him caused him to leave his relations and acquaintances and to seek out a more lonely existence in some place where he was quite unknown. This decision being made, he journeyed "at the command of God," first to Lutterworth, Northampton, Newlort-Pagnell, and came finally, in 1644, to Barnet. During these days he was often in great despair and questioned whether he had done rightly in leaving his parents and friends. In these periods of misgiving he consulted often with priests concerning his condition and sought thereby a remedy, which, however, he did not find. Driven by sheer desperation he continued to travel, and, after leaving Barnet, came to London where he remained for a short time only, having come now to a decision that he should return again to the home of his parents.[8]

Beginning of his travels

The return to his native village, however, was no cure for his mental ill, though his conscience was thereby somewhat stilled. He continued his visits to various priests, especially one Nathaniel Stevens, with whom he was wont to argue religious questions, and who, after Fox had enunciated certain beliefs, which will be mentioned later, became one of his most cruel persecutors.[9] Each succeeding experience with the priests was but a repetition of a former and it became clear to him that they saw nothing but the externals of his condition and had not the power to penetrate to the innermost complexities of his situation. According to his view their recommendations met only the demands of the ecclesiastics; his need was genuine and he was enabled to see the narrow limitations which hamper the activity of one man who attempts to parcel out salvation to another.

His return home

George Fox was now in his twenty-second year. It is pertinent that mention be made at this place of three fundamental beliefs or principles, whose truth, up to this time, had made itself manifest in his mind. The second of these is the one which, being so often misquoted, has become the basis for the belief on the part of many, that the Society was opposed to education.

---

[8]Fox, *Journal*, I, 51.
[9]*Ibid.*, 52.

1.   And the Lord opened to me that, if all were believers, then they were all born of God, and passed from death unto life, and that none were true believers but such; and though others said they were believers, yet they were not.

Three of
Fox's con-
clusions;
fundamental

2.   The Lord opened unto me, that being bred at Oxford or Cambridge was not enough to fit and qualify men to be ministers of Christ; and I wondered at it, because it was the common belief of the people.

3.   At another time it was opened to me, that God, who made the world, did not dwell in temples made with hands. . . . But the Lord showed me clearly that he did not dwell in these temples which men had commanded and set up, but in people's hearts; for both Stephen and the apostle Paul bore testimony that he did not dwell in temples made with hands, not even in that which he had once commanded to be built, since he put an end to it; but that his people were his temple, and he dwelt in them.[10]

These doctrines which he began to promulgate in 1647 were recognized as fundamental, and their influence is plainly to be seen in the organization and discipline of the society which finally resulted.[11]

It may well be mentioned here that though these tenets

But not
untried

were incorporated in the foundation principles of the Quakers, they were by no means new, in the sense that they had never been accepted, in part, at least, by any other group of people. J. Brown, writing concerning the Quakers, states that Caspar Schwenkfeld, a Silesian of high birth, had promulgated the same doctrines of *inner light, direct revelation* and the inadequacy of the sacraments at least two centuries before the time of Fox in England.[12] The dispersion of Schwenkfeld's adherents in 1547 led to the spread of their doctrines outside of Silesia, being embraced by a part of the Mennonite Church of Amsterdam, whence their entrance was made into England, and found acceptance in the minds of the Quakers.[13] This view is held also by other students of Quaker history,[14] and the similarity of doctrine is clearly seen in the statement of the Mennonite creed, as given by B. L. Wicks, a student of Mennonite history.[15] Further, it is

---

[10]*Ibid.*, 53.
[11]Myers, A. C., *Immigration of Irish Quakers into Pa.*, 5.
[12]Brown, in Traill, H. D., *Social England*, IV, 258.
[13]*Ibid.*
[14]Barclay, R., *Inner life of Religious Societies of the Commonwealth*, 77.
[15]Wicks, B. L., *The Amish Mennonites*, 13–18.

known that some of the earliest preachers among Quakers went to Amsterdam and vicinity and found there a kindly reception by a part of the people, making converts among both the Baptists[16] and the Mennonites.[17] An instance of their kindly attitude toward Quakers and also of the recognition given their belief on the part of the Quakers, is shown in the account by Thomas Chalkley, concerning his journey of some nine hundred miles in Holland, Friesland and Germany.[18]

Kindly reception given to Quaker ministers

> As I have had great peace and satisfaction in my travels in Holland and Germany, so, for inciting others under the like exercise, I may truly say that there is encouragement for faithful ministers to labor in the work of the gospel. I know not that I ever met with more tenderness and openness in people than in those parts of the world. There is a great people whom they call Mennonites, who are very near to truth, and the fields are white unto the harvest among divers of them, spiritually speaking.[19]

At Kriegsheim in the Palatinate Quaker exhorters like Ames and Rolfe, who had been sent out by the direction of George Fox, 1657, succeeded in winning converts among the Mennonites, though they were received unfavorably by the magistrates who fined those who offered to give them any entertainment.[20] It is from this same district that both Quakers and Mennonites made their voluntary departure and came to settle in Pennsylvania. Their prompt attention to school affairs on their first arrival is very similar to that of the Quakers, though in their case it was often the work of the laity, and not through the church organization.[21]

A still more extensive missionary journey was undertaken at a later date, 1677, by several Quakers, among them Fox, Penn, Furly, Barclay and Keith. They visited Brill, Leyden and Haarlem where they held meetings, preaching to both Quakers and Mennonites.[22] The tour continued up into the

Journey of Fox, Penn, Furly, Barclay and Keith

16Sewell, *Hist.*, I, 284.
17*Pa. Ger. Soc.*, IX, 166.
18Chalkley, *Journal, Friends Library*, VI, 27.
19*Ibid.*
20Besse, *Sufferings of the Quakers*, II, 450f.
21*Pa. Ger. Soc.*, IX, 401.
22*Pa. Mag. of Hist.*, II, 250; Seidensticker, *Erste deutsche Einwanderung in Amerika*, 29–33.

Rhine region where Penn and his party came into touch with members of the Pietist group. It is doubtless true that this journey and the impression which was made by Penn must have played an important part a few years later when he opened his colony to settlers on the well known liberal principles.

In the presentation of the foregoing material it has been pointed out: (1) how the doctrines of the Quakers were rapidly spread broadcast by the itinerant preachers; and (2) that there was a great similarity between Quaker and Mennonite in doctrine and belief.

Increased
number of
ministers

The work of spreading the new gospel, as instanced by the work of Ames and Rolfe in 1657, was carried rapidly forward; as early as 1654, seven years after George Fox had begun to preach, he had enlisted the services of some sixty preachers who travelled continually up and down the country.[23] Such a number of leaders bespeaks a considerable following, though we have no record of a census of the followers made during Fox's lifetime. Brown is apparently willing to accept Barclay's statement that by 1675 they numbered ten thousand in London and by the end of the century, sixty thousand.[24] It does not seem that this is too large an estimate. It can be estimated from the work of Besse on *Sufferings* that between 1650 and 1689 there were approximately fifteen thousand individual cases of "sufferings."[25] Since his work is compiled from "authentic records" it may be considered to be fairly accurate, though the errors, if any, would likely be to make the number too small rather than too large. As a matter of fact his collection includes some cases between 1689 and 1700, but the vast majority of them are from the period above stated. Certainly we must suppose that if such a large number actually came under the hand of English tolerance, then the total number of adherents very probably equalled or exceeded the estimate previously mentioned. Whatever objection may be made to the accuracy of these figures they may certainly be taken as fairly indicative of the growth of the sect; for that purpose they are intended.

The number
of adherents
estimated

---

[23]Brown, J. in Traill, *Soc. England*, IV, 259.
[24]*Ibid.*   [25]Besse, J., *Sufferings*, II, 539–638.

Just as the church discipline and organization are traceable to the hand of Fox, so also is the attitude on educational affairs. It has been said that the doctrine of the *inner light* made all education unnecessary, and this perverted idea has doubtless possessed even some members of Quakers to the extent that they came to regard learning as an instrument of Satan, a thing to be carefully avoided. However true this statement may have been of some members of the group, it certainly is not representative of the belief and practice of the Quakers as a whole. Some of the more ignorant may have interpreted the *inner light* to mean just that thing; but it is certainly true that such an idea was never expressed by George Fox, nor did it become the accepted belief of the organization, as is shown by their practices. The actual practice, educational, among Quakers is to be followed in this monograph. A later chapter will be devoted to a consideration of the views on education held by various individuals who have left some tangible monuments to their beliefs. In the present chapter, however, it is intended to indicate merely the position assumed by Fox in regard to the question at the outset of his labors.

Fox's doctrine the basis in their educational practice

As has been previously mentioned (page 2) George Fox had the advantage of only a limited education. Opposition to the higher education, if he exhibited such, might find an explanation in this fact, assuming that not having shared its delights and advantages, he chose to deprecate it altogether. From a study of his utterances and his actions throughout his career it seems, however, that the facts point rather to a true appreciation rather than deprecation of education. The evidence appears to support, in a very satisfactory manner, the following points:

1. That he placed a great emphasis on moral and religious training.
2. Education should be of practical value; apprenticeship education recommended.
3. That the establishment of schools was believed to be necessary.
4. The objection to classical training was its inadequacy to prepare for a minister of the gospel.

Fox's educational creed

5.   That the scope of education was not limited to Quakers alone, nor even to the Whites, but should include also Negroes, Indians and the poorer classes of society as well as the rich. The remainder of this chapter will be devoted to a brief consideration of the foregoing statements.

First, in regard to moral and religious instruction, it seemes hardly necessary to do more than state simply that he did urge moral education at all times.   His whole life being permeated with the desire to propagate his newly founded society, it certainly is to be expected that he would recommend and insist on instruction of that nature.   If proof be desired, however, it may be found in statements made from time to time, which are quoted below.   The system of moral education based on the utterances of Fox was chiefly a prohibitory one, and it might well be questioned whether the result would not be passive rather than active virtues.

.   .   .   .   in warning such as kept public houses for entertainment, that they should not let people have more drink than would do them good; and in testifying against their wakes and feasts, May games, sports, plays and shows, which trained up people to vanity and looseness and led them from the fear of God;   .   .   .   in fairs also, and in markets I was made to declare against their deceitful merchandise, cheating and cozening; warning all to deal justly, to speak the truth, to let their yea be yea and their nay be nay;   .   .   .   I was moved also to cry against all sorts of music, and against the mountebanks playing tricks on their stages, for they burdened the pure life and stained the people's mind to vanity.   I was much exercised, too, with schoolmasters and schoolmistresses, warning them to teach their children sobriety in the fear of the Lord, that they might not be nursed and trained up in lightness, vanity and wantonness.   Likewise I was made to warn masters and mistresses, fathers and mothers in private families, to take care that their children and servants might be trained up in the fear of the Lord; and that they themselves should be therein examples and patterns of sobriety and virtue to them.[26]

I was to bring them off from all the world's fellowship and prayings and singings, which stood in forms without power: .   .   .[27]

Prohibitions, moral, social and educational

These prohibitions and many others that were enunciated from time to time in his speaking and writing, were to be in time a part of the discipline of the organization, and were as

---

[26]Fox, G., *Journal*, I, 73; also 264–265.
[27]*Ibid.*, 71.

religiously imposed on all members as the ardor of the meeting and the difficulty of the task would permit. The cases coming up before the monthly meetings for discipline are largely composed of infringements of the regulations, which grew out of Fox's recommendations. These are, without question, of very ascetic nature. One instance which illustrates the incorporation of these ideals in the discipline of the organization may be cited in this connection.

Kept promi-
nent place
in the church

All Friends, train up your children in the fear of God; and as they are capable, they may be instructed and kept employed in some lawful calling; that they may be diligent, serving the Lord in the things that are good; that none may live idle and be destroyers of the creation, and thereby become burdensome to others, and to the just witness in themselves.[28]

Second, the emphasis placed on the values to be derived from a practical education, to be gotten, to a large degree, through a careful system of apprenticing the children of members to people, members if possible, who would also be careful in regard to their moral instruction, is unmistakable. The practice as recommended, indicated below, became the general rule in Quaker communities, as is adequately evidenced in the meeting records. In this connection, however, it should be kept in mind that apprenticeship education could be *legally* enforced.

Being in London, it came upon me to write to Friends throughout the nation, about putting out poor children to trades. Wherefore I sent the following epistle to the quarterly meetings of friends in all counties:

MY DEAR FRIENDS,

Let every quarterly meeting make inquiry through all the monthly and other meetings, to know all Friends that are widows, or others that have children fit to put out to apprenticeship; so that once a quarter you may set forth an apprentice from your quarterly meeting; and so you may set forth four in a year in each county, or more, if there be occasion. This apprentice, when out of his time, may help his father or mother, and support the family that is decayed; and in so doing all may come to live comfortably. This being done in your quarterly meetings you will have knowledge through the county in the monthly and particular meetings, of masters fit for them, and of such trades as their parents or the children are most inclinable to. Thus, being placed

Apprentice-
ship educa-
tion recom-
mended

---

[28]*Friends Lib.*, I, 129.

out with Friends, they may be trained up in truth; and by this means in the wisdom of God, you may preserve Friends' children in the truth, and enable them to be strength and help to their families, and nurses, and preservers of their relations in their ancient days. . . . For in the country you know, you may set forth an apprentice for a little to several trades, as bricklayers, masons, carpenters, wheelwrights, ploughwrights, tailors, tanners, curriers, blacksmiths, shoemakers, nailers, butchers, weavers of linen and woolen stuffs and serges, etc., and you may do well to have a stock in your quarterly meetings for that purpose. All that is given by any Friends at their decease (except it be given to some particular use, person or meeting) may be brought to the public stock for that purpose. This will be the way for the preserving of many that are poor among you, and it will be the way of making up poor families. In several counties it is practised already. Some quarterlies set forth two apprentices; and sometimes the children of others that are laid on the parish. You may bind them for fewer or more years, according to their capacities. . . . [29]

G. F.

London, 1st of 11th month, 1669.

The following lines, taken from the meeting records, are sufficient proof of the working out of this recommendation concerning apprenticeship education.

And executed in various meetings

It is agreed and concluded upon by this meeting, that the meeting take care of all Friends children that are left as orphans and unsettled, to inspect and see that all such be taken care of and settled in the best and suitablest manner, according to their capacity, that thereby they may discharge their duty and all such be eased by taking such due care.[30]

Third, the establishment of schools was believed to be necessary; for a proof of this attitude may be cited his action in regard to the establishment of schools at Waltham and Shacklewell.

Establishment of school advised

Then returning towards London by Waltham, I advised the setting up of a school there for teaching boys; and also a girls' school at Shacklewell, for instructing them in whatsoever things were civil and useful.[31]

This statement would certainly indicate a liberal attitude towards education. Fox himself makes no further comment on what the nature of the school was to be. His interest in these schools, it is asserted, never flagged, and many visits were made in behalf of their prosperity.[32]

---

[29]Fox, G., *Journal*, II, 76f.
[30]Min. Middletown Mo. Mtg., 9—2—1699.
[31]Fox, *Journal*, II, 57.   [32]*Friends Lib.*, I, 72.

Fourth, the popular idea that has at times prevailed, that Quakers objected to giving an education such as was enjoyed by other sects, was probably founded on a misunderstanding of certain statements made by Fox with regard to education. Let us examine some of these statements, and seek to learn his intended meaning.

But classical education not the first essential for ministers

I saw that to be a true believer was another thing than they looked on it to be; and I saw that being bred at Oxford or Cambridge did not qualify or fit a man to be a minister of Christ; what then should I follow such for? So neither these, nor any of the dissenting peoples could I join with, but was a stranger to all, relying wholly upon the Lord Jesus Christ.[33]

I was to bring people off from Jewish ceremonies and from heathenish fables, and from men's inventions and worldly doctrines, by which they blew the people about this way and the other way, from sect to sect; and from all their beggarly rudiments, with their schools and colleges for making ministers of Christ, who are indeed ministers of their own making but not of Christ; . . .[34]

They could not know the spiritual meaning of Moses; the prophets and John's words, nor see their paths and travels, much less see through them, and to the end of them into the kingdom, unless they had the spirit of Jesus; nor could they know the words of Christ and of his apostles without his Spirit.[35]

Then we came to Durham, where was a man come from London to set up a college there, to make ministers of Christ, as they said. I went, with some others, to reason with him and to let him see that to teach men Hebrew, Greek and Latin, and the seven arts, which were all but the teachings of the natural man, was not the way to make them ministers of Christ.[36]

These statements represent a small selection from many similar ones, and may be fairly taken as indicative of his position concerning this one point. They are the most drastic prohibitory statements made on the subject in all of his works. But even here we fail to find either (1) a condemnation of general or ordinary education or (2) a wholesale condemnation of classical education; indeed we read no objection to a minister's possessing a knowledge of classical authors, such as was the case of both Penn and Barclay, pro-

[33]Fox, *Journal,* I, 53.
[34]*Ibid.,* 72.
[35]*Ibid.,* 69.
[36]*Ibid.,* 327.

vided he possess also the "light."   His statements may be
summarized as follows:

1.   Classical training is inadequate as a preparation for
ministers of the gospel.

2.   Divine guidance is the one requisite for their preparation.

3.   There is no objection to the classical learning if it be
added to the qualification under (2).

Fifth, their conception of the scope of education did not
limit it to their own people alone, but extended it rather to
all peoples, Negroes and Indians, the rich and the poor.   This
is made perfectly plain in his address sent to the Governor
of the Barbados in 1671.

> Consider, Friends, it is no transgression for a master of a family to
> instruct his family himself, or for some others to do it in his behalf; but
> rather it is a very great duty incumbent upon them. . . . We
> declare that we esteem it a duty incumbent on us to pray with and for
> those in and belonging to our families; . . . . and to teach, instruct
> and admonish them; . . . now Negroes, Tawnies and Indians make
> up a very great part of the families in this island; for whom an account
> will be required by him who comes to judge both quick and dead, at the
> great day of judgment, when every one shall be rewarded according to
> the deeds done in the body, whether they be good or whether they
> be evil.[37]

The effect of the above statements must tend to convince
even the skeptical that any statement or belief, to the effect
that the founder of Quakerism was opposed to education, is
chiefly a myth based on either ignorance or gross misunderstanding.

SUMMARY

The origin of the Quakers and the organization and discipline of the Society are due almost entirely to the influence
which first came from the founder, George Fox.   He extended
his belief in his native country and even into foreign countries
by (1) preaching, (2) letters, (3) extensive travels on his own
part, and (4) through the agency of many capable men whom
he attracted to his service.   For this service the leading of the

[37]*Ibid.*, II, 105.

inner light was deemed the only preparation which was absolutely necessary. The society experienced a rapid growth in numbers and, due to the policy of its founder, laid great stress on the moral and practical education of their youth. A great similarity existed between the beliefs of Quakers and those of the Mennonites, both of which came to form a large part of the population of the colony of Pennsylvania. The Mennonite beliefs are thought, by some special students of their history, to have been the determining influence in forming those of Friends; but this is not clearly proven. It is pointed out, by certain references to utterances of George Fox, which to a great extent formed the basis for Quaker practices, that the common belief in their objection to education is erroneous. The system of moral education was exacting and full of sweeping prohibitions, and, in those respects, according to modern ideals, quite inadequate.

CHAPTER II

MEETING ORGANIZATION: ITS CONNECTION
WITH EDUCATION

An
organization
developed

The organization of meetings in the Society of Friends was based almost entirely on the recommendation of its founder, and still obtains without many variations from the type which was thus early begun. The organization thus planned was not developed completely at one time, but depended rather on the growth of the society in this or that section of the country. Meetings, as at first established, were not so specialized in their functions as they came to be later; there were those for worship and sufferings, the latter becoming in due time a specialized part of the yearly meeting, and for taking action in regard to poor members. The time was further occupied in disciplining those members who were not faithful to the doctrines of the church.

The place of
organization
in the estab-
lishment
of schools

It is of particular importance for us to understand the ordinary arrangement of the meetings and their relation to each other, since it was by virtue of this organization of the church that its schools were set up. Perhaps no other factor played so important a part in the success which was met with in setting up schools, as that through the organization of the meetings all localities were kept in closer touch with each other than would otherwise have been possible at that time. As it was, the local meetings were literally forced to listen to the school-proposition, even though they were in the backwoods of America, or inhabited the Barbados. The chief means of communication established were church letters, travelling ministers, representatives from the constituent meetings, and reports of general meetings which were distributed to all those belonging thereunto.[1]

---

[1]Letters, London Yearly Meeting, 4—10, 14—1717.

Originally the purpose of the church organization seems to have been twofold. It was realized that among those who became members some would be less constant in their behavior than others; hence some sort of oversight was necessary to keep each and every one in line. In the second place, there were many adherents in limited circumstances and the Quakers' belief made it imperative that these people be taken care of in the best manner possible.[2] Realizing the existence of these conditions among members, it was clear to Fox that a definitely organized meeting was necessary whereby (1) the necessary assistance could be extended to those in need, (2) discipline could be enforced for the maintenance of the religious life of the organization, and (3) new meetings could be officially established when and where they became necessary.

Purposes of the organization

The earliest mention that is made of a meeting established for these purposes is in the case of Balby, in Yorkshire, in 1658.[3] This statement is not exactly accurate, it seems, for we have also mention made of a general meeting, or what came to be known as a yearly meeting, as early as 1654 when one was held at Swannington in Leicestershire.[4] The meeting at Balby seems to have been of considerable importance and is frequently mentioned as one of the stopping places of George Fox. He recounts a meeting held at that place in 1660 "in a great orchard of John Killam's where it was supposed some thousands of people and Friends were gathered together."[5] The business of the yearly meeting seems to have been to devote some time to the affairs of the church; at any rate, this idea is expressed by Fox in writing of a similar meeting held at Skipton in 1660.[6] The characteristic of these meetings, that is always mentioned, is that they were attended by representatives from various towns and counties. The yearly meeting is still a representative body.

Early meetings established

The smaller meetings for worship were, of course, the first established. Aside from the question of worship, however,

---

[2] *Friends Lib.*, I, 68.
[3] *Ibid.*
[4] Fox, *Journal*, I, 179.
[5] *Ibid.*, 362.
[6] *Ibid.*, 363.

the development of the organization was from the larger unit
to the smaller. We have noted above the beginning of the
general or yearly meeting. As the sect grew in numbers, and
the labor of caring for these, sometimes in a physical sense
and again in the religious, increased, it became necessary to
have a finer organization, the smaller units of which would
reach the smallest communities. By 1665 there were
established (1) the *yearly* and (2) the *quarterly* meetings, and
in 1666 Fox recommended the establishment of a smaller
unit, the *monthly* meeting, saying:

> Then I was moved of the Lord to recommend the setting up of five
> monthly meetings of men and women in the City of London (besides the
> women's meetings and the quarterly meetings) to take care of God's
> glory, and to admonish and exhort such as walked disorderly or care-
> lessly, and not according to the truth. For whereas Friends had had
> only quarterly meetings, now truth was spread, and Friends were grown
> more numerous, I was moved to recommend the setting up of monthly
> meetings throughout the nation. And the Lord opened to me what I
> must do, and how the men's and the women's monthly and quarterly
> meetings should be ordered and established in this and other nations;
> and that I should write to those where I did not come, to do the same.[7]

Immediately after this, there is mentioned the establishment of monthly meetings in Essex, Suffolk and Norfolk,
Huntingdonshire, Nottinghamshire, Leicestershire and War-
wickshire and many others.[8] Three years later (1669) he
reports fourteen monthly meetings in the county of York.[9]
The rapid increase in the number of meetings and the extent
of territory covered by them is a fair indication of the phe-
nomenal growth of the society.

Following his resolve and subsequent exertions toward
setting up of monthly meetings, during which he made very
extensive campaigns, there came the great step which was
taken to organize all under the general leadership of a yearly
meeting, that of London. This was accomplished in 1672.[10]
This general meeting of ministers drew up a resolution or
minute to this effect:

Marginal notes:

Meetings develop from larger to the smaller

Number of monthly meetings set up

---

[7]Fox, *Journal*, II, 52f.
[8]*Ibid.*
[9]*Ibid.*, 67.
[10]*Friends Lib.*, I, 69.

It is concluded agreed and assented to by Friends present that for the better ordering, managing and regulating of the public affairs of Friends relating to the Truth and the service thereof, there be a general meeting of Friends held at London once a year, in the week called Whitsun-week, to consist of six Friends for the City of London, three for the city of Bristol, two for the city of Colchester and one or two from each of the counties of England and Wales respectively.[11]

London Yearly Meeting established

The meeting convened in the year following, in accordance with the above resolution.   Many of the duties performed by the General Meeting of Ministers were transferred to the representatives of the various meetings.   The ministers, though in fact subject to the approval or disapproval of monthly meetings, did not relinquish their oversight of each other.

The smallest unit in the organization was the *particular* or *preparative* meeting.   This meeting is not mentioned in all localities, though it is clear from Fox's statements that he recognized this as a part of the organization, for in a letter of 1669 he writes concerning the representatives of the quarterly meetings that,

The preparative meeting the smallest unit

none that are raw or weak and are not able to give a testimony of the affairs of the church and Truth, may go on behalf of the particular meetings to the quarterly meetings, but may be nursed up in your monthly meetings.[13]

This statement is given here merely for the purpose of pointing out how completely the ideas of Fox were embodied in even the smallest unit of church organization.   There is adequate proof of their existence in all sections occupied by the Quakers in Pennsylvania, and of their great importance in carrying out the details both of relief work for the poor, and in the establishment of schools.[14]

Details of organization worked out by Fox

There have been noted different phases of the development of the meeting organization.   When finally it was complete in all its parts, there existed a hierarchy of meetings, the lower and smaller units of which were subject to and under the

---

[11]Friends Lib., 117.
[12]*Ibid.*
[13]*Ibid.*, 125.
[14]Min. Horsham Mo. Mtg., 3—1—1797.
Min. Horsham Preparative Mtg., 12—20—1757.

direction of the higher. This resultant organization may be made somewhat clearer by means of a diagrammatical representation.

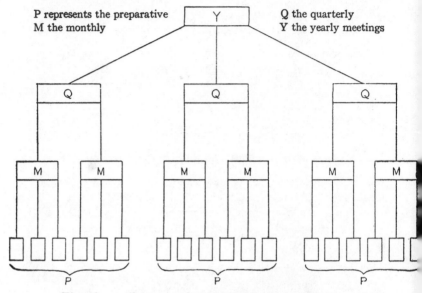

P represents the preparative
M the monthly

Q the quarterly
Y the yearly meetings

The above diagram represents the relation of the various kinds of meetings in the organization of the Society of Friends. The yearly meeting (Fig. 1, Y) is the general head of the entire organization. Its functions are of a general directive nature and its influence of very wide extent. For example, it will be shown a little later that the Yearly Meeting of London issued, very early, certain communications concerning education which were sent to each meeting belonging to the London Yearly Meeting. In the same manner it exercised its influence along other lines than education. There is no special virtue in the number of meetings represented above; for example, the three Q's do not mean that each and every yearly meeting had three quarterly meetings under its care. The number is not specified. In the case of the Philadelphia Yearly Meeting there are at present nine quarterly meetings and two half-yearly meetings.[16] The same variation is also true in the number of monthly meetings in a quarter, Caln Quarterly having only one monthly meet-

Functions of yearly meeting

---

[16]Friends Yearbook, 1917, 16f.

ing, while Western Quarterly has six.[16]   The same is true as
to the number of preparative meetings.

The quarterly meeting is representative of the monthly
meetings which comprise it.   Its functions are chiefly directive and advisory, though it may often occur that a bad case
of discipline may be turned over to it by the monthly meeting.
In the case of school regulations, its chief concern was to pass
on the recommendations of the yearly meeting to the monthly
meetings and to repeat them frequently, that the lower
meetings might be stirred up to action.[17]   It was also through
the quarterly meetings that the reports on the conditions of
schools in the monthly meetings were collected and sent to
the yearly meeting.   It was also quite customary for the
monthly units to pass any of their decisions on a matter up to
the quarterly unit for its formal approval or disapproval.
Especially is this marked in educational affairs, and particularly in the Philadelphia Quarter.[18]   This is most marked in
the earliest years after establishment, and is due, no doubt,
to a lack at that time of a very close differentiation in the
functions of the meetings.

Functions of the quarterly meeting

The monthly meetings are primarily the business units of
the organization.   Before them come all cases of care for the
poor, apprenticing of children, enforcement of discipline,
establishment of schools, requests for permission to marry, to
remove to a new location and still many others.   They may
settle some of these finally, or they may act in connection
with their superior meeting as mentioned above.

Monthly meeting the business unit

The preparative meeting is the smallest organization unit
and has its finger on the pulse of the local community at all
times.[19]   Officially it acts as the agent of the monthly
meeting in carrying out the details of any piece of work that
must be done, and which the monthly meeting is willing to
delegate thus far.[20]   Thus in the case of Horsham, for
instance, the business of the schools in the scope of the preparative meeting is turned over to it and their organization

Function of the prepara- tive meeting

---

[16]Friends Yearbook, 1917, 16f.
[17]Min. Phila. Q. Mtg., 9—4—1728.
[18]*Ibid.*, 6—30—1689.
[19]Many of the local preparative meetings are now closed.
[20]Min. Horsham Prep. Mtg., 1—27—1783.

and maintenance are under the care of its school committee.[21] The preparative meeting is at all times cognizant of breaches of discipline among its members and responsible to report such to the monthly meeting for settlement. One might go to great length to enumerate and explain all the detailed duties of each of these branches of the organization, but it is believed sufficient has been said of them, to make their action in educational matters intelligible.

We have noted, somewhat briefly to be sure, the organization and interrelation of the meetings in the Society of Friends. It is now necessary to point out what connection existed between this organization and the program put forward for the establishment of schools. This will be done by the presentation of certain extracts from meeting records which seem in all cases to have been responsible for kindling an interest in education in near and distant meetings, and keeping that interest alive by virtue of many advices until some material results were forthcoming. The selections presented are not continuous; they are chosen because they are representative and illustrative of the point in question.

The Yearly Meeting of London was established (see page 17) in 1672. Consistent with the purpose of its establishment, as then stated, it began at once to busy itself with certain important problems of the church. Among the first

Attention of yearly meeting to education in 1690

that received a considerable amount of attention was the education of the youths of members in the society, which was, of course, soon extended to include others. For instance, in 1690, there is given out this educational advice.

And, dear Friends, it is our Christian and earnest advice and counsel to all Friends concerned (so far as they are able or may be capable) to provide schoolmasters and mistresses who are faithful Friends, to teach and instruct their children, and not to send them to such schools where they are taught the corrupt ways, manners and fashions of the world and of the Heathen in their authors and manners of the heathenish gods and goddesses. . .[22]

And again in the year following we find the following advice:

---

[21]Min. Horsham School Com., 1792–1816, one vol.
[22]Min. London Yearly Mtg., 4—9, 11—1690.

We are glad to hear that care is taken in some places, according to former advices, for the providing of schoolmasters and mistresses who are faithful Friends to instruct Friends' children in such method as Truth allows. And we desire that Friends may go on in the care to provide such education and schools, for the advantage of their children and posterity.[23]

1691

More specific instructions follow in 1695.

And it is desired . . . to take special care for the good education and order of Friends' children in God's holy fear, . . . and also to see that schools and schooolmasters who are faithful Friends, and well qualified, be placed and encouraged in all counties, cities and great towns, or places where they may be needed; and that such schoolmasters, as much as may be, sometimes correspond with one another for their help and improvement in such good and easy methods as are agreeable to the Truth and the children's advantage and benefit; and that care be taken that poor Friends' children may freely partake of such education, in order to apprenticeship.[24]

1695

At a much later date, 1745, very similar instructions are found among those issued.

And, dear Friends, though frequently and repeated advices have been given from this meeting, respective of the education of our youth in sobriety, godliness and Christian virtues; yet, this being a matter of very great moment for the welfare of the present and future generations, we think it our incumbent duty again to recommend an especial care therein. . . . We also recommend to schoolmasters and mistresses, to educate the children committed to their charge, in the frequent reading of those sacred writings and such other good books as tend to their instruction in true Christianity; whereby their minds are in danger of being corrupted and led aside from the way of truth and holiness.[25]

and 1745

A casual reading of the above statements, or any of numerous others like them, will suffice to point out to what great extent they are similar to the statements of Fox and other Quakers who were interested in education.* For convenience, the content of these extracts from the yearly meeting minutes may be summarized in something like the following:

1. To educate morally, according to Friends' standards.
2. To train the individual in some practical employment.

---

[23]Min. London Yearly Mtg., 4—1, 4—1691.
[24]*Ibid.*, 3—13, 17—1695.
[25]*Ibid.*, 4—7—1745.
*See first chapter.

They are accompanied by:

1. Select schools.
2. Teachers of approved morality.
3. Selected subject matter.
4. Apprenticeship training.
5. Schools to be in all communities, the stronger assisting the weaker.[26]

The influence of these fundamental ideas about education is clearly reflected in the type of schools that were first set up in England. Those recommended by Fox at Waltham and Shacklewell in 1667, for both boys and girls, represent the first attempt.[27] At a later date, 1702, Clerkenwell was established under the oversight of London and Middlesex Quarterly Meetings, and in the latter part of the century the Ackworth School, founded by John Fothergill in 1779.[28] In all the schools established, of which those mentioned are representative, there is always found this primary emphasis on *moral* and *useful* training.[29]

The great influence of English Quaker education on that in America was made secure by virtue of the very intimate relation between the meetings in both countries; this relation being constantly maintained through the traveling ministers, and tracts and epistles sent out by the yearly meetings. The same alertness, characteristic of London Yearly Meeting in these affairs, was likewise assumed by the Burlington and Philadelphia Meetings, from whence came numerous advices. As concrete evidence of this close relation existing, and the consequent communications, a few extracts thereof are inserted.

Influence
exerted by
means of
ministers,
epistles and
tracts

There was brought to this meeting (Middletown Monthly) the last London printed epistle, which was read, containing sundry weighty advices and exhortations with some comfortable account of the prosperity of the Truth in divers places, as also the extracts of our last yearly meeting (Philadelphia) wherein is recommended amongst other things, a half collection for the next year, and some proposals concerning the settling of schools in the country. . . .[30]

---

[26]Min. London Yearly Mtg., 4—10—1718.
[27]Fox, *Journal*, II, 57.
[28]*Bib. of Ackworth School* (Eng.), p. VII.
[29]*History of Ayton School*, 1f.
[30]Min. Middletown Mo. Mtg., 11—6—1750.

That these letters of advice were not mere formalities but were really seriously considered and acted upon favorably or unfavorably, as in the first case below, is shown adequately in the following:

This meeting taking into consideration the proposals of last yearly meeting concerning the settling of schools in the country, are of the opinion that the method proposed will not answer for the Friends who live remote from each other in the country. . .[31]

In the case of Darby Monthly Meeting, later in the century, there is an instance in which the recommendations of the yearly meeting (1778) are followed most minutely in the reorganization.

Had definite results

In consideration of improving our school, agreeable to the recommendations of the last Yearly Meeting in 1778, and subsequent advices down to this time having been spread in this meeting and so and several remarks made thereon, pointing out the advantages which may arise therefrom to the present rising and succeeding ages, and the loss sustained for the want thereof, tending to animate a desire to pursue the interesting prospect. It is therefore now agreed that in future five Friends be appointed and called the overseers of the Darby School, three of whom shall be deemed a sufficient number to transact any business within their appointment, viz.: to have the oversight of and visit the school, examine the progress the scholars make in their learning, remark thereon as appears to them necessary; inspect the teachers' conduct, and from time to time as occasion may be, with the approbation of the meeting, agree with and employ a teacher or teachers, and on sufficient cause appearing, discharge any such teacher or teachers, as also any unruly scholars who cannot be brought to submission to the rules and orders of the school; hear and determine upon all differences relative to the school which may arise between any teacher and employer, take into consideration and endeavor out after some eligible plan for raising a fund for the benefit of the school and as way shall open for it, pursue the same accordingly, and every matter and thing tending to promote a settlement for a school agreeable to the recommendations before cited; and as some of our deceased brothers have made donations to this meeting for the benevolent purpose of schooling children of the poor, therefore, the aforesaid overseers are hereby empowered and directed to receive and collect from the trustees thereof for the time being, the interest arising from the said donations, dispose thereof agreeable to the intentions of the Donors, and when necessary, advise and assist the trustees in taking better securities for the principal, and as future donations may be made for the benefit of the school, the overseers are directed

---

[31]Min. Middletown Mo. Mtg., 6—1—1751.

to extend care therein, as the same shall become necessary, and keep fair minutes of all moneys received and expended and other matters of importance which come before them, to be produced in this meeting when called for, and preceding the quarterly meeting in the 8th month annually make to this meeting a clear statement of the amount received, expended and remaining in hand and outstanding and of the capital under their care; what donations made within the year past and for what purposes; and of such other matters as they may judge needful to enable this meeting to transmit the true estate of the school to the Quarterly Meeting, and as a fundamental of their proceedings they transcribe a copy of their minutes, together with such other writings as are necessary for their government in what is now constituted their cares.[32]

A committee was accordingly appointed and directed to choose their officers, that their business might be begun at once and properly performed.

In addition to the advices sent out in the form of letters from the yearly sessions, the meeting also furthered regularly the distribution of books, tracts and pamphlets, usually the expression of prominent Friends, such as, for example, Penn's *Advice to His Children*, Barclay's *Apology*, Sewell's *History of Quakers*, Barclay's *Catechism*, Turford's *Grounds of a Holy Life*, and many others of similar nature. Works of this kind were frequently sent over in lots, sometimes for free distribution, or to be sold to members; as witness the following:

Works of Penn, Barclay, Sewell, Turford, and others distributed

Joseph Kirkbride and Walter Faucit, having been lately in London upon the service of Truth, did subscribe for 100 of Barclay's *Apologies* on behalf of this yearly meeting, which the said meeting approves of; and agreed that Samuel Carpenter pay for them out of the yearly meeting stock and distribute them to each meeting according to their proportion of books that they usually receive, that so they may be given away by the several meetings for the service of truth.[33]

Sam Nixon informs the meeting that he brought from last quarterly meeting ten small books, entitled *Reflections and Maxims*, wrote by William Penn and printed for the use of schools, which he desired us to take the care of and to apply to the use intended as occasion may require.[34]

Produced at this meeting, 6 Barclay's *Apologies*, 12 Richard Davis' *Journals*, 7 Daniel Stanton's *Journals*, 4 Hugh Turford's *Grounds of a*

[32]Min. Darby Mo. Mtg., 1—28—1790.
[33]Min. Phila. Yearly Mtg., 7—24—1708.
[34]Min. Richland Mo. Mtg., 3—21—1793.

Holy Life, 8 Barclay's *Catechisms;* 37 books under care of Thos. Pickering, Thos. Watson, and Robert Kirkbride—to lend to the poor or others, as they think useful.[35]

The foregoing presentation of conditions within the church organization, their method of interaction, has been made so that the reader may understand that whatever activities may be later noted among the Quakers in Pennsylvania in connection with the establishment of schools, were intimately connected with and were in fact the result of the English influence.

SUMMARY

The form of organization of the meeting in the Society of Friends was due to the needs then existing, and was planned, even to the smallest unit, by the founder of the society. The chief purposes of the organization, when first begun, were (1) moral and religious discipline of members, (2) assistance to the poor among their number, and (3) to protect themselves against the oppression of outsiders (function of the meeting on sufferings). The functions of the higher meeting (yearly) were chiefly advisory in character, while those of the lower meetings (preparative) were to work out the details. Educationally, the yearly meeting exercised an influence very early by its frequent recommendations and the literature sent to the smaller individual meetings. This rôle was likewise assumed by the Burlington and Philadelphia Yearly Meeting.[36] This close relationship between the meetings of different order and the educational influence is in part shown by extracts taken from the meeting records.

---

[35]Extracts Buckingham Mo. Mtg., 12—2—1776.
[36]The two localities at the first establishment constituted but one yearly meeting, which met at each place in alternate years.

CHAPTER III

EDUCATIONAL IDEALS OF QUAKER LEADERS

Criticism
inevitable;
beneficial

Any institution one may name has its adverse critics. The basis of their criticism is often ill-defined; it is sometimes fact, sometimes imagination; it may spring from a knowledge of truth, or possibly from ignorance.

Some criti-
cism based
on misunder-
standing

Quakerism has had many critics and the effect of wise criticism may be seen in some of the changes from the old to the modern Quakerism. Much of that which was unjust and without foundation of fact, failed to have any effect whatever. But though the effect on the institution may have been nil, it occurs in some cases that the criticism still lives in the popular mind and is accorded a good degree of authenticity. By those better informed it may not be so considered. It is with one of these criticisms, concerning the attitude of Quakers toward education, that we are chiefly concerned in this chapter. Due chiefly to a misinterpretation of the doc-

Certain
doctrines

trine of *inner light* and its application, which was mentioned in the first chapter, there arose an erroneous conception of the Quakers' attitude towards education. This conception is not always constant; it varies now to this side, now to that, but does not cease to persist. In order that this criticism may be put as clearly as possible before the reader, use is made here of a quotation from the works of S. H. Cox, at one time a member of Friends, who expresses with clearness the opinion of a very considerable group of critics.

The criticism
offered by
S. H. Cox

But there is one feature of the system of Friends which deserves a recognition here—its inimical regard to classical and scientific learning. I do not say that all Friends are thus hostile, or that they are all alike hostile to liberal learning but I charge this hostility on the system. That such is its character, appears from the denunciation, the indiscriminate proscription of Barclay, and that not in a few places in his book. It appears in the general hostility of Friends to all colleges and seminaries where the elevated branches are thoroughly taught. Not one young Friend out of five hundred, even in this free country, ever obtains a liberal education in fact or in name; certainly never becomes graduated in the arts at any chartered institution, and where an instance occurs, it is always attended with special difficulties. They have no college of liberal science in the world! Some, I know, of the suspected worldly sort in Philadelphia have proposed and would have forwarded so excellent an object, but they were always awed into despondency by the unlettered, all-knowing light within. And in this, their obsequiousness was quite consistent, for if schools, academies, and universities are all in their nature wrong, and as such forbidden of God, it is certainly right to desist totally and at once from the prosecution of their cause! Incidental evils they will always include, but the system is not chargeable with these, unless in its nature it approves and fosters them. There will always be, perhaps, hypocrites at the communion table but christianity does not make them, and the purest ministry of the gospel will often become a savor of death unto death, but sinners themselves and not such a ministry are to blame for the consequence. And so the best organized system of intellectual education that the world has seen has often presented the appalling spectacle of profligate and wicked students perverting its privileges. But what of that? Shall we burn our colleges? Why not our primary school houses too? What beneficient institution, what bounty of the blessed God is not perverted and abused in this naughty world. . . .[1]

I cannot leave this matter without remarking the power of education especially with Friends. Their mode of education is the making and the keeping and the secret of their sect. They subdue the infant conscience with the direct rays of the inward light. They identify all divinity and right in the associations of their children with the light within and it friendly fruits. Here the spell commences that grows with their growth and strengthens with their strength. Investigation is much akin to skepticism and is devoutly precluded—but what worse skepticism it is to suppose that investigation could raze the foundation of our faith. They must take everything for granted or see it in the light. They must wear a ridiculous cut and color of clothes, such as are orthodox or common to the clanship and use the plain language and act like Friends, and then if they feel awkward or foolish, if their garb appears ridiculous to themselves, if their manner expose them to jeering and affront, if they are insolently struck (as I have often) in the street by worthless boys and cursed as a "Quaker," if their effeminate holy whine is profanely mocked, as it often is by saucy passengers, and if a thousand other inconveniences accrue, especially if they are sometimes asked for one good reason for such singularity in gratuitous oppositon to mankind, they must just bear it all for righteousness sake, not be afraid of the cross, but remember early Friends how much more they endured in the same cause.

---

[1]Cox,S. H., *Quakerism*, 56–57; for similar criticism, see Bugg, Francis, *The Quakers Detected*, etc.; also Bowden, *History*, II, 35, recognizes the criticisms made.

Now much of this which they call a guarded education, is just the worst kind of sorcery. It is a fascination and religious tyrannizing over the blighted attributes of mind. It is a system exactly calculated to prostrate every noble, courageous and manly sentiment, and to transmute a fine ingenuous boy into a sorry, sly, and often simulating creature in the form of a man.[2]

It is not necessary to discuss directly the views set forth in the above quotation, as they are stated clearly enough in the author's own language. However, in the following pages, there will be presented the views on education of as many prominent Friends as space will permit, that in so doing they may be considered in connection with the remarks of their critics and a just comparison made. In presenting the views of Quaker educators reference may be made to salient points in the criticism, which seem out of keeping with the ideas set forth and without foundation as matters of fact.

Contrast Cox's statements above with those of early Quakers in regard to education

There are quite a number of men, in the brief period studied, who stand out clearly and express themselves definitely in favor of education, though they do not consider it the first requisite for a minister of the gospel.[3] From this number it will be feasible to select only a few for the chief consideration, relegating the remainder to a place of comparative unimportance and incidental notice. The work of George Fox, though he was poorly educated, had a remarkable effect on the educational work of the society. But it is not necessary to review that in the present chapter as it has been presented in the first.[4]

Only a few of the leaders statements to be considered

By far the most familiar of all characters in Quaker history is that of William Penn. And to his influence must be attributed largely the hearty interest in education shown, not only in Philadelphia, but also in the surrounding communities. He was well educated, but it is not desired to make a case for or against him on the basis of his education; let us judge by his written or spoken expression and actual procedure in practice. No attempt is made to prove or disprove his contentions as to what was right or wrong, necessary or unnecessary in education. The questions asked in his case and the

---

[2]Cox, S. H., *Quakerism*, 142–3.
[3]This point was further explained in Chapter I.
[4]pp. 7ff.

others that follow is: What did they approve or disapprove of in education?

Not only in works that might be called strictly educational did Penn give educational advice, valuable alike to youth and to parents, the directors of youth. His advice to his children on the value of diligence and its necessity for success, and the propriety of frugality, even in the homes of the rich, embodies many of the most essential principles in education at any time. It is especially applicable to the education of the man of business, emphasizing the importance of the practical duties in life. Some pointed statements are especially worthy of repetition.

Penn recommends practical virtues

> Diligence . . . is a discreet and understanding application of onesself to business; . . . it loses not, it conquers difficulties. . . . Be busy to a purpose; for a busy man and a man of business are two different things. Lay your matters and diligence succeeds them, else pains are lost. . . . Consider well your end, suit your means to it, and diligently employ them, and you will arrive where you would be. . . .[5] Frugality is a virtue too, and not of little use in life, the better way to be rich, for it hath less toil and temptation. . . . I would have you liberal, but not prodigal; and diligent but not drudging; I would have you frugal but not sordid.[6]

Diligence

Frugality

This bit of philosophy is educational in its bearing in very much the same way as that of Benjamin Franklin.

In the letters to his wife and children, referring to the care for their education, he is more specifically concerned with actual school education.

> For their learning, be liberal. Spare no cost, for by such parsimony all is lost that is saved; but let it be useful knowledge such as is consistent with truth and godliness, not cherishing a vain conversation or idle mind; but ingenuity mixed with industry is good for the body and the mind too. I recommend the useful parts of mathematics, as building houses, or ships, measuring, surveying, dialing, navigation; but agriculture especially is my eye. Let my children be husbandmen and housewives; it is industrious, healthy, honest and of good example, . . .[7]

School education recommended; the useful emphasized

His preference, as might be expected from an Englishman of that time, was for a tutorial system of education. His

Private tutors desired

---

[5]Penn., *Advice to his Children* in vol. of tracts, II, 20.
[6]*Ibid.*
[7]Penn., *Letters to Wife and Children; Tracts on Moral and Religious subjects*, pub. 1822, 6f.

reasons therefore seem to have been based chiefly on moral
grounds.

> Rather have an ingenious person in the house to teach them, than
> send them to schools; too many evil impressions being received there.[8]

The above quotation alone would seem to be adequate
proof that Penn did not oppose education, but urged it for
others and in his own family.   But still more convincing and
irrefutable evidence is found in the preamble to this school
charter, whence an extract is taken.

> Whereas, the prosperity and welfare of any people depend in great
> measure upon the good education of youth, and their early instruction
> in the principles of true religion and virtue, and qualifying them to serve
> their country and themselves, by breeding them in writing and reading
> and learning of languages, and useful arts and sciences, suitable to their
> sex, age and degree; which cannot be effected in any manner or so well
> as by erecting public schools for the purposes aforesaid, therefore. . . .[9]

Public educa-
tion essential
for the wel-
fare of a
people

If, as must be admitted, the previous statement points out
the lack of any opposition to the ordinary rudimentary education that is necessary for the everyday walks of life, the
last one certainly does the same in reference to his attitude
towards a higher classical education.   Moreover, this is not
a mere skeleton of words never clothed with the flesh of
action.   The principles set forth in the charter were actually
incorporated in the work of the schools established in Philadelphia, and we find them maintaining a classical school for
languages and higher mathematics.[10]   The practical elements
received the just emphasis which belonged to them; it was
necessary that the boys and girls be made able to earn a
living and be at least ordinarily intelligent citizens.   The
example of Philadelphia was followed by other communities;
practical needs were given the first consideration and a higher
classical education offered when it became possible.   Not
only were these studies, which we would term higher education, mentioned by Penn and other writers among Quakers,
but they were taken up and recommended by the yearly
meeting.   For example, in 1737, the minutes recommend
that as opportunity can be found, children should be privi-

His ideals
expressed
in action

Yearly meet-
ing recom-
mend French
High and
Low Dutch,
Danish, etc.

[8]Penn., *Letters to Wife and Children; Tracts on Moral and Religious
subjects*, pub. 1822, 6f.
[9]*Friends Library*, V, 208.
[10]Minutes Philadelphia Mo. Mtg., 7—30—1779, 151.

leged to learn "French, High and Low Dutch, Danish, etc."[11]
This particular recommendation was made by the meeting
because of a felt need.[12] If then in case of a need for a particular subject, they were willing to recommend that it be
taught, can it be truly said that they opposed all education?

It may be well to examine Barclay, since it is with him and
his writings that Cox takes issue. In his *Apology for Chris-*
tian Divinity Vindicated is to be found a very clear statement   Barclay's
of his position on the subject, and he voices it as the principle   position
of the whole society as well. He seems to be answering   defined
some critic, who has taken him to task for his educational
views:

> He goes on after his usual manner saying, I inveigh against all human
> learning that has been made use of any ways in Theology; but where he
> finds this asserted I know not, whether the words he would declare it   In his
> from, to wit: that man hath rendered the plain and naked truth   *Apology*
> obscure and mysterious by his wisdom, will bear such a consequence is
> left to the reader's judgment. But he thinks he has found out our
> secret design of being against learning and schools of learning, which is
> neither our affirmation nor our principle, but his own false supposition.
> We would, saith he, have all those banished, that we might more easily
> prevail with our errors. But methinks the man should be more wary
> in venting his own false imaginations, unless he would bring some ground
> for them; for his assertion is so far untrue, that if he had been rightly
> informed, he might have known that we have set up schools of learning
> for teaching of the languages and other needful arts and sciences,[13] and
> that we never denied its usefulness; only we denied it be a qualification
> absolutely necessary for a minister, in which case alone we have opposed
> its necessity.[14]

Another character of very great importance in this connection is Anthony Benezet. Born, 1713, at St. Quentin in
France, of "an ancient and respectable family" he spent his   Benezet's
early years in France and then in Holland, whither his father   early life and
had fled for refuge.[15] A few months were spent in Rotterdam   education
and the family then moved to London where the father
entered into the mercantile business and retrieved to some
extent his fallen fortunes. This enabled him to give Anthony

---

[11]Extracts London Yearly Meeting Minutes and Advices, pub. 1802,
124.
[12]Necessary for use of missionaries in foreign fields.
[13]Schools established in England.
[14]Barclay, *Apology*, 11.
[15]Vaux, *Memoirs of Benezet*, 10-11.

sufficient education to qualify him for that business, for
which, however, he seemed to evince but little taste. Being
of a very religious nature, he became a member of Friends at
about fourteen years of age, and in that society found the
field of his whole life's activity, which was chiefly educational.[16] Considerable space will be devoted to his work in
respect to the education of Negroes, so that will be entirely
omitted in this place.[17] He was a voluminous writer, producing chiefly tracts and letters, and a great majority of these
have a definite educational bearing. Because of the great
number of them it is impossible really to do them justice,
but an attempt will be made to state a few brief theses for
which he unchangingly stands.

First, education is a religious and social duty.[18] It is
exceedingly interesting to notice that he looks upon education
as in the first place a governmental function, *if the governments of this world were influenced by true wisdom, they would
make the proper education of youth their first and special care;*[19]
but since governments have neglected to do this, it occurs to
him that it is a service for which Quakers are remarkably well
fitted. |It is a service for which the wage is very small and
which secures no return of special social favors for the laborer.
But they, being a quiet people, not wishing to gain great
wealth or to shine in social positions, can find their sphere of
activity in the education of the youthful members of society.

Second, a special care in the education of the poor is urged.[20]
This should become the duty and secure the interest of the
well-to-do public spirited man, for if the upper class does not
safeguard it, they cannot be educated. The poor child
represents so much unimproved property, the owner being
unable to improve it, which, if taken over by philanthropists,
may become of some consequence to himself and perform
great services for society at large. Such a movement would,
besides being a great aid to the poor and uneducated, be also
a worthy occupation for those who at present have nothing

Marginal notes:

Education
a function of
government,
but often
neglected as
such; hence
individual
effort
necessary

Children
represent
"capital";
they must
be educated

---

[16]Vaux, *Memoirs of Benezet,* 13.
[17]Chapter on Negro Education, pp. 235f.
[18]Letter to Samuel Fothergill. *Friends Library*, IX, 220.
[19]*Ibid.*, 221.
[20]*Ibid.*

but time and money to spend. It would help them to realize that there is something real in the world, something greater than wealth and broader than religious denominations. The heart of Benezet knew no bounds; in his philanthropy he included all classes.

Third, a definite stand is made for higher standards for teachers.

> I do not know how it is amongst you, but here any person of tolerable morals, who can read and write, is esteemed sufficiently qualified for a schoolmaster; when indeed, the best and wisest men are but sufficient for so weighty a charge.[21]

He endeavors to show that the work of a teacher is pleasant and should interest a better class of masters than it has in the past. The experiences of Benezet in the school work were of most pleasant nature. Not only by his own statement, but judged also by the accounts given in his memoirs by Robert Vaux, it seems that he was unusually kind and sympathetic as a master, which won him the greatest respect of his pupils.[22] The tasks of schoolteaching are only unpleasant when being performed merely for the sake of the wage obtained. Those who attempt to teach large numbers for the sake of a large income find it disagreeable; they form the class of teachers against whom he would discriminate.[23] Add to these three principles, his great contribution toward the freedom and education of the Negroes, his long life of service, and we have all for which he lived. It is stated that he had no private life; at any rate it sinks into oblivion in comparison with his interest and active work in public philanthropies.[24]

The educational influence of John Woolman in regard to Negro and Indian education will be mentioned in another chapter,[25] but concerning education generally he was equally outspoken, and being a member of some consequence he was able to make his influence felt. Like Benezet, he regarded education as a social duty, both to each individual and to the community of individuals. This duty could not be per-

John Woolman, his position in regard to education

---

[21] *Ibid.*
[22] Vaux, *Memoirs of Benezet*, 15-16.
[23] *Friends Library*, IX, 221.
[24] Vaux, *Memoirs* 105.
[25] See chapter on negro education, pp.234f.

formed by immoral tutors and schoolmasters, for the pupil
could be made to rise no higher than the master; so the
result would be an immoral society.[26]   The responsibility,
in the last analysis, for the right conduct of schools falls upon
the parents. If they are indifferent, nothing can be accomplished for the schools, for the whole community is no better
or more insistent in its demands than the individuals constituting it.   For this reason he urges individual philanthropy
to come to the aid of the schools, which are badly neglected;
those who possess wealth can do no better, for, as he says:

Meditating on the situation of schools in our provinces, my mind hath,
at times, been affected with sorrow, and under these exercises it hath
appeared to me, what if those that have large estates were faithful
stewards, and laid no rent or interest nor other demand, higher than is
consistent with universal love; and those in lower circumstances would
under a moderate employ, shun unnecessary expense, even to the
smallest article; and all unite humbly in seeking the Lord, he would
graciously instruct and strengthen us, to relieve the youth from various
snares, in which many of them are entangled.[27]

If to this list of advocates of education, it is necessary to
add others, mention should be made of Henry Tuke, George
Whitehead, and William Crouch.   In defending certain
differences between the Quaker doctrine and that of other
denominations, the former discusses this one, *in not considering human learning essential to a minister of the gospel.*[28]   The
reasons adduced are chiefly biblical; the knowledge of human
literature is not recommended by the New Testament as
being necessary for a minister, and this is considered conclusive proof.   Moreover, it is pointed out that Paul, though
a well educated man, disclaimed the value of his education
for that service, and wished always to appear to the people
as an unlettered man of God.[29]   But Tuke goes on to explain
that though it is not essential for a minister, learning is not
unesteemed nor its usefulness slighted.[30]   Members are
desired to direct their attention to education, for a right use
of it may promote religion and benefit civil society.[31]   That

The responsi-
bility of
tutors and
parents

Tuke, White-
head, Crouch
as advocates
of education

[26]Woolman's *Works*, 305–6.   [27]*Ibid.*
[28]Tuke, *Works*, III, 95 ff.
[29]Corinthians, Chap. 2:1-5.
[30]Tuke, *Works*, III, 95 ff.
[31]*Ibid.*

the use of Latin and Greek is not decried may be seen in the work of Penn and Whitehead, who were both scholars, and whose works are full of classical references and illustrations. In one instance their chief argument against swearing is produced from certain references to the works of Socrates and Xenocrates, pointing out that the Greeks were aware of a higher "righteousness excelling" that of the legal Jews.[32] The same point of view with reference to a knowledge of the classics is taken by William Crouch, as is understood at once by this statement:

> They acknowledge the understanding of languages, especially of Hebrew, Greek and Latin, formerly was and still is very useful, yet they take them not therefore to be necessary to make a minister nor so profitable as that one unacquainted with them must be styled an idiot, illiterate and of no authority.[33]

Moreover, from various sources one is assured that a classi-cal education was not abhorred by the Quakers of Philadelphia. The work offered in the classical school was for any one who had the ability to do it and its attainment was encouraged by Friends. The higher education was for girls as well as for boys, as we may judge from reading the journal kept by Sally Wister (or Wistar), a Quaker girl of the days of the Revolution.[34] She attended the school kept by Anthony Benezet,* which was one of the highest class, moral and literary, and patronized by the best classes of the citizens. Extracts from her *Journal* indicate that her education had not been limited to the mere rudiments, but that she enjoyed also an elementary knowledge, at least, of Latin and French.[35] This sort of education was clearly not uncommon among Friends and it was not the object of opposition on their part. It must, however, be kept in mind that the Quakers never confused education necessarily with true Christianity.[36] Religion in this life and the salvation of one's soul in the next was a problem which concerned the poor as well as the rich, the untutored as well as the learned. How could the demands

The Latin School of Philadelphia exemplifies contention of those quoted the above

---

[32] *The Christian Quaker*, 181.
[33] Crouch, W., *Collection of Papers of*, 183.
[34] Wister, Sally, *Journal*, 13–14.
*Established 1754 (M. P. C. S., I, 117.)
[35] *Ibid.*
[36] Phipps, *Original and Present State of Man*, 90.

be greater for one than the other; the same tests had to be met and passed by all, the educated one received no favors though more might be expected of him.[37]   Education was looked upon as an asset which might be turned to great use for Christianity, but the lack of it was never a bar to Christianity.[38]   On the other hand, education might easily become, according to the Quakers' views, a definite hindrance to Christianity.[39]

Education an asset; but apt to be perverted

It would be quite improper in connection with this subject to fail to mention the scheme, Utopian in that day, which was conceived in the mind of Thomas Budd, for the development of a system of education for Pennsylvania and New Jersey. At the very outset it seems more comprehensive than anything suggested by any other leader, and in fact it embodied so much that it was quite beyond the limit of expectation for either of the colonies.   Thomas Budd, though not at first a member of Friends, became convinced of the justice of their principles and joined the society before the year 1678.[40] He was a man of affairs and became greatly interested in the colonization of Pennsylvania and New Jersey, whither he soon came as a colonist himself.   At that time it was equally true, as at the present, that if a scheme or undertaking was to be put through, it must be made as attractive as possible to the prospector.   The attempt to do this called forth a considerable exercise of individual initiative, and one result was the educational plan outlined by Thomas Budd and published in Philadelphia in 1685.   The details of the scheme as outlined are deemed of sufficient interest and importance to warrant their reproduction here.

Scheme of education suggested by Thomas Budd

Children to be in public school seven years or more

1.   Now it might be well if a law were made by the Governors and General Assemblies of Pennsylvania and New Jersey, that all persons inhabiting the said provinces, do put their children seven years to the Public School, or longer, if the parent please.

To receive instruction in the arts and sciences and to learn a trade

2.   That schools be provided in all towns and cities, and persons of known honesty, skill and understanding be yearly chosen by the Governor and General Assembly, to teach and instruct boys and girls in all the most useful arts and sciences that they in their youthful capacities may

---

[37]Phipps, *Original and Present State of Man*, 65.
[38]*Ibid.*, 90.
[39]*Ibid.*
[40]Budd, *Good Order Established*, p. 9.

be capable to understand, as the learning to read and write true English and Latin, and other useful speeches and languages, and fair writing, arithmetic and bookkeeping; the boys to be taught and instructed in some mystery or trade, as the making of mathematical instruments, joinery, turnery, the making of clocks and watches, weaving, shoemaking or any other useful trade or mystery that the school is capable of teaching; and the girls to be taught and instructed in spinning of flax and wool, and knitting of gloves and stockings, sewing, and making of all sorts of useful needlework, and the making of straw work, as hats, baskets, etc., or other useful art or mystery that the school is capable of teaching.

3. That the scholars be kept in the morning two hours at reading, writing, bookkeeping, etc., and other two hours at work in that art, mystery or trade that he or she most delighteth in, and then let them have two hours to dine, and for recreation and in the afternoon two hours at reading, writing, etc., and the other two hours at work at their several employments. *[Eight hours per day allotted to studies and chosen trade]*

4. The seventh day of the week the scholars may come to school only in the forenoon, and at a certain hour in the afternoon let a meeting be kept by the schoolmasters and their scholars, where good instruction and admonition is given by the masters to the scholars and thanks returned to the Lord for his mercies and blessings that are daily received from him, then let a strict examination be made by the masters, of the conversation of the scholars in the week past, and let reproof, admonition and correction be given to the offenders, according to the quantity and quality of their faults. *[Regular school work five and one-half days per week; moral instruction on Saturday]*

5. Let the like meetings be kept by the school mistresses, and the girls apart from the boys. By strictly observing this good order our children will be hindered from running into that excess of riot and wickedness that youth is incident to, and they will be a comfort to their tender parents. *[Similar arrangement for girls educated separately]*

6. Let one thousand acres of land be given and laid out in a good place, to every public school that shall be set up, and the rent or income of it to go towards the defraying of the charge of the school. *[Land endowment for schools]*

7. And to the end that the children of the poor people, and the children of Indians may have the like good learning with the children of the rich people, let them be maintained free of charge to their parents, out of the profits of the school, arising by the work of the scholars, by which the poor and the Indians as well as the rich, will have their children taught, and the remainder of the profits, if any be to be disposed of in the building of the schoolhouses and improvements on the thousand acres of land, which belongs to the school.[41] *[Indians and the poor to be educated free of cost]*

The author does not claim to be entirely original in his scheme, having been influenced, he says, by a similar thing

---

[41]Budd, *Good Order Established*, p. 43 ff.

described by Andrew Yarenton in a book, *England's Improvements by Sea and Land*.[42] His chief interest seems to be in the benefit to be derived for the commercial life of the colonies, and for that reason there is accordingly a great stress on the industrial education. By this introduction of the industrial schools, spinning for example, in the larger cities and the preparation of children at an early age for participation in that great occupation, the production of linen cloth could be made equal not only to the domestic demands but also a considerable margin for the foreign trade.[43] It is pointed out that the colonial consumer pays twice as much for his purchase as its cost of production in France or Germany, and that he pays this extra cost into the coffers of the English merchants. This profit should accrue to the home merchants.

The industrial and commercial values to be derived are pointed out

The educational and also the industrial scheme is to receive the backing of the colonial government. It is recommended that laws be passed for the encouragement of linen manufacturers and that farmers "that keep a plow" should sow an acre of flax and two of hemp, with which to supply the manufacturers.[44] Educational support by the government was not secured, as is amply evidenced by the unsurpassed development of private and parochial schools of all denominations. The churches were the sponsors for education. It is worthy of note, however, that the elements emphasized by Budd, (1) education in the arts and sciences for all those capable of it, (2) industrial education for a trade for every one, (3) moral and religious training, and (4) equal educational opportunities for poor and rich or otherwise unfavored classes, are the same as those urged officially by the Quakers.[45]

Scheme to be encouraged by the government

Essential points urged in the scheme

Far from receiving governmental support, it was necessary that the schools be supported by individual or small group enterprise. The society recognized this, and it is stated in the organization of the church that the duty of the monthly meeting is to provide *for the subsistence* of the poor and *for their education*.[46] Furthermore it is recommended that all

The lack of governmental support; supplied through meetings of Quakers

[42]Budd, *Good Order Establishsd*, p. 43ff.
[43]*Ibid.*   [44]*Ibid.*
[45]*Ibid.*   *Friends Library* I, 435.
[46]*Summary of Doctrines of Friends*, 23–24.

special bequests of Friends be kept as a distinct fund for the purpose originally intended by the donor, and that if expended for any other purpose, it must be again made up by the quarterly meeting.[47]   One of the most frequent uses designated, judging from the records, seems to have been the educational.[48]

The reader may have perused the foregoing pages with more or less interest; a curiosity may have been aroused concerning the present-day attitude of Friends, educationally. Have they experienced any considerable change?   The institutional evidences of their continued interest are familiar enough to the educationist.   But what is the attitude within the schools: Is instruction stiff and more formal there than in the public schools, and what can be said of the progress among the teachers?   To answer all of these questions and similar ones is not the purpose of this present work.   And in the following excerpt, taken from an expression drawn up by a body of teachers, it is not hoped to find conclusive proof of this or that, but perhaps it may be taken as a fairly reliable indication of the present professional attitude.

Have Quaker schools kept pace with the public?

The teachers' subjects are *not Mathematics, nor Latin, nor Scripture, nor Quakerism*—they are boys and girls.   The information imparted is, in a sense, a minor matter: the growth of the mind that assimilates it is all-important—growth in keenness, efficiency and power. . .

The pupil as an individual to be emphasized

To the Society at large we would put forward this view that the principles urged above are deserving of careful consideration in making any forward move.   The quality of the teaching given in our schools is in a measure in the hands of Friends; they have raised admirable buildings in many places—these are a small matter compared with the character of the staff.   The freedom of the teacher, which is in indispensable condition of excellence is a gift they can grant or withhold. And that we who are responsible for the term of school life may have the best chance and the best reward, we would press upon Friends the need of laying foundations and awakening interest in the days of childhood, and of turning to best account the powers of those who go forth from our schools.[49]

Well-equipped teachers needed; and their academic freedom essential

---

[47]*Friends Library*, I, 135;   Accounts of expenditures from the J. Walton Fund, II, p. 1.   (Richland Monthly Meeting.)
[48]*Ibid.*
[49]*Religious Instructions in Our Schools.*   No. 9 of a vol. of pamphlets.

SUMMARY

This chapter treats of the attitude of Friends towards education. At the beginning there is presented a criticism of S. H. Cox, which is a concrete example of the type of criticism referred to in these pages. Following this there are presented the educational views of several Friends,—Penn, Barclay, Benezet, Woolman, Whitehead, Crouch, Tuke, and Thomas Budd, in order that the reader may judge of the truth or error presented in the criticism. The chief points made in Cox's criticism are: (1) hostility of the Quaker system to classical education, (2) general hostility of the Friends to colleges and seminaries of learning, and (3) that the "light within" was sufficient without any education.

From the material next presented it is shown that: (1) Penn recommended both practical and higher education, (2) useful arts and sciences are recommended to be taught in public schools, (3) the classics were introduced as a part of the curriculum in the Penn Charter School, and also in other schools established by the society, (4) Barclay explains that the society holds a classical education not absolutely necessary for a minister, though it is useful, (5) the learning of languages is recommended by the London Yearly Meeting, (6) education is advocated by Benezet as a religious and social duty; the education of the poor and unfortunate classes and races is urged; a higher education for schoolmasters is recommended, (7) Woolman urges the education of Negroes and Indians as a social duty; the responsibility is placed on the individual, (8) Crouch states that Hebrew, Greek, and Latin are recognized as useful and are not opposed when taught for that purpose, (9) Budd, one of the early Quakers in Pennsylvania, introduced a very comprehensive and Utopian scheme for (a) industrial education and (b) higher education, proposing to organize it under the control of the General Assembly, and (10) indications are that progress, within the teaching body in Friends' institutions, is quite comparable with that of other institutions, though there is no attempt to produce conclusive evidence either to that effect or the contrary.

Summary
of Cox's
position

Summary
of points
maintained
by certain
Quaker
leaders

CHAPTER IV

EDUCATION IN PHILADELPHIA*

On ye 27th day of October, 1682, arrived before ye Towne of New Castle from England, William Penn, Esqe., whoo produced twoo deeds of feofment for this Towne and twelve myles about itt, and also for ye twoo lower counties, ye Whoorekills and St. Jones's—wherefore ye said William Penn received possession of ye Towne ye 28th of October, 1682.[1]

It is probable that Penn reached Philadelphia in the latter days of October or the early part of November,[2] though no student of Philadelphia history has yet been able to settle the question of the day absolutely.   Tradition says he came up the river in an open boat and landed at the landing on Dock Street near the new tavern, the Blue Anchor, which had just been erected by George Guest, a Quaker.[3]   The formal ceremony of transferring the territory which had been arranged between Penn and the Duke of York before leaving England,[4] was accomplished with the Duke's commissioners, Moll and Herman,[5] and the official debut of Pennsylvania in colonial society was no longer a hope but a reality.

The date
of Penn's
coming
disputed

The foundation of the colony's educational institutions had, however, not been delayed till the formalities of "making" a colony were over.   Education received early consider-

---

*In this chapter a chronological organization is followed.

[1]Quoted from Watson, *Annals*, I, 15.   (From New Castle Records.) (Proud's statement of the 24th is said by some to be a typographical error.)   The writer has, however, examined Proud's MS. notes on the *Rise and Progress of the City of Philadelphia* in which he writes: "The Honorable Proprietary and Governor of Pennsylvania, William Penn, first arrived at New Castle, on Delaware, in October 24th, 1682."   He also states "after the 11th month (January) with the assistance of his surveyor general, Thomas Holmes, he first began to lay out the plan of the City of Philadelphia."   (MS. No. 10, p. 1.)   (These two statements point the difference of opinion among scholars, which is still unsettled.)

[2]Jenkins, *Memorial Hist.*, I, 39.

[3]*Ibid.*

[4]*Ibid.*, 30.

[5]*Ibid.*, 37.

(41)

Education
provided for
in first
Frame of
Government

ation in the Frame of Government which was drawn up from England by Penn and agreed to on April 25, 1682, before he prepared to depart for Pennsylvania.[6] In that document it is clearly set forth that education was the function of the civil authority, though the intentions of the author were not realized fully for more than a hundred and fifty years.[7] The same idea is present in each of the three Frames of Government which were drawn up; the first, April 25, 1682;[8] the second, April 2, 1683;[9] and the third, November 7, 1696,[10] under Governor Markham. The instrument drawn on April 2, 1683, contained in part the following stipulations, which bear the impression of the Quaker ideal of education.

The
provisions

Tenth. That the Governor and the Provincial Council shall erect and order all public schools and encourage and reward the authors of useful sciences and laudable inventions in the said provinces and territories thereof.

Eleventh. That one-third of the Provincial Council residing with the Governor from time to time shall, with the Governor, have the care and management of public affairs relating to peace, justice, treasury and improvement of the province and territories, and to the good education of the youth, and sobriety of the manner of the inhabitants therein aforesaid.[11]

The plan for education as above set forth was not destined to be the one followed consistently for more than a century and a half of development, though throughout the first decades the relations between the schools of Friends and the governing Council were very close.[12] It is significant that the first school was actually ordered by the Council, in keeping with Penn's provisions. About one year after Penn's arrival in Philadelphia the educational problem came to the attention of the Council and received decided recognition, as the

Quaker
Council
provides a
school

following witnesses:

The Governor and Provincial Council having taken into their serious consideration the great necessity there is of a schoolmaster for the instruction and sober education of the youth in the town of Philadelphia,

---

[6]*Col. Rec.*, I, XXVI.
[7]Pub. Sch. established by law, 1834.
[8]*Col. Rec.*, I, XXVI.
[9]*Ibid.*, I, XXXVI.
[10]*Ibid.*, LXVI.
[11]*Ibid.*, XXXVI.
[12]For example, E. Flower's School; Friends' petition.

sent for Enock Flower, an inhabitant of said town, who for twenty years past has been exercised in that care and employment in England, to whom having communicated their minds, he embraced it upon the following terms: to learn to read English 4s by the quarter, to learn to read and write 6s by the quarter, to learn to read, write and cast accounts 8s by the quarter; for boarding a scholar, that is to say, diet, washing, lodging, and schooling, ten pounds for one whole year.[13]

Thus the first impetus to education in Pennsylvania came through properly constituted governmental authority. The Council records show that the interest in educational affairs was maintained for some time. In the month following a law was proposed for making several sorts of books for the use of persons in the province, and also recommended that care be taken about "Learning and Instruction of youth, to witt: a school in the arts and sciences."[14] This interest in, and the close relation of the Council to, education were not long continued however; for this there is no satisfactory explanation, though it is very clear that the attitude on the part of the government did change.[15] This change is evidenced in the policy as outlined by the Charter of 1701, in which there is no reference made to education or the responsibility of the Governor or Council therefor.[16] To the writer it seems that the withdrawal of the Council from any very active participation in the affairs of education may have been due to two reasons: *first*, the willingness evinced by private interests to establish schools and thus take over to themselves the duties of educators (evidenced by the establishment of Keith's school by Friends in 1689 without the assistance or advice of the Council);[17] and *second*, the urgent details of establishing a new government, which occupied their first attention.

Additional provisions or books

Charter of 1701 does not refer to education as did the former ones

If further proof of the withdrawal of the colonial government from the active establishment of schools, and of the fact that they did accept and recognize the assistance of private agencies is desired, it is to be found in various acts of legislation of the first half century. Specific instances of such

---

[13]*Col. Rec.*, I, 36.
[14]*Ibid.*, I, 93.
[15]See Charter of 1701, *Col. Rec.*, II, 54.
[16]*Ibid.*
[17]G. S. P. P., II, 154 (Min. Phila. Mo. Mtg., 5—26—1689.)

permissive legislation were the acts of May 28, 1715,* and also of February 6, 1730–1.† This legislation is chiefly concerned with granting privileges to purchase and hold land and erect buildings for the use of institutions stated therein, among which schools are mentioned. In this connection the statute of 1715, which evidences the facts stated above, is quoted.

> Be it enacted by Charles Gookin, Esq., by the royal approbation Lieutenant-Governor, under William Penn, Esq., Proprietary and Governor-in-Chief of the Province of Pennsylvania, by and with the advice and consent of the freemen of the said provinces in General Assembly met, and by the authority of the same, that it shall and may be lawful to and for all religious societies or assemblies and congregations of Protestants, within this province, to purchase any lands or tenements for burying grounds, and for erecting houses of religious worship, *schools* and hospitals; and by trustees, or otherwise, as they shall think fit, to receive and take grants or conveyances for the same, for any estate whatsoever, to and for the use or uses aforesaid, to be holden of the lord of the fee by the accustomed rents and services. And be it further enacted by the authority aforesaid, that all sales, gifts or grants made to any of the said societies, or to any person or persons in trust for them, or any of them, for or concerning any lands, tenements or hereditaments within this province, for and in any estate whatsoever, to and for the use and uses aforesaid, shall be and are by this Act ratified and confirmed according to the tenor and true meaning thereof, and of the parties concerned therein. And where any gifts, legacies or bequests have been or shall be made by any person or persons to the poor of any of the said respective religious societies, or to or for the use or service of any meeting or congregation of the said respective societies, the same gifts and bequests shall be employed only to those charitable uses, or to the use of those respective societies or meetings, or to the poor people to whom the same are or shall be given or intended to be given or granted, according to what may be collected to be the true intent and meaning of the respective donors or grantors.

The first meeting of record

On "11th month, 9th, 1682," the Friends met and enacted business relating chiefly to the sick, a meeting house, purchase of books and such other details of importance, but made no reference to schools or the education of youth.[18] This remained true for all meetings till 1689,[19] the chief part of

---

Stat. at Large of Pa., III, 37–38.
†*Ibid.*, IV, 208–210.
[18]*Ibid.*, I, 252. (Phila. Min.)
[19]When they established the school with Keith as teacher.

business in the meantime having to do with either (1) strictly religious affairs or (2) raising money for the poor and the orphans. The absence of any remarks or any plans for schools from 1682 to 1689 is more easily understood when it is recalled that the school under Enock Flower was set up in 1683.[20]   There is no evidence to prove definitely that Flower continued as schoolmaster during the whole of this time, but (1) the absence of any record of change, (2) no record of schools kept by the Friends Meeting, (3) the fact that he was a teacher of long experience (twenty years) and probably as satisfactory as any to be found, and (4) the absence of keen competition on the part of neighboring places to draw him away, would lead one to believe it probable that he remained there for the greater part of the period at least.

The probable
length of
Flower's
tenure as
teacher

In 1689 Friends determined to establish a school, designed to meet the demands of rich and of poor,[21] which does not seem at all strange since they were known to have been supporting their poor and the orphans by subscriptions since their first establishment.[22]   The transaction of the business relating thereto was performed in the monthly meeting and referred to the quarterly meeting (higher) for its approval. The following extract from the records of the meeting gives the result of their decision:

Friends being to encourage a school in this town, and in order hereunto they have agreed with George Keith to assure him a certain salary of 50 pounds per year to be paid quarterly, with house rent, convenient for his family and school, with the profit of his school for one year, and for two years more to make his school worth to him 120 pounds per year, if he shall think fit to stay in this place, the said George also promiseth to teach the poor (which are not of ability to pay) for nothing. The abovesaid Keith having heard the proposals of Friends, readily assented and agreed thereto, his salary beginning from the time school begins. It is agreed that it be also mentioned to the next Quarterly Meeting for their concurrence with the same, as also agreed that Anthony Morris give notice to the several monthly meetings in this county.[23]

Friends
school set
up under
Geo. Keith

The number of children who attended this school is not known, but it is clear that it grew rapidly. In January,

---

[20]Michener, *Retrospect of Quakerism*, 243.
[21]G.S. P. P., II, 154 (Phila. Min.); Proud MS. No. 3, p. 115.
[22]*Ibid.*, I, 252. (Phila. Min.)
[23]Min. Phila. Mo. Mtg., 5—26—1689.

succeeding the first establishment, the new master complained of the "inconvenience and straitness" of his school and Anthony Morris and Samuel Carpenter were appointed to consult with Robert Turner for a more convenient situation.[24]

The first interpretation of "straitness" would undoubtedly be that it was crowded, and that might well have been true without there having been an increase in the size of the school; more conclusive proof of the rapid increase in numbers is to be found in the fact that Thomas Makin was hired as usher to assist Keith,[25] probably about February, 1690.[26] A more convenient room for the school was arranged for with John Fuller at thirteen pounds per year, three pounds more than was paid for the first.[27]

In the 3rd month, 1691, Keith made known his intention of leaving the school,[28] whether because of dissatisfaction with the school itself or the beginning of the feeling against the Quakers which resulted in his rupture with them,[29] it is not known, and recommended to the meeting the appointment of his usher, Thomas Makin, to take his place.[30] It was Keith's desire to leave on 4th month, 10th and he may have discontinued teaching at that time, but it appears that his account against the meeting was not settled until the eleventh or the twelfth month, 1691.[31] According to his suggestion concerning Makin, the meeting appointed a committee to consult with him,[32] the outcome of which was a satisfactory agreement. It would appear from numerous references to the subject, that the matter of getting the subscriptions and keeping them paid was a chief source of trouble, which required their constant energies and attention.[33] In 1693 Thomas Makin brought in a bill against the meeting for £12/15/7, which was still owing for his services as usher in 1690.[34]

Margin notes:
A larger school needed

Makin hired as usher

Thomas Makin recommended by Keith to be master

Makin chosen

---

[24]Min. Phila. Mo. Mtg., 1—28—1690.
[25]*Ibid.*, 3—29—1691.
[26]*Ibid.*, 2—26—1690.
[27]*Ibid.*
[28]*Ibid.*, 3—29—1691.
[29]Jenkins, *Memorial Hist.*, I, 99.
[30]Min. Phila. Mo. Mtg., 3—29—1691.
[31]*Ibid.*, 11—29—1691.
[32]*Ibid.*
[33]*Ibid.*, 3—29—1691; 9—27—1691; 11—29—1691; 7—29—1692.
[34]*Ibid.*, 4—30—1693.

The last four years of the century saw greater strides made in the better establishment of education as a system. In 1696 it was agreed that there should be established four meetings a year, the chief function of which was the religious education of the youth in the principles of Friends.[35] Steps were shortly taken for the establishment of the so-called "free school." Penn had written to Thomas Lloyd, President of the Council, in 1689, advising that a grammar school be set up (that of George Keith)[36] and it was this same school which in 1697 the meeting desired to make a "free school." On 10th month, 31st, 1697:

Penn said to have written letter to Lloyd about the school

> A paper for the encouragement of a free school was this day read, whereupon Samuel Carpenter and James Fox are desired to treat with Daniel Pastorius and Thomas Makin concerning the same, and — they desire the Friends of the town to meet together this day week, about the 1st hour at this meeting house to consider further of it, and that Daniel Pastorius and Thomas Makin be present.[37]

In the month following (11th month) Samuel Carpenter reported to the assembly that the committee had met with Daniel Pastorius and Thomas Makin and agreed to pay each of them forty pounds per year for keeping school.[38] The means of support was the familiar subscription blank, Samuel Carpenter and James Fox being the first appointed to take them. School was to begin the first of the following month, in the room over the meeting house, which had been prepared for that purpose.[39] In the 12th month a petition was sent to the Governor and Council, requesting the ordaining and establishment of the "Public School." The text of the petition is as follows:

Pastorius and Makin in the school

> The humble petition of Samuel Carpenter . . . in behalf of themselves and the rest of the people called Quakers, who are members of the Monthly Meeting, . . . showeth that it has been and is much desired by many that a school be set up and upheld in this town of Philadelphia, where poor children may be freely maintained, taught

Petition to Council to incorporate the school

---

[35]Min. Phila. Mo. Mtg., 8—30—1696; 7—25—1696.
[36]Janney, *Life of Penn*, 347; Clarkson's *Penn*, II, 53; although biographers and historians mention this letter written to Lloyd, no student has yet been able to produce it or tell where it is. It is hoped that their search will be rewarded.
[37]Min. Phila. Mo. Mtg., 10—31—1697.
[38]*Ibid.*, 11—28—1697.
[39]*Ibid.*

and educated in good literature, until they are fit to be put out as apprentices, or capable to be masters or ushers in the same schools. And forasmuch as in the laws and constitution of this government it is provided and enacted that the Governor and Council shall erect . . . . public schools . . . . reward the authors of useful sciences and laudable inventions . . . . therefore, may it please the Governor and Council to ordain and establish that in the said town of Philadelphia a public school may be founded, where all children and servants, male and female, whose parents, guardians and masters be willing to subject them to the rules and orders of the said schools, shall from time to time with the approbation of the overseers thereof for the time being, be received and admitted, taught and instructed; the rich at reasonable rates, and the poor to be maintained and schooled for nothing. And to that end a meet and convenient house or houses, buildings and rooms may be erected for the keeping of the said school, and for the entertainment and abode of such and so many masters, ushers, mistresses and poor children, as by orders of said meeting shall be limited and appointed from time to time. And also that the members of the aforesaid Meetings . . . . make choice and admit such and so many persons as they think fit, to be masters, overseers, ushers, mistresses and poor children of the said school, and the same persons . . . . to remove or displace as often . . . . as they shall see fit. And that the overseers and the school aforesaid, may . . . . be . . . . in name and deed, a body politic and corporate, to have continuance forever by the name of the Overseers of the Public School founded in Philadelphia at the request of the people of God called Quakers. And that they, the said overseers, may have perfect succession, and by that name they and their successors may hold and enjoy, all lands, tenements and chattels, and receive and take all gifts and legacies as shall be given, granted or devised for the use and maintenance of the said school and poor scholars, without any further or other license or authority from this Government in that behalf; saving unto the chief Proprietary his quitrents of the said lands. And that the said overseers by the same name shall and may, with consent of said meeting, have power and capacity to devise and grant by writing, under their hand and seal and of said lands and tenements and to take and purchase any other lands . . . . for . . . . advantage of said school. And to prescribe such rules and ordinance for the good order and government of the same school . . . . successively, and for their and every of their stipends and allowances, as to members of the said Meeting for the time being . . . . shall seem meet; with power also to sue and to be sued, and to do and perform and execute all and every other lawful act and thing, good and profitable for the said school, in as full and ample manner, as any other body politic or corporate more perfectly founded or incorporated, may do.[40]

---

[40]*Col. Rec.*, I, 499.

This request was immediately granted by the Council,[41] and the school thus incorporated in 1697.[42] In 1701 Penn confirmed its incorporation by the following charter:

The petition granted and charter issued by Penn in 1701

WILLIAM PENN True and absolute Proprietary and Governor in Chief of the Province of Pennsylvania and territories thereunto belonging. To all to whom these presents shall come sendeth greeting. *Whereas* Charles the Second, late King of England by his letters patents bearing date the fourth day of March in the three and thirtieth year of his reign did grant unto me my heirs and assigns the said Province And Absolute Proprietary thereof with full power to me by the assent of the freemen there to make laws for the good and happy government of the same with divers other powers preheminsures jurisdictions, privileges and immunities therein specified. *And Whereas* I with a great colony of the People of God called Quakers for the free enjoyment of liberty of our consciences in matters of religion as of other privileges and advantages in the said patent granted as well to me the said Proprietary and Governor as also to the said people did transport ourselves unto the said Province and at our own risk costs pains and charges settled and planted the same the soil also of the said Province being first by me purchased of the Indian Natives. And forasmuch as by the laws of the said Province since enacted the Governor and Council have power to erect and order all public schools of literature and science *And Whereas* Samuel Carpenter —Edward Shippen—Anthony Morris—James Fox—David Lloyd— William Southby and John Jones in behalf of themselves and the rest of the said people called Quakers Members of their Monthly Meeting at Philadelphia in the said Province by their petition to the Governor and Council of the said Province and territories at Philadelphia the tenth day of the twelfth month Anno Domini one thousand six hundred ninety seven (eight) set forth that it was the desire of many that a school should be set up and upheld in the said town of Philadelphia where poor children might be freely maintained taught and educated in good literature until they should be fit to be put apprentices or capable to be masters or Ushers in the said school requesting the Governor and Council in the said petition to ordain that at the said town of Philadelphia a Public School might be founded where all children male and female whose parents guardians or masters might be willing to subject them to the rules and orders of the school should from time to time with the approbation of the overseers thereof for the time being be received or admitted taught and instructed the rich at reasonable rates and the poor to be maintained and schooled for nothing. *And* that to that end a meet and convenient house or houses buildings or rooms might be erected for the keeping of the said school and for the entertainment and abode of such and so many Masters Ushers Mistresses and poor children as by the

[41]*Col. Rec.*, I, 499.
[42]*Ibid.;* Janney, *Life of Penn*, 347.

order and direction of the said Monthly Meeting should be free from time to time limited and appointed and also that the members of the aforesaid meeting for the time being might at their respective monthly meeting from time to time make choice of and admit such and so many persons as they should think fit to be Overseers Masters Ushers Mistresses and poor children of the said school and the same person or any of them to remove and displace as often as the said meeting shall see occasion, and that the overseers and school aforesaid might forever thereafter stand and be established and founded in name and in deed a body politic and corporate to have continuance forever by the name of the Overseers of the Public School grounded in Philadelphia at the request cost and charges of the people of God called Quakers. And that the said Overseers might have perpetual succession, and by that name they and their successors forever, have hold and enjoy all the lands tenements and chattels and receive and take all gifts and legacies that should be given granted or devised for the use and maintenance of said schools and poor scholars without further or other license or authority from the government on that behalf. *Saving* unto the Chief Proprietary his quit rents out of the said lands and that the said Overseers by the same name might with consent of the said Meeting have power and capacity to demise and grant by writing under their hand and common seal any of the said lands and tenements and to take and purchase any other lands and tenements and hereditaments for the best advantage of the said schools and to prescribe such rules and ordinances for the good order and government of the said school and of the masters ushers mistresses and poor children successively and for their and every of their stipends and allowances as to them members of the said monthly meeting for the time or the major part of them should seem meet, with power also to sue and be used and to do perform and execute all and every other lawful act and thing good and profitable for the said school in as full and ample manner as any other body politic and corporate more perfectly founded and incorporated might do and by the said petition which I have seen may more fully appear whereupon my then lieutenant Governor and Council did grant and order that the said schools should be founded and erected with the incorporation privileges and powers as desired   *Now* forasmuch as those of the said petitioners that are living have made fresh application to me in Council for confirming the said lieutenant Governor and Councils order and grant upon the said petition which being well weighed and considered by me I greatly favor the good inclinations and just and laudable desires and conscientious regards of the said petitioners and people for the education instruction and literature of their children and posterity and more especially their care and concerns for the poor on that behalf. . . .

Therefore Know Ye that pursuant to the powers to me granted as aforesaid and to the laws of the said Province already enacted I have (by and with the consent of my Provincial Council) granted and confirmed all and every request matter and thing . . . contained in the said petition and do by these presents for me my heirs and assigns grant ordain and establish that the said Public School shall be erected and founded, and I do grant, ordain and found the same to be kept forever hereafter in the said town of Philadelphia or in some convenient place adjacent as the overseers of the said school for the time being shall see meet and I do likewise grant and ordain that in the said school all children and servants as in the school petition requested shall from time to time (with approbation of the said Overseers) be received admitted taught and instructed as in the same petition is mentioned and desired and to the end that all meet and convenient houses, rooms, chambers and buildings may be erected for keeping of the said schools and entertainment of the masters ushers mistresses and poor children to be therein admitted as hereinafter mentioned.   I do by these presents for me my heirs and successors grant and ordain that from the day of the date of these presents for-ever hereafter the members of the Monthly Meeting of the said People called Quakers in the town of Philadelphia for the time being shall have full and absolute power and authority and the same power is hereby given unto them in their respective monthly meetings from time to time to make choice of and admit such and so many persons as they shall think fit to be Overseers Masters Ushers Mistresses and poor children of the said school and the same persons or any of them to remove and displace as often as the said Meeting shall see occasion and likewise that the said Overseers shall have like powers and authority (with the direction and consent of the said Meeting) from time to time to frame and erect or cause or procure to be framed and erected such and so many houses and buildings as they shall see meet for the use and service of the said schools.   *And* moreover I do by these presents for me my heirs and successors grant and ordain that the overseers and schools aforesaid shall forever hereafter stand and be established and founded and are hereby founded erected and established in name and in deed a body politic and corporate to continue forever by the name of *The Overseers* of the Public School founded in Philadelphia at the request cost and charges of the People of God called *Quakers*.   And also that they the said overseers shall have perpetual succession and by the said name they and their successors shall forever have hold and enjoy (to the use of the said school) all the messuages lands tenements hereditaments goods and chattels and receive and take all gifts and legacies already given granted and devised or that shall be hereafter given granted or devised to the use and maintenance of the said school and masters ushers mistresses and poor scholars thereof without further or other leave license authority or power whatsoever from me my heirs or successors or from this government or any therein on that behalf saving unto me my heirs and successors the respective quit rents and other duties and payments out of the said messuages lands tenements and hereditaments and every of them reserved and payable in and by their several original grants and patents and furthermore I do by these presents for me my heirs and successors give and grant unto the said

Overseers by the name aforesaid full power license and authority to give grant bargain sell alien enfeoff or demise with the consent of the said meeting by writing under their hands and common seal (or the hands and said seal of so many of them as shall make a quorum) to such person or persons his or her heirs or their heirs executors administrators and assigns as shall be willing to purchase or rent the same all or any of the aforesaid messuages lands tenements and hereditaments goods and chattels and likewise to purchase receive and enjoy all or any other messuages houses lands tenements and hereditaments for the best advantage of the said school. *And also* to frame make and prescribe such rules orders and ordinances for the good order and government of the said school and of the masters ushers mistresses and poor children thereof successively and for their and every of their stipends salaries and allowances as to the members of the said Monthly Meeting for the time being or the major part of them (in their respective meetings) shall seem meet with power also to the said overseers by the name aforesaid to sue and be sued and to do perform and execute and suffer to be done all and every other lawful act and thing good and profitable for the said school in as full and ample manner as any other body politic or corporate more perfectly founded and incorporated may and can do. And I do for me my heirs and assigns ordain and grant that the said school and the masters ushers members officers and scholars and all other persons placed or to be placed in the said school shall forever hereafter be accepted and freed from all visitation punishment and connection to be had used or exercised by any person or persons whatsoever other than the said Overseers for the time being and their successors *In Witness* whereof I have hereunto set my hand cause the Great Seal to be affixed dated at Philadelphia the five and twentieth day of the eighth month in the thirteenth year of the reign of William the third over England etc. King etc. and the one and twentieth of my government Anno Domino one thousand seven hundred and one 1701. Recorded the 5th 10th 1701.[43]

WM. PENN.

For Aaron K. DUNKEL,
    Sec'y of Internal Affairs,
       W. B. HUSTON.

Rechartered in 1708, and 1711, extended privileges

The charter of 1701 was confirmed and enlarged by another of 1708,[44] according to which the corporation was to consist of fifteen persons (Quakers) by the name of "The Overseers of the Public School, founded in Philadelphia, at the request of, cost and charges of the people called Quakers." The

[43]William Penn's Charters for the Public School, pp. 1–8.
(A certified copy from charter in Patent Book two (2) page 202, in dept. of internal affairs, Pa.)
[44]*Ibid.*, pp. 11–19.

charter of 1711[45] contained extended privileges* and also provided that the election of new members of the board of overseers should be the right of the overseers themselves, thus constituting them a self-perpetuating corporation,[46] From this the reader might expect that the school at once became independent of the Friends' meeting, but this did not occur, since the original members or overseers were Friends and continued to appoint Friends as their successors. Reports on the various details of the business of the school continued to come into the monthly meeting, but it is not to be considered that we find there a complete story of its existence.[47] In 1699 it was found that the affairs of the school took too much time in meeting and therefore it was decided that Friends in the care of schools and press should meet on sixth day before monthly meeting, transact their business and keep a record thereof in books provided for the purpose.[48]

Made a self perpetuating corporation

The affairs of the school continued much the same as though no charter had been requested or granted. The records lead one to think that the growth was very rapid. Pastorius and Makin had become the masters in 1697 and by 1699 the indications are that "mistresses" were also employed,

---

[45]William Penn's Charters for the Public School, pp. 21–31. (See also Robert Proud's MS. papers, No. 175, p. 57.)

*In 1757 more extended privileges were desired and the following petition was sent to the Representative Assembly:

To the Rep. Assembly.

That some doubts having arisen whether from the terms of our charter we are authorized to apply any part of the estate under our care to these purposes, out of the limits of the city and county of Philadelphia.

We therefore are inclined to apply for your assistance in furthering a design of such public utility and request you to permit us to bring in a Bill for the confirmation of our present charter and enlarging the powers thereby given us, by extending them as far as to authorize our applying a part of the estate under our care towards erecting and maintaining schools on the same foundation in other parts of this province.

(P. C. S. M., I, 185)

[46]*Ibid.*, 29f; Janney, *Life of Penn*, 348.

[47]There are, no doubt, records at 304 Arch Street, which would be of great importance for a detailed history of the schools; permission to search for such records was refused at the time of this compilation. The minutes of the overseers of the P. C. S. offer a considerable amount of material history in some respects.

[48]These are the records referred to in (47).

Mistresses
employed in
schools

money being turned over to Anthony Morris to "pay the schoolmasters' and the mistresses' salaries."[49] This is the first mention made of women as teachers. Pastorius having severed his connections with the school in 1701 steps were taken to fill the vacancy, it being decided that the newcomer should show his ability by competing with the one remaining master, Thomas Makin.[50]

Cadwalader
to fill
vacancy
made by
Pastorius'
leaving

Griffith Owen . . . recommended John Cadwalader as a person very fit for an assistant in the school, and it being proposed a good method for the better improvement of the scholars that they be equally divided between them for trial to see which of them best discharged their duty, there having been great complaint of former neglect. The meeting approves thereof and desires the said Griffith to acquaint John Cadwalader thereof, and that he may have twenty pounds for a half year for a trial, as the former master had, and Anthony Morris is desired to show Thomas Makin this minute for his information in the matter.[51]

MASTERS AND MISTRESSES FROM 1700 TO 1800

Nothing like a complete or connected story can be given with reference to the masters and mistresses of this period, due to a lack of adequate available records. In August, 1701, Thomas Makin announced his intention of leaving the school and requested that his accounts be settled.[52] John Cad-

Makin plans
to leave
school

walader, who had been his assistant since 1700, was interviewed as to his ability to undertake the headship of the school; intimating if he thought himself fit, he would be further considered.[53] There is no direct record of how Mr. Cadwalader rated himself as teacher, but he was continued in the capacity of master. He found the limited salary[54]

Cadwalader
becomes
headmaster

almost too small for the support of his family and upon his request it was soon raised to fifty pounds per year.[55] At the same time the salary of a mistress, Olive Songhurst, whom we meet for the first time and with scant introduction, was increased five or ten pounds. The prospect of a higher salary

---

[49]Min. Phila. Mo. Mtg., 1—31—1699; 5—26—1700.
[50]Makin became principal in the school when Pastorius left in 1700.
[51]Min. Phila. Mo. Mtg., 1—29—1700.
[52]*Ibid.*, 8—31—1701.
[53]*Ibid.*
[54]Forty pounds a year.
[55]Min. Phila. Mo. Mtg., 1—27—1702.

does not appear to have attracted him much for we learn of his intended separation from the school in May, 1702. It is not clear that he did actually sever his connection therewith at that time, for in June, 1703, it was desired that John Cadwalader, schoolmaster, be paid ten pounds that was left by Robert Jones for the use of the Public School.[56] This sum may have been for other services such as copying, which he frequently performed,[57] but it is more probable that he was convinced of the advantages of remaining at a salary of fifty pounds per year, with the additional sums paid for the copying work.[58]

Salaries increased

John Every's connection with the school as usher is first announced in April, 1702, when he made demands for an increase of salary to thirty pounds, which was agreed to.[59] He remained there nearly two years and then departed, making a place for Thomas Makin, who returned at his request, agreeing to accept the salary previously paid to Every. These two masters, Makin and Cadwalader, appear to have been employed continuously until 1706, when they decided the school could not furnish a competent living for both of them and Cadwalader accordingly left.[60] There were further suggestions considered at that time and Friends appointed to endeavor to secure a qualified master from England. So far as the meeting's minutes record, it seems that Thomas Makin was the only master employed from 1706 to 1708, when it was suggested that Jacob Naylor be employed as a teacher.[61]

John Every, usher

Makin returns

Jacob Naylor suggested for teacher

The duties of the schoolmasters were by no means limited to the routine of the schoolroom. They were required to be careful of their several scholars and often had to do police duty among them during the meetings on first day.[62] The master's only hope for any respite from the imposition of such duties was to stand firmly for his rights, else he might have been given charge of all the children in the meeting. John Walby, a master, when asked to perform a similar service,

Extra school room duties

---

[56]Min. Phila. Mo. Mtg,. 6—27—1703.
[57]*Ibid.*, 9—26—1703.
[58]*Ibid.*, 4—26—1702.
[59]*Ibid.*
[60]*Ibid.*, 1—29—1706.
[61]*Ibid.*, 9—26—1708.
[62]*Ibid.*, 3—27—1709; 1—26—1725.

made answer that "he would take care of his own scholars, but did not care to undertake any further."[63]   His objection was sustained and another Friend endeavored to perform the task.

William Robbins

In 1711 William Robbins** came to wield the rod in Friends School, having requested permission to keep school in a part of the Friends' schoolhouse, which was "granted for the present."[64]   It cannot be determined how long he remained in that capacity, but the following year it was proposed that Richard Warden be allowed to teach school in one end of the schoolhouse, and it is quite probable that he filled the place of Robbins.[65]   On the other hand, if Robbins did leave at that time he had returned again to the school in 1715.[66]   Thomas Makin had in the meantime severed his connection with the school, but not permanently.   Seven years after the employment of Richard Warden (1719) a vacancy occurred and a committee was appointed to visit the overseers requesting them to take action regarding the vacancy.[67]   From this it may be judged that the overseers were at times remiss in their attention to their trust.   The overseers were set in action, and Thomas Makin was secured to fill the place, provided he would agree to teach six children of the poor and give up the house when Friends ordered him to do so.[68]   He doubtless filled a minor position at this time, though he was offered a better one, later in 1722, provided Richard Brockden were willing to leave it, which does not appear to have met with the said Brockden's approval.[69]   Of Richard Brockden little is known, save that he had been schoolmaster at Byberry about 1710 or 1711.[70]   In 1724 William Robbins† mentioned above as a teacher some years

Richard Warden

Thomas Makin

Richard Brockden

[63]Min. Phila. Mo. Mtg., 3—29—1730.
**The minutes of the overseers, 12—8—1712, make known hat Robbins was teaching at that time, I, 3.
[64]*Ibid.*, 3—27—1711.
[65]*Ibid.*, 2—25—1712.
[66]*Ibid.*, 8—28—1715.
[67]*Ibid.*, 11—29—1719; the vacancy was made by the departure of William Robbins out of the Province (P. C. S. M., I, 5.)
[68]*Ibid.*, 5—29—1720.   [69]*Ibid.*, 2—27—1722.
[70]Min. Abington Mo. Mtg., 4—25—1711.
†Robbins was put in charge of the school at this time, on the initiative of the monthly meeting, as the overseers recognize in their minutes of 4—3—1725, 42; they acquiesced therein.   (P. C. S. M., I, 11.)

earlier, applied for a place as master. It was agreed that he be allowed to teach on the condition that he would agree to teach at least four children for the use of the house, if ordered to do so.[71]

It is quite probable that for most of the ten years preceding 1730 the school was under the charge of three or four masters just mentioned, Robbins, Brockden, Makin and Warden. They shifted quite often, that is certain. In 1730 mention is made of a John Walby as master; but no further account of him is given.[72] Thomas Makin's career as teacher very likely came to an end in that period, as he was getting aged, though he may have taught up to the time of his death. An account of his death is given in the *Weekly Mercury* of 1733.[73]

From 1730 there is only an occasional mention made of the masters employed at the public school, until we come to the period about 1770 when the names were occasionally given in committee reports on the condition of the schools. However, with the fourth decade came a period of real greatness, for in 1742† began the services of Anthony Benezet, of whom considerable mention is made elsewhere, who continued in the public school till 1782.[74] He had throughout his life been interested in the Negroes and for several years previous had cherished a desire to work in their schools. His request, in that regard, was accordingly granted in 1782, after John Houghton relinquished that position.[75] He continued to teach the Negro school, until the time of his death two years later.[76] In 1748 Robert Willian came from England for the purpose of keeping Friends school, and was accordingly accepted into their meeting, having produced the customary certificate from his home meeting at Scarborough in York-

Margin notes:
J. Walby

Death of T. Makin

Anthony Benezet employed 1742

Robert Willian master in 1748

---

[71]Min. Phila., Mo. Mtg., 2—24—1724.
[72]*Ibid.*, 3—29—1730. Walby was engaged by the overseers in 1730 to teach (3—29—1730) the three r's and to "well instruct" four children for the use of the schoolhouse. (P. C. S. M., I, 14).
[73]*Am. Wek. Mer.*, Nov. 29—1733; Rec. Births and Burials, Phila., Mtg., A, 321.
†Benezet was employed in 1742 to teach arithmetic, writing, accounts, and French and to teach 15 poor children. (P. C. S. M., I, 33.)
[74]Simpson, *Lives of —*, 52; Min. Phila. Mo. Mtg., 5—31—1782, 28.
[75]Min. Phila. Mo. Mtg., 5—31—1782, 28.
[76]Simpson, *Lives of —*, 52.

shire.[77]   The next mention of a new master in the ranks is
concerned with Josai, who married in 1763.[78]   Encouragement was at all times given to women as teachers, mention
having already been made to their employment as early as
1699.[79]   In 1764:

Ann
Brientnall
establishes
small school

The meeting being informed that Ann Brientnall is desirous of keeping
a small school for the instruction of Friends children only in reading and
sewing and not being at present able to hire a place suitable for the
purpose, requests the use of a vacant lower room in one of the alms-
houses, and Friends approving her proposal, it is agreed that she may
make use of one of these rooms for that purpose until she can accommodate herself elsewhere, or it may be wanted (for other purposes).[80]

The recommendations of the Yearly Meeting of Philadelphia in 1778,[81] produced a very beneficial effect upon the
school affairs in all of its monthly meetings.   Thereafter,
reports were sent in, bad, good and indifferent, which were
much superior to anything that had been done previously,
though they were still too infrequent and abbreviated in
regard to information contained.   A digest of the report of
1779 follows, which shows the number of teachers in the
several schools at that time:[82]

Schools
reported
in 1779

1.   The Grammar School was presided over by John
Thompson who also taught writing and arithmetic.

2.   John Todd taught reading, English, writing, arithmetic and some branches of mathematics.

3.   Another master was Joseph Yerkes, who taught the
same branches as Todd.

4.   George Smith taught reading, writing and arithmetic
to the children of Friends and others.

5.   Anthony Benezet at this time was employed in teaching the Girls' School in which were received also the children
of other denominations besides Friends.

---

[77]Min. Phila. Mo. Mtg., 6—26—1748, 64.   It appears that John
Fothergill and John Hunt in London had signed a contract with Willian
teaching in the school, on behalf of John Kinsey and Israel Pemberton
in Philadelphia.   He was to be employed one year at 150 pounds (Pa.
currency) and the expense of his journey to the city.   He was to teach
Latin and Greek and "other parts of learning."   (P. C. S. M., I, 64).

[78]*Ibid.*, 11—25—1763, 188.

[79]See page 54.

[80]Min. Phila. Mo. Mtg., 5—25—1764, 234.

[81]Min. Phila. Yearly Mtg., 10—1778, 408 ff.

[82]Min. Phila. Mo. Mtg., 7—30—1779, 151.

6. Sarah Lancaster taught the younger children of both sexes the rudiments of learning, and other branches suitable to girls.

7. Rebecca Jones and Hannah Cathrall taught together in the same school, which was for girls, a large number of them poor.

8. A school for younger boys and girls of various societies was taught in Pine Street by Essex Flower.

9. Spelling and reading were taught the younger children by Ann Rakestraw.

It appears from the meeting's records that these masters and mistresses were all Friends, and that the schools which they taught were under the direction of the overseers of the public school.[83] Five years later another report was prepared and presented on the state of schools. At the later date several new names are found among the teachers.[84]

1. The Latin and Greek Grammar School is under the direction of Robert Proud, the historian.†

2. John Todd still continues in his old place.

3. Isaac Weaver teaches boys reading, writing, and arithmetic.

4. Sarah Lancaster continues in her old position as teacher of young children.

5. William Brown, engaged in teaching a girls' school.

Schools and teachers reported in 1784

The five schools above mentioned were under the direction of the school corporation of overseers, and poor children were taught there free of expense. The committee also reported on five other schools, whose masters and mistresses were either Friends or made the professions of that religious society.[85]

---

[83]Min. Phila. Mo. Mtg., 7—30—1779, 151.
[84]*Ibid.*, 1—30—1784, 123 ff.
†Our attention is first called to Robert Proud in 1759, when Israel Pemberton made known to the Board that he had received a letter from J. Fothergill of London recommending him (Proud) as "a person well qualified to instruct our youth in divers branches of learning." A number were named to speak with him, saying they were unanimously agreed to employ him. Proud was thus employed till 1770 when he resigned. (P. C. S. M., I, 334, and I, 175).
[85]*Ibid.*

Other
schools
reported

1. Mary Harry, teaching in Charters Alley.
2. Joseph Clarke, teaching in the girls school.
3. Mrs. Clarke (wife of Joseph).
4. Ann Marsh, teaching about fifty girls.
5. Mary McDonnell, teaching fifteen children.

This report of 1784 is the best during the century which gives a clew to the members in the teachers' ranks. The growth from a school employing one teacher to a system employing ten does not seem great when measured by our present standards of increase, but for that century it is significant of rapid growth. Many of the teachers were people of no great importance, whose names were probably never known outside of Quaker circles; others were distinctly well known. In 1799 we find one other Quaker schoolmaster mentioned, Richard Hartshorne. The idea of a boarding school for Friends' children had received quite an impetus about 1791, due largely to the interest and influence of Owen Biddle,[86] and by 1799 the school was ready to begin operations.[87] Richard Hartshorne was chosen to serve as its first superintendent and with the permission of the Monthly Meeting of Philadelphia moved to Westtown in 1799.[88]

Richard
Hartshorne
superintend-
ent of the
new school
established
at Westtown

SUPPORT OF THE SCHOOLS

From the very beginning of the schools in Philadelphia their primary means of support lay in *voluntary subscriptions*.

Three chief
means of
support

We have already seen that this was the accepted means of raising money to maintain the poor and orphans,[89] and also to build their meeting houses; it was quite the natural way, really about the only way then familiar to them for maintaining their school system. As the meeting grew and the schools also increased many members were led to believe that it was advisable to endow them with *legacies*. This being in accordance with the recommendations of the Yearly Meetings of London and Philadelphia,[90] it became quite a common

---

[86]Min. Phila. Mo. Mtg., 4—25—1791, 111.
[87]Wickersham, 91.
[88]Min. Phila. Mo. Mtg., 4—25—1799, 217.
[89]G. S. P. P., I, 252.
[90]A collection of Christian and Brotherly advices, 1753 (found in most of the depositories for records).

procedure in Philadelphia, as also in the other monthly meetings. Their third means of support was the *rate* which was paid by all children whose parents were able to bear the expense of their education.

As has been stated, subscriptions were made voluntarily, though they might be rigorously solicited, enough at least to make some feel uncomfortable who did not contribute when they were able. There are instances which might be considered as mandatory though such cases are very rare. One such occurred in 1701 when, Tobias Dinnock desiring a certificate, the meeting reported there was nothing to hinder it save that he had not paid anything toward the school.[91] This does not mean that he had to subscribe but it was doubt- less unpleasant pressure to have brought to bear on one. Subscriptions were usually made and paid at the subscriber's convenience, or on a date which he designated when making the subscription. Though this was ideally satisfactory it often failed to work out just at the right time, so it was neces- sary to appoint a committee to go out after the subscriber and get that which he had promised to pay. The first record of a committee appointed on a service of this kind was in 1691. The work of such committees was continued throughout the century, and the following extract will indicate very well their function, without further explanation or reference.

Subscrip- tions urged, but not compulsory

Subscription method not entirely satisfactory

> Whereas several of the subscriptions towards the school are unpaid, the Meeting beng engaged for the same, they have requested Alexander Beardsley, Anthony Morris, Francis Rawles, John Delavall and Samuel Richardson to use their endeavors to get what is unpaid of the said sub- scriptions, and they are desired to pay what money they receive unto Robert Turner and give account thereof to the next Monthly Meeting.[92]

The rates paid by parents in the earlier years of their colony are seen in the establishment of Flower's school in 1683.[93] The next references made to the amounts paid for instruction, under the rate system, are in the report of the school com- mittee of the Overseers in 1784.[94] Flower received four

Rates charged

---

[91]Min. Phila. Mo. Mtg., 8—31—1701.
[92]*Ibid.*, 3—29—1691; similar references, *Ibid.*, 1—31—1699; 6—30— 1700; 3—30—1701.
[93]See page 43.
[94]Min. Phila. Mo. Mtg., 1—30—1784, 123ff.

shillings per quarter for teaching reading, six shillings for reading and writing, and eight for reading, writing and casting accounts; if by the year, then everything was furnished for ten pounds. In 1784 Isaac Weaver received thirty shillings per quarter for teaching the same subjects which Flower had taught for eight.[95] William Brown also received the same amount for the same subjects which he taught the whole day.[96] Joseph Clarke was teaching for thirty shillings. For instruction in the three R's it appears that the general tendency for the cost in 1784 was about twenty-two shillings higher than it was in 1683.* Small children were taught generally at about fifteen shillings per quarter, or half the customary price for older pupils whatever that might be. The general custom was that in cases where the school corporation sent poor children to a teacher they were admitted for a lesser rate than the others; if fifteen shillings were paid by others, then ten shillings might be paid for the poor children, schooled at the trustees' expense. These prices for teaching among the Quaker masters are quite comparable with those demanded by other private masters in the city at about the same dates.[97]

As was cited previously in this work,[98] the practice of making special donations, bequests and legacies was urged by the yearly meeting as a proper means of support for the schools or other institutions. These recommendations of te yearly meeting which were written in the form of letters, were

Special bequests and legacies recommended and their probable effect

transmitted to the quarterly meetings and through them reached all members of the monthly and preparative meetings in the compass of the general assembly. It cannot be doubted that they were a very important means to instill a desire to give to a worthy cause, and the very similar procedure in all monthly meetings seems to indicate that they constituted the most effectual means for getting anything definite done towards establishing any permanent foundation.

---

[95]Min. Phila. Mo. Mtg., 1—30—1784, 123 ff.
[96]*Ibid.*
*The reader will recall, however, that in 1874 the real was far below the face value.
[97]*Pa. Gaz.*, 1772, No. 2285; *Pa. Gaz.* and *Wk. Advt.*, 1783, No. 2782; *Pa. Gaz.* and *Wk. Advt., Supplement,* 1784, No. 2811.
[98]See page 60, note 90.

Nothing in the way of a complete survey of various legacies and donations given to the schools in Philadelphia will be attempted here, even granting that it might be interesting enough, but a few of them will be treated briefly. The first example of this individual philanthropy came before the monthly meeting in 1699, when the will of John Lineham was read, by which he proposed to leave "twenty pounds for the use of the public school."[99] This sum was not to be expended at once for present needs but was to be kept as a "stock forever for that use." Two members, John Kinsey and Ralph Jackson, were ordered to pay in the said amount that it might be turned over to Edward Shippen the treasurer. Other legacies were left by Robert Wade[100] and Mary Richards.[101] In regard to the former there was trouble about getting it settled, which lasted for many years.[102] The above names are only a few of the many who are mentioned by the minutes up to 1700 as having left donations for the school. There were indeed many others. In that year (1702) it was considered advisable that an account be kept of all legacies which had been granted to the use of the public school, as also those granted for the poor. Isaac Norris was appointed to prepare this account. Its purpose was probably to straighten out the tangle into which some of them had fallen (especially that of Robert Wade) and that one man might be held responsible for the expenditure of funds. No funds were to be paid out for the use of schools by Norris, except on the order of the overseers. Funds for the poor might be expended at the order of the monthly meeting.[103]

Will of John Lineham

Legacies of Wade and Richards

The appointment of some one to see that an account of legacies be kept, resulted in some investigation of those already granted. It appears that that of Robert Wade, who probably died before 1686,[104] had not been paid at all according to the stipulation of the donor, which stated that £5 should be paid yearly for the use of the school. The first

[99]Min. Phila., Mo. Mtg., 3—26—1699.
[100]*Ibid.*, 12—28—1702.
[101]*Ibid.*, 11—29—1702.
[102]*Ibid.*, 1—28—1707.
[103]*Ibid.*, 11—29—1702.
[104]No record of his death is found in Records of Births and Deaths beginning with 1686.

record of a payment of the £5 was in 1699.[105] David Lloyd
and John Jones were accordingly appointed to attend to
it.[106] Their success does not seem to have been very marked
as in 1704 the minute again urges them to treat with John
Wade (brother) concerning the legacy.[107] This was done,
but their efforts met with a refusal to pay the money,[108] so a
committee of three Friends was appointed with others to

**Trouble over
the R. Wade
legacy**

advise whether it should be sued for or not. Such activity
continued without any significant variant features until 1707,
when it was proposed by those "concerned," presumably his
brother, to buy off the legacy. Having been unpaid for
several years past, it was considered best that something be
gotten out of it, so a committee of three of the overseers was
appointed to treat with the buyers and make as satisfactory
terms as they could.[109] The minutes point to the fact that
it was not settled to any one's satisfaction. In 1712 it was
still before the meeting and again in 1727 the overseers are
directed to use "their care to get the legacy left by Robert
Wade secured."[110] Among other legacies, obtained more
easily, was one devised by Jonas Langford, which was brought
to the attention of the meeting in 1711. The amount of it
was £50 in Antigua money.

The Public School, established by charter, was not the only
recipient of such permanent endowments. The Negro

**Negro school
likewise
received
gifts**

School was a popular and proper object of philanthropy and
was benefited by bequests very early after its establishment
in 1770.[111] The first donation came in 1771 when £2, Pennsylvania currency, were given to Israel Pemberton and
Anthony Benezet or their executors to be appropriated for
the promotion of the school for Negroes, and to be paid to
such trustees as might be appointed to the care of the said
school.[112] In the year following another legacy of £10 was

---

[105]Min. Phila. Mo. Mtg., 2—28—1699.
[106]*Ibid.*, 12—28—1702.
[107]*Ibid.*, 4—30—1704.
[108]*Ibid.*, 7—28—1704, 420.
[109]*Ibid.*, 1—28—1707.
[110]*Ibid.*, 11—26—1727-8.
[111]See page 243f.
[112]Min. Phila. Mo. Mtg., 4—26—1771, 444.

left for the instruction of the Negroes, and paid to Richard Blackham, treasurer of that institution.[113] Anthony Benezet at his death left a considerable sum as a legacy, which, added to the amount of salary which was still owing him for services in the said school, had amounted by 1800 to £103 and 4s.[114] The amount of other donations to that institution up to date amounted to £117/5/11.[115]

In addition to the ways already mentioned there was also occasional recourse to a *bond* issue for raising funds, but the last was not common, being used only in emergency cases. The first example of it, which has come to the writer's attention, was in 1701, when it had been decided to build a school house and the work being begun, a lack of funds occurred which prevented continuing. To meet this emergency it was agreed that the committee having charge of the financial matters should "take up 100 pounds upon interest for one year, giving bond jointly for the same and this meeting does engage to indemnify them for the payment."[116]

Funds also raised by bonds, rarely

BUILDINGS AND GROUNDS

Various items on buildings and grounds occupy a considerable amount of attention on the part of the monthly meeting though the minutes are usually of general nature. The place of Keith's school (1689) was doubtless no more than an ordinary house procured for the use of his family and the school at the same time.[117] This proved satisfactory only for a short time, and to remedy Keith's complaint (1690)[118] of its "straightness" another more convenient room was arranged for by the committee with John Fuller for the rent of £13 a year. The former had cost but ten.[119] It is likely that the school continued to be held in the same house, others similarly, for about seven years; there is, at any rate, no mention of change of place or location for that period of

Place of first school

[113]Min. Phila. Mo. Mtg., 12—25—1772, 145.
[114]*Ibid.*, 11—2—1800, 300.
[115]*Ibid.*
[116]*Ibid.*, 9—28—1701, 315.
[117]*Ibid.*, 5—26—1689, 154.
[118]*Ibid.*, 1—28—1690, 163.
[119]*Ibid.*, 2—26—1690, 164.

School in
loft of the
meeting
house

time.   At the end of that time the meeting made preparation to receive the school into the "inner chamber over the meeting house," the expense of fitting it up being paid out of the meeting's stock.[120]   It was in this school in the loft of the meeting house that Daniel Pastorius and Thomas Makin first taught the school together.[121]   The meeting house served thus as schoolhouse until early in the year 1698, when property was purchased for the purpose, the meeting minute of the transaction being as follows:

Property
purchased
for the
Public School

Whereas Friends have purchased an house and lot of Lionell Brittain for the service of the public schools, according to that has already been agreed to by this meeting, and the said purchase is approved, and David Lloyd is desired to draw the writings for confirmation of the same unto Edward Shippen until he be secured the money, and then he to reconvey it again for the use aforesaid.[122]

First record
of house
built for
school

In 1701 we find the first record for building a house for the sole use of the school, presumably on the lot previously purchased by the meeting.[123]   Robert Burrough and Nathaniel Edgcomb were appointed to get the subscription for the building and pay to Anthony Morris, who was to agree with suitable workmen for the building.[124]   The dimensions, "20 feet wide by 60 feet long," were, at first consideration, thought to be satisfactory, but it was finally decided to build it 24 feet by 60 feet.[125]   The work was at first to be supported by subscriptions, but before its completion it became necessary to issue bonds for the amount of £100.[126]

Property
acquired
by gift

The acquisition of property, this time by gift, continued. In 1701, Daniel Lloyd reported that a deed for the lot in High Street, given by Samuel Carpenter to Friends for the use of the free school, was signed to the said Samuel, and the meeting directed him to get another drawn to the overseers of the school.[127]   It might easily appear that the new schoolhouse, just proposed, was to be built on this lot and not that pre-

---

[120]Min. Phila. Mo. Mtg., 11—28—1697, 227.
[121]*Ibid.*
[122]*Ibid.*, 2—29—1698, 229.
[123]*Ibid.*, 2—25—1701, 292.
[124]*Ibid.*, 3—30—1701, 294.
[125]*Ibid.*, 4—27—1701, 298.
[126]*Ibid.*, 9—28—1701, 315.
[127]*Ibid.*, 11—30—1701, 322.

viously purchased of Lionell Brittain. After due consideration it seems, however, that the greater weight is in favor of
its having been built on the Lionell tract. The minutes show
that as late as 2d month, 24th, 1708, the deed for the lot from
Samuel Carpenter to the meeting had not been drawn up.[128]
But as was previously mentioned, Anthony Morris had been
told to engage workmen (3d, 30th, 1701)[129] and the statement
that £100 had to be raised by bond to carry on the work
(2nd month, 28th, 1701)[130] would indicate that the work had
actually been begun and was perhaps well towards completion
by the end of that year. It seems quite impossible that any
such building program would have been carried on so long
before the transfer of property was properly drawn up and
signed. The years 1704 and 1705 are busy with the details
of getting several pieces of property, purchased and received
as gifts, confirmed by the commissioners of property.[131]
Late in 1705 it is stated:

> All is done, viz.: a patent for a front lot, a High Street lot and
> twenty acres of liberty land and also a patent for a bank lot. . . .
> But this meeting house, ground and schoolhouse ground, being only in
> the name of Edward Shippen, in case of mortality, Friends think there is
> a necessity for a speedy reconveying thereof to more hands and for the
> particular use intended . . . . desired that the said Edward
> Shippen may convey them to Samuel Carpenter, R. Hill and Anthony
> Morris, being the persons in whose name the Patents are granted unto,
> adding the names of all the overseers of the Free School in the part
> belonging to the said school.[132]

Property confirmed

Some light is thrown upon the interior arrangement of the
school. In 1712 Thomas Griffith was ordered to pay
Christer Thomason 12 for "making" a stove in the schoolhouse,[133] presumably an old fashioned brick stove, such as a
few years later was condemned by William Robbins as being
"injurious to many of the scholars."[134] Mr. Robbins proposed that a "chimney might be erected," and Samuel
Preston was appointed to have it done, if not inconvenient

Heating facilities

[128]Min. Phila. Mo. Mtg., 2—24—1702, 329.
[129]See page 60.
[130]See page 66.
[131]See the minutes from 1704 and 1705, pages 420 to 463, various items.
[132]Min. Phila. Mo. Mtg., 10—28—1705, 463.
[133]*Ibid.*, 2—25—1712, 222.
[134]*Ibid.*, 8—28—1715.

or expensive. He reported that it would be a greater charge than represented and would hardly answer the end proposed nearly so satisfactorily as an iron stove, which he had thought necessary and had accordingly had set up, to be removed however if the meeting did not approve of his action.[135]   The charge for the iron stove was £7.[136] Such items as the foregoing were brought up in the monthly meeting which appointed some one to attend to this or that detail; as the schools grew these were left more in the hands of the school committee or overseers, who reported occasionally thereon.

An iron stove placed in the school

This tendency on the part of the meeting to turn over the details of management to the overseers came to a head about 1725,* when it was agreed by the meeting that all titles to the schoolhouses and other property be conveyed the overseers of the public schools and a minute be drawn up relating to such decision.[137]   In the month following, the minutes of the committee's report were made referring to the transfer:

Overseers assume greater responsibility

Anthony Morris, Ebenezer Sorge, Samuel Powell and Jones being appointed by the Monthly Meeting of Philadelphia the 2—30—1725, to meet with the overseers of the public school, do acquaint them that the said meeting being concerned for the promotion of the public school have unanimously agreed that the title of the school house and ground with the lots, tenements . . . . now in the tenure of Evan Owen and Thomas Cannon with all the other titles of real estate and annuities appertaining to the public school, be vested in the overseers thereof and desire for the future distinct accounts may be kept of all legacies and donations made to the said schools in order that the same may be duly applied pursuant to the intentions of the donors respectively.

Titles to property to be transferred to the overseers

Then follows a minute of the overseers stating their appreciation of the meeting's coöperation in the work of the school.

The Monthly Meeting of Philadelphia expressing the same kind inclination to encourage that at first led them to erect the public school and to procure the same to be established by the proprietor's charter, as it is now under the care of the present overseers, having thought it neces-

An account of funds to be made

---

[135]Min. Phila. Mo. Mtg., 9—25—1715, 10f.

[136]*Ibid.*, 10—30—1715, 11.

*The overseers of the school had kept a regular record of their meeting in regard to schools, since 1712; they were, however, closely associated with the monthly meeting in the school affairs.   (P. C. S. M., I, first record in 1712.)

[137]*Ibid.*, 2—30—1725, 119.

sary that an exact account should be taken of all the benefactions intended by the several donors for the use of the said school, the moneys or effects whereof might have come under the direction of the said meeting. In order thereunto appointed some friends to adjust the said accounts with the overseers, which being carefully done, it appears the meeting has received of such benefactions as aforesaid for the use of the school the sum of £226. . . . and that they expended in the building the school house which was begun, carried on and finished under their care and direction the sum of £264 and 3d, whereby the meeting is in disburse for the public schoolhouse, above what they received in the sum of £37/15/3, which last sum or balance they were pleased freely to . . . . grant and release to the said school, together with the lot belonging to it and all those (equipages) and tenements now in the occupation of Evan Owen and Thomas Cannon with their appurtenances and all the rents, profits and issues thereof, and have accordingly ordered the persons who are by legal deeds or instruments vested with the right to the said tenements in trust for the meeting to (grant) and absolutely convey the said schoolhouse and . . . . with the lots and grounds on which they stand and appurtenances to the overseers of the school, to be held by them and their successors for the use of the public school founded by charter in the town and county of Philadelphia in Pennsylvania, forever.[138]

This transfer was at once acknowledged by the overseers in a minute of the same date, and Thomas Griffiths and John Goodson were desired to execute the proper papers conveying the properties to the said overseers of the public schools, which was accordingly done before the next meeting (4th month, 1725).[139] — Papers to be executed conveying the properties

By this time (1733) the old building erected in 1701 was badly in need of repairs, but on a closer examination it was decided more economical to pull down the old and build a new one, more convenient, on the north side of the school lot.[140] — New building proposed

The work was begun immediately, though a lack of funds hindered its completion for some time.[141] The demand for an increase of building space seems to have been regular and urgent, indicating a healthy growth of the system. In 1740, when the consideration for a new meeting house came up, it was decided to build it large, "with chambers over it commo- — and begun / New meeting house built large to contain school rooms

---

[138]Min. Phila. Mo. Mtg., 3—28—1725, 121 ff.
[139]*Ibid.*, 4—25—1725, 124.
[140]*Ibid.*, 12—22—1733-4, 142.
[141]*Ibid.*, 4—25—1736, 271.

dious for school rooms."[142]   In 1744 the overseers, finding the old school building inconvenient in divers respects, requested the monthly meeting to name a committee to confer with them on a plan, location and dimensions of a new building. Michael Lightfoot and twelve others were named.[143]   The committee decided to locate the building on the south side of the lot devised by William Forest, the dimensions to be about 60 feet by 35 feet in the clear and two stories high, also a cellar under it, rising three feet above the surface of the ground. This quite pretentious building was not to be finished entirely at this time.   The plan was to enclose all of it and finish the interior as the size of the school demanded.[144]

For twelve years apparently no further building projects were launched.   Then the overseers appealed to the meeting

New school building requested on the Fox lot

for permission to erect a school on the middle of the lot left to them by George Fox.   This was agreed to by that assembly and a committee named to remove the present incumbent of the lot who had not paid the rent for some years past.[145] Their next building was begun, not for the purpose of a place of instruction, but as investment: It was proposed to the monthly assembly in 1760 that several houses be erected on the schoolhouse lot fronting Chestnut Street, expenses defrayed out of the treasury of the overseers, for the purpose

Tenement buildings erected on lots as an investment for the school

of increasing the yearly income of the property.[146]   The suggestion was well received and the liberty granted to erect one or more such houses.[147]   In 1767 the accommodations for the Girls' School, being unsatisfactory, the overseers of the school requested permission to have the chamber of the meeting house fitted up as a place for them, which was taken under consideration by a committee of the meeting appointed for that purpose.[148]

The Negro School, established 1770, was first housed in a building rented for that use,[149] in which it continued for

---

[142]Min. Phila. Mo. Mtg., 5—25—1740, 318.
[143]*Ibid.*, 10—28—1744, 378.
[144]*Ibid.*, 11—25—1744, 379.
[145]*Ibid.*, 8—27—1756, 243.
[146]*Ibid.*, 4—25—1760, 248 ff.
[147]*Ibid.*, 6—27—1760, 259.
[148]*Ibid.*, 11—27—1767, 199.
[149]*Ibid.*, 6—29—1770, 398.

nearly a year. The plans for a permanent school made a building for that purpose desirable, and in 1771 the committee on education of the Negroes requested that a house be built on the lot where the alms-houses were situated, which was granted.[150] This house was occupied by the school until charge of it was assumed by Anthony Benezet (1782), who held the school in his own house.[151]

In the foregoing pages we have mentioned some of the facts of the establishment and development of the school in Philadelphia, with reference to (1) founding, (2) support, (3) masters, (4) properties, buildings and grounds. It is deemed advisable to omit from this chapter any presentation of curriculum, excepting as that has been mentioned at a few places, reserving such presentation to a chapter comprising all the schools established in Pennsylvania. As a fitting close to the previous discussion of the century's development, we present, almost entire, one of the reports returned by the committee of the meeting, which in a fair way will tell the reader more about the growth up to, and the status of the system in 1784, than will any discussion. Portions of the report are discussed in other chapters.

The schools under their direction and care within the limits of this meeting, are:

(1) One under the tuition of Robert Proud, by whom about 30 boys are instructed in the Latin and Greek languages and some branches of the mathematics; his salary is fixed at £250 per annum, having an usher who is allowed £80 per annum, at the expense of the estate under the care of the overseers. The present £6 per annum for each scholar for which he accounts to the said overseers and has for one year past received one Guinea entrance to his own use and charges 5/ for fuel. We had some conversation with him on the case necessary to guard against the use of such books, whose contents have a tendency to prepossess the youthful minds with sentiments unfavorable to the Christian faith and the true spirit of the gospel; which appears had his attention, having observed a care therein agreeable to what the occasion requires. In this school are read Barclay's *Apology* in Latin and the Testament in Latin and Greek. The overseers have enjoined the attendance of the scholars who are chiefly members of our own religious society, at our meeting on the fifth day of the week, but it had not been sufficiently observed.

---

[150]Min. Phila. Mo. Mtg., 1—25—1771, 430.
[151]*Ibid.*, 5—31—1782, 28.

(2)   One under the care of John Todd, in which are taught reading, writing, the English Grammar, Arithmetic and some other branches of the mathematics. It consists of 88 boys on this list, for 83 of whom he has 20/ per quarter, 2/6 for pen and ink, 5/ for fuel; on the entrance of each 15/ except where the parents or guardians are not of ability to afford it, the other 5 being put to him by the school corporation, he teaches for 10/ per quarter. He remarked there are each day about 70 together. The master appears careful to observe good order in his school and frequently attends our meeting on the 5th day with his scholars. He also kept a night school in the winter season consisting of 82 scholars.

(3)   One by Isaac Weaver consisting of about 28 boys, being limited to 10/ per quarter, 2/6 for pen and ink and 5/ a year for fuel, he takes no entrance fee and teaches reading, writing, and arithmetic, and is careful to keep good order in the school, also frequently brings his scholars to the meeting fifth day.

(4)   William Brown teaches girls reading, writing and arithmetic, language, 8 whole days at 30/ per quarter 14 in mornings 15/ per quarter 13 in afternoon 15/ per quarter and for some time has been in the practice of taking 7/6 entrance fee, except for those placed with him by the school corporation—he represents some difficulty in enforcing the rules and regulations provided for the schools on account of the greater number of his scholars children of persons not professing with us.

(5)   Sarah Lancaster has a school for young children of both sexes consisting of about 64 scholars of whom:

35 attend whole days at 15/ per Q.

18 attend, sent by school corporation, 10/ per Q.

11 attend half days, also sent by them, 7/6 per Q.

Also pay for fuel. She teaches both sexes to spell and read and the girls to sew and appears to have an orderly school.

In all the foregoing schools, which are under the direction of the school corporation, 41 poor children are taught at their expense. We also visited the following schools, the masters and mistresses of which are either members or make profession with our religious society, but are not immediately under the care of the board. (I give here only a digest of their report).

(1)   Mary Harry.
  School in Charters Alley; 15–16 children at 15/ per Q.
  Income is about 40 pounds per year.
  Not a Friend but attends our meetings.

(2)   Joseph Clarke.
  School in Fifth St.; about 30 girls.
  Curriculum—reading, writing and arithmetic.
  For 25 he receives 30/ per Q. and others gratis.

(3)   Mrs. Clarke (wife) and Joseph Clarke.
  Same house; 15–16 boys reading; and the girls, sewing at 15/ per Q. each; they try to attend our fifth day meetings.

(4) Anna Marsh.

  50 (approximately) girls and boys.

  Taught reading, and the girls, needlework; 20/ per Q.

  Each has a right of membership with Friends.

(5) Mary McDonnell.

  15 young children at 15/ per Q.

In the most of the schools there are nearly one-half if not more of the children of the people of the societies and we wish Friends children may not be too frequently excluded for want of room, evident inconvenience being very observable in the present mixed state of schools, it is much to be desired that a more select mode of education could be effectually promoted; in the meantime it would be well that master be not too lax in the observance of the rules.[152]

The other item of very great interest, though not in reality immediately connected with the schools in Philadelphia, concerns the establishment of a boarding school, which was to be founded and planned after one of the oldest and largest schools of the society, the great Ackworth School in England.[153] The project was greatly encouraged by Owen Biddle, who (6th month, 10th, 1790) published a pamphlet of 52 pages in which the plea for such a school was elaborated.[154] A committee was appointed to confer with him, and reported they wished to present their wishes also to the other monthly meetings of the city,[155] and they concurring, to present the wishes of the monthly meetings to the quarterly and so on to the yearly meeting.[156] The report, when presented to the other two monthly meetings, met with favor,[157] and it was accordingly agreed (1792) to bring the matter before the quarterly meeting.[158] The approval of the quarterly and yearly meetings* in the time immediately ensuing resulted in the plans being set on foot for a subscription of £5000 and which was made open to all members of the yearly meeting in whatsoever quarter; the amount of these,

Boarding school encouraged by Owen Biddle

Approved by quarterly and yearly meetings

[152]Report of Committee in Phila. Mo. Mtg. Min. 1—30—1784, 123 ff.
[153]See Thompson, Henry. *A History of Ackworth.*
[154]This pamphlet may be seen in H. S. P., Philadelphia.
[155]Min. Phila. Mo. Mtg., 4—25—1791, 111.
[156]*Ibid.*, 6—24—1791, 118.
[157]*Ibid.*, 7—27—1791, 123.
[158]*Ibid.*, 1—27—1792, 140.
*Minute, Yearly Meeting, held in Philadelphia, 9th and 10th mos. 1794.

in 1797, was £247/10.[159]. The school established at Westtown on the tract of land purchased by the yearly meeting,
was opened in 1800,[160] with Richard Hartshorne as the first
superintendent.[161] Rules and regulations for its conduct had
been drawn up by a committee appointed by the yearly meeting in 1794.*

Rules drawn
up therefor

OTHER SCHOOLS IN PHILADELPHIA COUNTY

The date of the first school in Byberry has not been
definitely determined, though it can surely be placed at a very
early period in its history, as early as 1710 or 1711. Richard
Brockden, who later taught school in Philadelphia,[162] was a
teacher in the school at Byberry, for a minute of Abington
monthly meeting states in the 4th month of the later year
that "At this meeting Richard Brockden, late schoolmaster
at Byberry, had a certificate granted him in order to go to
England."[163]

First school
probably as
early as 1710
or 1711

This would indicate that the said Richard had been teaching at Byberry, and it is quite probable that he had, but it is
not conclusive evidence that he did so. About the middle
of the eighteenth century the Byberry Meeting became very
active in schooling the children of poor Friends. This movement, it seems from all records found, was due in large
measure to an apportionment received from a legacy left by
William Carter to the charge of Abington Meeting, for the
schooling of the children of Friends in poverty.[164] In 1755,
it was:

Greater
activity
near middle
of century

. . . . agreed that Horsham, Germantown, Byberry meetings
shall have 40 shillings each for the ensuing year, and Oxford twenty
shillings, Abington three pounds for the same time, (of the annuity left
by William Carter) in order that the same may be employed in paying
for the schooling of such children as the said meetings may think proper
objects thereof if they find any, and the Friends of the said meeting are

[159]Min. Phila. Mo. Mtg., 7—28—1797, 158.
[160]See history of Westtown School.
[161]Min. Phila. Mo. Mtg., 4—26—1799, 217.
*Minute, Yearly Meeting, held in Philadelphia, 9th and 10th mos.
1794.
[162]Min. Phila. Mo. Mtg., 1—3—1722, 83.
[163]Min. Abington Mo. Mtg., 4—25—1711, 73.
[164]*Ibid.*, 1—27—1749, 50.

desired to see that the same be well applied and that the children who partake of the benefit thereof do go regularly to school.[165]

The money thus devised to the meeting was in the care of the committee appointed by the same, whose duty it was to receive requests and to investigate all cases where help was requested or found to be necessary. The accounts of the said committee were audited at a period when necessary by Friends appointed especially for that purpose.[166] This form of philanthropy became very popular here, as in other meetings, almost every meeting bearing forward a new record of it. In 1758 James Thorntown and Giles Knight reported that they had received of James Paul (treasurer of Abington Monthly Meeting) the sum of £6, part of the donation left for the poor children's schooling, and had applied £2/5 of the same to that use, leaving a remainder of £3/15 in the hands of Knight.[167] In 1770 the records run in this manner:

Donations under care of trustees, used for schooling poor

It appears that Phillip Wells stands in need of some of the moneys that were given to the use of schooling poor Friends children; Thomas Townsend is therefore ordered to pay forty shillings of the money in his hands.[168]

Though very few references are made throughout the early period of the schools, it is quite certain from the nature of these reports on education of the poor that the schools were continued regularly. When the yearly meeting began to demand reports on the condition of the schools, there was on stir about the matter whatever, the first report being that those who have our school under care "report that it is in good order."[169] The requests coming into the preparative meeting for information on schools, were referred to the standing school committee.[170]

The standing committee performed all duties in connection with the school, with the exception of certain cases of difficulty, where it was necessary to call on the meeting for assistance, at which time that body coöperated with them

Case of schools under standing committee

[165]Min. Abington Mo. Mtg., 8—215—755, 151.
[166]Min. Byberry Prep. Mtg., 4—24—1793.
[167]*Ibid.*, 8—23—1758.
[168]*Ibid.*, 12—6—1770.
[169]*Ibid.*, 7—25—1787.
[170]Min. Abington Mo. Mtg., 5—21—1788.

through specially appointed committees.[171]   The Byberry
Preparative Meeting was, of course, not independent in this
matter of school organization; their place was very much in
accord with that suggested by a committee report to the
various preparative meetings in 1790:

General plan
for encour-
agement of
better schools

We of the committee appointed to attend the preparative meetings
with the extracts in order to spread the concern of our last yearly
meeting, have attended to the appointment and taken into due consideration that part of them relating to schools, and being desirous to adopt
it in so far as our present circumstances will admit, and in order to
encourage any charitably disposed persons who may incline in their last
will and testament or otherwise to give or bequeath something towards
so laudable a purpose as to raise a certain fixed union for the support of
schools, it is our desire that it may be safely counted to the care of the
preparative meetings, he or she appointing, if they see fit, their own
trustees and that Friends earnestly endeavor to provide for the schoolmasters a house lot, ground, etc., either purchasing or renting, whenever
it may be necessary, and that our minds being deeply impressed with a
sense that a guarded religious education of the rising youth is a matter
of great importance it is our sense of judgment that Friends within the
compass of this meeting should be pressingly urged to consider the
necessity of employing conscientious and pious persons as schoolmasters,
being members of a religious society and that the preparative meeting
continue to appoint committees from time to time as occasion may
require to have the care and oversight of such schools and that they
visit the respective schools at least once in six weeks to see that good
order be observed, and for the encouragement of the children in their
learning, and render an account thereof to the preparative meeting once
in six months. Signed the 28th of the 4th month, 1790.

By SAMUEL GUMMERE, SILAS WALMSLEY, THOS. WALMSLEY,
JOHN TOWNSEND and NAYLOR WEBSTER.[172]

In the month following the reception of these suggestions
from the monthly meeting's committee, the Byberry school
trustees made the following report on the conditions of the
schools, and the nature of their own activities.

Byberry
report on
schools

We, the trustees appointed by the meeting to have the care of the
schools under the direction of the meeting, do inform, agreeable to our
trust, we have several times met within the year past at the school in
order to encourage the children in their learning, also to see that good
order be kept by the master and children and we believe this a good
measure complied with, and we further inform, that we have en-

[171]Min. Abington Mo. Mtg., 10—22—1788.
[172]*Ibid.*, 6—23—1790.

deavored to comply with the intentions of the donor, by distributing the donations of William Carter, by schooling such children as we apprehended proper objects and have engaged as many as to take most of the money now in hand. (Clerk asked to give the committee a copy of the monthly meetings extracts that they comply with the regulations concerning schools.)[173]

The gist of their report six months thereafter is as follows:[174]

Summary of a later report

1. The trustees have met several times at the school in the last six months.

2. Afternoons are usually spent hearing the scholars read and in examining their learning.

3. The masters keep strictly the rules, which the trustees have laid down.

4. We believe the school is kept in good order.

In 1792 it was considered necessary to enlarge the schoolhouse to make adequate facilities for the increasing number of children. The committee appointed on the subject decided there should be an addition of ten feet for the length; their suggestion was approved and a subscription begun to carry forward the work as speedily as could be done.[175] Thomas Walmsley was appointed to have oversight of the work.[176] The status of the school at the end of the century is stated in the report to Horsham Monthly Meeting, as follows:

School house to be enlarged

We have one school under the care of the meeting, to which our members send their children, except some Friends who live remote. It is supported by subscription; the tutor is a Friend and we believe endeavors to discharge the important trust committed to him. The children of such as are in straightened circumstances are schooled by donations left for that purpose—A committee appointed by the meeting frequently visits the said school and reports the state thereof.[177]

School's status at end of century

GERMANTOWN

It has already been mentioned that Francis Daniel Pastorius taught in the Friends School at Philadelphia during the period from 1697 to 1700.[178] While in the school at Phila-

Pastorius in Philadelphia

---

[173]Min. Abington Mo. Mtg., 7—21—1790.
[174]*Ibid.*, 1—26—1791.
[175]*Ibid.*, 6—20—1792.
[176]*Ibid.*, 7—25—1792.
[177]Min. Horsham Mo. Mtg., 3—29—1797; Min. Byberry Prep. Mtg., 3—22—1797.
[178]Phila. Mo. Mtg., 1—29—1700.

delphia it appears that he left his residence at Germantown vacant and took up his abode in the city. The following letter, written by his children, to their grandfather in Windsheim, indicates their longing for their "own home" at Germantown and the tedium of their school days in the Philadelphia school.

Wir Wünschen gar offt bey dir zu seyn /ach dass du hier wärest und in unserm Hause zu Germanton Wohntest /welches einen schönen Obsgarten hat/ und der Zeit leer stehet/ indeme wir zu Philadelphia wohnen /und täglich 8 Stunden lang in die Schul gehen müssen / ausgenommen den letzen Tag in der Wochen/ da wir Nachmittag daheim bleiben dörffen.[179]

Early school at Germantown

The school at Germantown was opened on January 11, 1702, though Dr. Seidensticher thinks that this must have been preceded for some time by an evening school.[180]

Contributors

The first overseers chosen were Aret Klincken, Peter Schumacher, and Paul Wulff.[181] Those who contributed voluntarily to the school were: Anton Loof, Peter Schumacher, Paul Wulff, Jacob Delaplaine, Jonas Potts, Isaak Schumacher, Walter Simons, Levin Herberdink, Johann Bleikers, Dirck Jansen . . . Johannas Umstett, Heifert Papen, Jan Lensen, Peter Bon, Hermann Bon, Dirck Keyser, Claus Tamson, Gerhard Ruttinghusen (and two others whose names can not be deciphered).[182]

Patrons of the school

The patrons of the school for the first year were: Aret Klincken, Reinert Tysen, Tünes Künders, Wilhelm Strepers, Paul Kästner, Reinier Hermans, Abraham op de Graeff, Christian Warmer, Arnold van Vossen, Johann Cunrad Codweiss, Cornelis Sivert, Aret Küster, Jan Doeden and Lanert Arets.[183]

Tuition

The school admitted both boys and girls for instruction. The amounts paid by voluntary contributors varied from 2/ to 15/ per year, while the tuition charged was from 4d. to 6d. per week.[184] The evening school was intended for those

---

[179]Quoted from Learned, *Pastorius*, 181.
[180]*Der Deutsche Pioneer*, III, 56.
[181]*Ibid.*
[182]*Ibid.*
[183]Learned, 182.
[184]*Der Deutsche Pioneer*, III, 56.

who were forced to work during the day time, or for others who, because of their age, could not enter the regular day school.[185] Among the patrons from 1706–1708 there are to be found a great number of English names,[186] which may no doubt indicate that the school under the German master was recognized by English inhabitants to be of very high standard. His experience in Philadelphia would speak for that. Evening school

Some question has been raised as to whether Pastorius taught the school in the English or the German tongue. Though in his manuscript it is found that he did use somewhat broken English,[187] we know that he taught the English school at Philadelphia, where most of the children were English.[188] The majority of his pupils at Germantown were, of course, German,[189] and doubtless German was spoken between them and the teacher at times. The fact, however, that the titles of Pastorius' school books were written in English, is pointed out by Seidensticker as an indication that the language of the province was given preference in the school.[190] It is also to be noted that the General Court had in 1696 ordered that the minutes of the Ratsbuch be transscribed into English, lending further evidence to the idea that the importance of the official language was recognized.[191] The length of continuation of the Friends' school at Germantown is not known, though it seems likely that Pastorius may have continued in its service till the time of his death, or at least until 1718.[192] The school probably taught in English

SCHOOLS AT EXETER MONTHLY MEETING

Exeter Monthly Meeting, established 1737, being set off from Gwynedd Monthly,[193] did not have any schools under their jurisdiction at a very early date. The first indication that the subject of education was being seriously considered

---

[185]*Der Deutsche Pioneer.*
[186]*Ibid.*, 57.
[187]See MS. collection of Pastorius. H. S. P.
[188]See page 77f.
[189]*Der Deutsche Pioneer*, III, 56.
[190]*Ibi l.*
[191]Learned, 185.
[192]*Der Deutsche Pioneer*, III, 58.
[193]Bunting, *List of Records for Phila. Yr. Mtg.*, 21.

was about 1758 when youths' meetings were established, two
each year, one at Exeter and the other at Maiden Creek.[194]
These youths' meetings, sanctioned by the quarterly meeting,[195] and another at Robeson several years later,[196] were the
first steps taken for education of youth, and controlled by the
meeting.   It is true, there was a school (day school) even at
this time situated near Samuel Lea's, as we learn from a chance
reference,[197] but though it was attended by Friends' children
in part, it was neither controlled by them, nor under the
monthly meeting.   This condition lasted until the recommendations of the yearly meeting of 1777 and 1778 caused the
monthly meeting to look into the educational situation.

In accord with the recommendations concerning "the
proper education of youth" published in these years, and sent

out, the meeting at Exeter appointed Samuel Hughes, Abel
Thomas, Benjamin Pearson, Mordecai Lee, James Thomas
and John Scarlet to take the question under their consideration.[198]   For two years and a half the substance of the reports
of the above named committee and its successors, was to the
effect that not much had been accomplished.[199]   In 1781 the
committee reported they had visited the preparative meetings
(two of them), and recommended to them the careful consideration of the youths' education, under good moral tutors.[200]
A year later, the committee was released, having, according to
reports, accomplished nothing.[201]   Those delegates who
attended the quarterly meeting in 1783, brought back new
advices, and were directed to furnish each preparative
meeting with a copy and request a report on school conditions
among them;   at the following monthly assembly more of

the preparatives were ready to report.[202]   Despairing of any
report, unless of their own making, the monthly meeting
appointed a committee of nine men to visit all the prepara-

[194]Min. Exeter Mo. Mtg., 10—16—1758, 301.
[195]*Ibid.*, 11—30—1758, 307.
[196]*Ibid.*, 4—27—1774, 212.
[197]*Ibid.*, 4—29—1762, 430;   7—26—1764, 519.
[198]*Ibid.*, 2—25—1778, 309;   12—30—1778, 336.
[199]*Ibid.*, 5—26—1779, 346;   7—28—1779, 350;   11—24—1779, 361;
11—29—1780, 383.
[200]*Ibid.*, 8—29—1781, 436.
[201]*Ibid.*, 8—28—1782, 474.
[202]*Ibid.*,11—26—1785, 503.

tives and report what they thought of their schools.[203]
They produced the following statement.

Most of the committee appointed two months ago to take into consideration and report the state of schools have given attention to the service; and divers of us have attended each of the preparative meetings belonging to this meeting and after a time of conference thereon, 'tis agreed to report, there is no school within the village of Exeter Preparative Meeting under the care of Friends; But we are of the mind that it is necessary that one be established there; and although work has been begun, yet we have but little expectation of its accomplishment in a short time; Report of the committee
No school of Exeter Preparative

That there is a . . . . school at Maiden Creek kept by Thomas Pearson, a Friend, who is at present engaged for a year, has 15 scholars entered for that time and 8 quarterly ditto scholars at the rate of 40/ per annum for each, which is under the direction of three overseers chosen by the employers; The school house built on a piece of ground belonging to a Friend which contains about five acres. There is likewise a school at Reading kept by Benjamin Parks and wife in their own house; they are members of the society and have about 50 scholars; such as spell at 7/6 and others at 10/ per quarter but is not under the direction of the meeting, nor are there any overseers chosen to superintend the same, yet we are of the mind a school established there under proper regulations and care of the monthly meeting, might be useful and deserves encouragement. A school at Maiden Creek

School at Reading

The schools within the verge of Robeson Monthly Meeting are kept by a person who inclines to go to our meetings, has about 20 scholars, amounting to about £34 per annum. Endeavors are also used to get a school established there upon a better plan and near the direction of the yearly meeting, but how far they may be successful is at present unknown. We do therefore recommend the whole to the notion of alleviation of the Monthly Meeting as a matter wherein friends are deeply interested. School at Robeson

Which we submit to the Meeting.

Amos Lee, Thomas Lightfoot, Samuel Hughes, Fannie Ambree, Owen Hughes, (which was approved by the Monthly Meeting, and decided that the substance be made a report to the Quarterly Meeting—The Committee to be continued to the service of Schools and report in the future).[204]

Maiden Creek was at this time (1784) making earnest efforts to meet the standards set by the general meeting. In the eleventh month they requested a number of persons to be named to whom they might give a deed of trust for the ground Maiden Creek secures land for school

---

[203]Min. Exeter Mo. Mtg., 2—25—1784, 307.
[204]*Ibid.*, 4—28—1784, 510f.

agreed upon for the use of their school.[205]   Three were suggested and the deed and declaration of trust accordingly drawn up.   Efforts in the meantime had been made towards establishing a school at Reading and a committee to conduct a subscription for that purpose named.[206]   Help was solicited from the yearly meeting, but James Pemberton answered for that body that there was no money to be spared at the time, so Reading was advised to·build such a house as their circumstances would permit.[207]   Near the close of 1787 those having direct charge thereof made the following report of their progress:

Attempt to establish school at Reading

We the committee appointed to have the school education of youth under care, have given close attention to a school proposed to be opened in a short time at Reading by Caleb Johnson, in a house now in building by Friends there, and nearly finished, which we are of the mind should be under particular care and direction of the monthly meeting; and that it may be well that a committee be thereby appointed to superintend and monthly to visit said school; we have also drawn up and agreed on certain rules to be observed and attended to by the employers, master and scholars concerned therein for the regulation and well ordering thereof: which we have ready for the examination and inspection of the monthly meeting if thought necessary.   All which we submit thereto.   Signed on behalf of the committee, Francis Parvin. . . .   Which minute being read was allowed of and it was directed that a copy thereof be kept in open view in said school and that the original be lodged among the meeting papers;   Benjamin Pearson, Samuel Jackson, John Mears, Francis Parvin, Johannes Lee, Jr., and James Iddings are appointed to have the said school under care and visit it once a month or oftener as necessity may require and report of their care. The former committee is continued.[208]

Committee report on Reading school

After the school had been in progress two years, Samuel Jackson reported that it "appeared to be in an increasing way"[209] but its prosperity was not to be long continued.   In 1705 it was reported "discontinued,"[210] and no reason assigned for it excepting "the situation of the Friends there" which, taking into consideration the shortage of funds when it was begun, we may infer, had reference to the financial situation.

School discontinued

[205]Min. Exeter Mo. Mtg., 11—24—1784, 524.
[206]*Ibid.*, 2—28—1787, 39.
[207]*Ibid.*, 6—27—1787, 50.
[208]*Ibid.*, 10—31—1787, 60f.
[209]*Ibid.*, 2—26—1789, 122.
[210]*Ibid.*, 1—28—1795, 283.

The action of the monthly meeting in regard to it was left entirely to their own judgment.[211]

SUMMARY

In this chapter we have considered the schools of Philadelphia (city and county), and also those at Exeter Monthly Meeting, which belonged to the Philadelphia Quarter.

Scope of chapter

Education in the Quaker colony was initially provided for in the instrument of government, drawn up before the Proprietary left England; in accord with said provisions the first school (Flower's) was set up by the Council in 1683.

Education to be function of government

Thereafter, however, the initiative was usually taken by the Quaker meeting, which in 1689 set up a school and in 1697 applied for a charter under the laws of the province. This petition was granted and Penn gave the first charter in 1701. Later charters, in 1708 and 1711, granted extended privileges; by the last one the body of overseers were made self-perpetuating, and thus as independent of the meeting as they wished to be. The letter said to have been written to Thomas Lloyd, which credits Penn with suggesting the school of 1689, has not yet been discovered.

First school

School established by monthly meeting

Overseers made independent

The earliest masters were Keith, Makin, Pastorius, and Cadwalader. Mistresses were mentioned in connection with the schools from about 1699, Olive Songhurst being the first one named. Salaries were not high and seem in some cases to have hardly sufficed for the family of the master; increases were made upon complaint. Extra duties for the teacher included keeping charge of the boys and girls in meeting. From 1689 to 1779 the system increased from employing one to one which required nine. In 1784 ten were reported.

Earliest masters and mistresses

Growth of system

Philadelphia Friends' schools were first supported by (1) *rates* and (2) *subscriptions*, while (3) *legacies* and *special gifts* soon came to form a considerable item in their support. Bequests were also a factor in the support of the Negro School. Funds were occasionally raised by bond issues, and derived from tenements built on school property.

Means of support

---

[211]Min. Exeter Mo. Mtg., 2—25—1795, 285.

Schools were first held in rented property and in the meeting house, but in 1698 steps were taken to purchase property of Lionell Brittain for the use of schools. Property

was received as a gift from Samuel Carpenter in 1701. The first record of a schoolhouse was the one to be begun in 1701. In accord with their charter rights the power and independence of the overseers increased. In 1725 the monthly

meeting conveyed to them all money and the titles for all school property. The Negro School was provided with a building in 1771. The end of the century is marked by the establishment by the yearly meeting of a Boarding School at Westtown in Chester County.

The exact date of Byberry's first school is not determined; but must have been early, since Richard Brockden is reported to have been schoolmaster there in 1711. School activity, however, seems to have increased greatly near the middle of the century. The school was under the care of a standing committee, which was to visit schools every six weeks and make two reports thereon each year. Poor children were schooled by the trustees of the school funds.

Germantown school began in 1702, though perhaps an evening school existed before that date. Pastorius continued in this school as master, at least until 1718. The official language used in the school was probably English. The names of the first patrons were all German; a large number of English names among them in 1708 is an indication of how the school and its master were regarded.

In 1758 youths' meetings were established by Exeter, but no school committee was appointed until 1778. This committee accomplished nothing and made no report of value. By a report of 1784, Maidencreek, Reading, and Robeson were

credited with one school each, which measured up in some ways to the desired standards. Exeter had none. The Reading School was discontinued in 1795.

The total number of schools reported at Philadelphia, Germantown, Byberry, and Exeter monthly meeting, was fifteen.

CHAPTER V

SCHOOLS OF BUCKS COUNTY

The establishment of schools in Bucks County will be discussed (1) under the head of the monthly meetings therein situated and (2) in the order of their establishment in point of time. The several monthly meetings and their dates of establishment, respectively, are as follows: Falls, 1683; Middletown, 1683 (known as Neshaminy until 1706); Buckingham, set off from Falls, 1720; Wrightstown, set off from Buckingham, 1734; and Richland, set off from Gwynedd (in Montgomery County) in 1742.[1] Of these meetings, all were a part of Bucks Quarterly Meeting save Richland, which belonged to that of Abington.[2]

Schools of five monthly meetings to be discussed

The first way in which the early Quakers usually looked after education was to arrange for a useful apprenticeship suitable to the individual, which was calculated to enable him or her to earn a living. The moral training was always considered when an apprentice was to be placed. The placing of youths as apprentices was in the charge of Friends appointed by the monthly meeting. The early records of Falls Monthly Meeting show them active in regard to this type of education. In 1704 this report was made before the meeting.

Apprenticeship looked after by meetings; placed among Friends

A complaint having been made to this meeting that the children of Abraham Clement are not placed out to the satisfaction of Friends, it is the mind of this meeting that the Friends formerly appointed do take care to speak with Samuel Carpenter and Benjamin Collins about them, and make report to next meeting.[3]

A similar one of 1714 points out the continued interest and attention in that respect.

---

[1]Bunting, pp. 30, 31, 33, 32, and 28 respectively; also first volumes of the respective Records.
[2]*Ibid.*, 28.
[3]Min. Falls Mo. Mtg., 11—3—1704, 128.

> It being proposed to this meeting that there is a necessity of some Friends being appointed to take care about placing out John Linton's children as apprentices, therefore this meeting doth appoint Joseph Kirkbride, Thomas Watson, Jr., and Joseph Fell to care about placing them out.[4]

Another phase of education, more particularly the moral, was cared for in the youths' meetings, which were established at intervals, usually not more than four or five times during the year. It was the practice for the youths' meetings to be established by the quarterly meetings, in conjunction with representatives of the monthly meetings. In 1713, Bucks Quarterly took up the re-establishment of those within their limits, and ordered them accordingly, as the following extract states.

Moral education in youths' meetings;

> It being thought necessary by this meeting that the youths' meeting be once a year at Buckingham, once a year at Bristol and but once a year at Falls and once at Middletown, therefore agreed that they be on the days . . . . etc.[5]

established by Bucks Quarterly

To locate the date of the first school at Falls is difficult; it seems impossible to do so from the information to be gleaned from the records. We may be certain, however, that there was a school in the neighborhood at a very early date, though we can hardly determine the year. In 1730 the following request was made of the meeting:

Question as to early school at Falls

> Some Friends of Falls Meeting requested to have the use of the old schoolhouse, and it wanting repairing, they would repair it at their own charge, which is left to be considered at next meeting.[6]

The presence in their vicinity, of an old schoolhouse which, moreover, needed repairs before it could be used, would indicate that a school had been there for a number of years. Taking fifteen years as a very moderate span for the life of the building, before it should need any considerable repairs we could state with a good degree of assurance that the school building had probably been built not later than 1715, and that the school dated back to that time at the very latest.[7]

---

[4]Min. Falls Mo. Mtg., 10—1—1714, 195.
[5]Min. Bucks Q. Mtg., 12—25—1713.
[6]Min. Falls Mo. Mtg., 7—2—1730, 282.
[7]The fact that Falls Meeting recommended Buckingham Friends to build a schoolhouse in 1706 (Bucks Quarterly Records, 3—30—1706) would seem to favor the view that they themselves were supplied.

But at the next meeting this encounters a very dangerous obstruction. That meeting, referring to the request of the seventh month, second, speaks of "the request about having *the old meetinghouse*," instead of, *old schoolhouse.*[8] It further mentions that it was desired for the purpose of a school.[9] From this it appears that the truth of our above conclusion depends upon the accuracy of the records for seventh month, second, 1730 and for eighth month, seventh, 1730. If the record of the first date is correct our conclusion is unfounded and the date for the first established school can probably be placed about 1730, or shortly thereafter.[10]

Contradiction in the minutes of Falls

The records for the next thirty years reveal but little of the activities of the schools in Falls Monthly Meeting, though we are led to believe them in continuance, but perhaps not regularly. In 1759 the meeting had agreed to allow a house to be built on their grounds for the accommodation of a school master, but the house was not built there, since Mahlon Kirkbride had already purchased some adjoining ground on which there was a house built for that purpose.[11] The said Kirkbride offered to convey the same property to some Friends, in trust for the meeting, and Robert Lucas, Story Kirkbride, Mahlon Kirkbride, Jr., Jonathan Palmer, Jr., and Edward Bayly, Jr., were appointed to receive the conveyance. This is the first record of any permanent benefaction received. In 1783 the urgent *Advices of the Yearly Meeting* being brought to their attention,[12] a committee was appointed which reported the results of their investigation up to that time in the following manner.

House for masters' accommodation proposed in 1759

Property conveyed to trustees for use of schools

We, the committee appointed, in the first month 1779 respecting the institution of schools for the instruction of our children in useful learning, having conferred together . . . . agree to report that we have divers times met and had this important matter under our . . . . consideration, and are desirous that this important subject and necessary care should meet with every proper encouragement and improvement; and we may inform the meeting that there have been several improvements made on the lot of ground lately purchased from Samuel

Report of school committee

---

[8]Min. Falls Mo. Mtg., 8—7—1730, 284.
[9]*Ibid.*
[10]*Ibid.*, 5—4—1733.
[11]*Ibid.*, 1—31—1759.
[12]*Ibid.*, 12—3—1783, 358.

Ground pur-
chased for
use of school

Rhoads for the advantage of the school and benefit of the master, and that the committee have endeavored to encourage and pay for the schooling of such poor children as are in the limits of the school kept at or near this place whose parents are in low circumstances and are willing to accept thereof. We have likewise extended our consideration and views to the schools belonging to the other preparative meetings, and although the circumstances of things at present do not afford so promising and encouraging a prospect as we could desire, yet we are desirous that every proper encouragement may be afforded to promote the good and necessary work, therefore, we are free to propose to the meeting's consideration that of having a standing committee appointed for this

Standing
committee on
education
recom-
mended; and
visitation

purpose by the monthly meeting, and that each preparative meeting should likewise appoint a committee for the like purpose that should have this important matter under their consideration in order to promote this so necessary care in their respective meetings; and that the said meeting's committee should at proper and suitable times visit the several preparative meetings' schools and unite with the said preparative meetings' committees in affording and giving such help and assistance as to them from time to time may appear necessary in order to promote this so good and necessary a work and care. Signed at the desire and on behalf of the committee, by James Moon.[13]

Monthly
meetings'
committee
to join
those of the
preparatives

In accord with the above report the monthly meeting urged each preparative meeting to appoint a committee on schools; the monthly meeting named James Moon, John Merrick, Jonathan Kirkbride, William Satterthwaite, William Bidgood, Jr., John Stapler and Joseph Gillingham to join with those of the preparatives for that service.[14] Five months thereafter they reported,

Three schools
reported

The three several schools kept within compass of our respective preparative meetings are conducted in some measure under the care of a committee of Friends appointed for that purpose and that the several teachers are members of our society.[15]

The three preparative meetings were Falls, Makefield, and Bristol, the last named being transferred to Middletown in 1788.[16] Wakefield Meeting was considerably assisted by help from private sources; they reported to the monthly meeting in 1787:

Individual
aid

We hereby inform the monthly meeting that lately there has been a house built on the ground belonging to Makefield Preparative Meeting

---

[13]Min. Falls Mo. Mtg., 2—4—1784, 363.
[14]*Ibid.*, 3—3—1784, 366.
[15]*Ibid.*, 8—4—1784, 376.
[16]Bunting, 37.

for the accommodation of a school master, chiefly at the expense of Bernard Taylor, which he is desirous should be under use for that purpose, to be subject to a moderate yearly rent to be paid to Friends of that meeting for the use of the said meeting: the said house to be their property and under the care and the direction of said meeting with the advice and assistance of the Falls Monthly Meeting as occasion may require.[17]

In 1790 a committee of the quarterly meeting was appointed to confer with those of the monthly meetings on schools, hoping that the union of all might be more productive of results than all working separately.[18] In 1794 plans were set on foot for a new schoolhouse at Falls Preparative, said house to be two stories in height and about twenty-two feet by thirty.[19] It was to be placed "near the line" of the meeting's land at the west end of the meeting house. The monthly meeting was to pay £75, the employers who are members, £75, and the school committee £50 from the money arising from donations left for the purposes of schools. The house was not built until 1799, due to some unknown delay; its dimensions were twenty-four by twenty-six feet, one story high, with a cellar of the same dimensions.[20]

New building proposed at Falls; not built till later

In 1797 the attention of the monthly meeting was called to the proposals of the yearly meeting for the founding of a boarding school.[21] Copies of the printed rules proposed for its government had been received, and a committee was appointed to distribute them and to take subscriptions from any who were interested to contribute.[22]

Attention called to the boarding school

The problem of school support occupied a considerable part of Falls Meeting's time. The means of support were here, as in others already mentioned, (1) *subscriptions*, (2) *donations* and (3) *rates*. In 1760 it was considered necessary to appoint a committee of fourteen members to take an inventory of all legacies and donations, lands and benefactions which had been left to the meeting.[23] Some had been given for definitely stated uses; and others allowed the application

Support of schools in Falls Monthly

[17]Min. Falls Mo. Mtg., 8—8—1787, 440.
[18]*Ibid.*, 2—3—1790, 52.
[19]*Ibid.*, 12—3—1794, 169.
[20]*Ibid.*, 9—4—1799, 283.
[21]See page 73f.
[22]Min. Falls Mo. Mtg., 1—4—1797, 217.
[23]*Ibid.*, 4—2—1760.

to be determined by the members of the meeting. It was the will of the assembly that the committee appointed should especially determine what funds might be applied to the use of the schools. They reported at the next meeting that the legacy left by Elinor Bryner might be applied to the use of schools, along with those given definitely for that purpose.[24] The method by which the funds were to be applied to that use were indicated in the suggestions of the committee at a later meeting, as follows:

A committee to have oversight of education of the poor

> We . . . . are of the opinion that the most that can be done at present, will be to appoint Friends to have the care of the schools and to examine what poor children may be amongst us, they being the proper objects of the charity designated by the givers of the money, and that the said Friends have power to agree with a master to teach such children; and also to draw orders for the payment thereof out of the interest arising from the money appropriated to the use of schools. Nominated seven Friends for that service and submitted the names and the report to the monthly meeting. The Friends above named are appointed to that service with the powers therein mentioned and are desired to lay an account before the monthly meeting at least once in each year and oftener if the meeting shall see fit to call for it.[25]

Such a plan as here indicated was consistently followed throughout the century in regard to school support. The interest on legacies had to be paid annually.[26]

Rhoads proposes to sell land for a school; considered

In 1781 the meeting was advised that Samuel Rhoads of Philadelphia had offered to sell four acres of ground adjoining the schoolhouse lot, to be used for the promotion of the school, and the benefit of the schoolmasters.[27] The consideration asked was £60, and Rhoads and his two brothers-in-law, Joseph Pemberton and Samuel Pleasants, offered to donate £20, making it cost the meeting but £40. The committee on school support was directed to consider this proposal. Bristol Preparative also received very valuable assistance for the use of poor children's schooling, in the bequest of £50 Pennsylvania currency which was left them by John Baldwin of Philadelphia.[28] The great concern of

---

[24]Min. Falls Mo. Mtg., 5—7—1760.
[25]*Ibid.*, 7—2—1760.
[26]*Ibid.*, 9—6—1780, 278.
[27]*Ibid.*, 10—3—1781, 304.
[28]*Ibid.*, 9—3—1783, 354.

the meeting for the best expenditure of these donations for educating not only the poor Whites but also the Negroes, is seen in their minute of 1787.[29]   Careful account was kept and the accounts frequently audited, sometimes at the request of individuals.[30]   In 1790 the committee reported their concerns as follows:

> We the committee appointed by the monthly meeting to have the care of schooling poor children; also to have the distribution of the interests accruing on the several donations given for that use, have given attention to the service to which we were appointed: and the schooling a considerable number of children has accordingly been paid for, but as it is allowed that a change of the teacher at times may be useful or advantageous to a school, we are united in the sentiment that if such a change was to take place in the school kept at this place, it would be a means whereby the school might be considerably enlarged and the design and end of the several donations left for the use of the said school more fully answered. (Report submitted and accepted and the committee continued to the further service.)[31]

Report of committee on education of the poor

The establishment of these permanent funds was frequently expressed by the numerous committees as the most important consideration for the execution of the school idea. They attempted again and again to provide a uniform means of establishing such funds, but due to the unequal circumstances of the several meetings it was impossible to do so.[32] The uniform plan was kept as an ideal to be striven for and recommended to the quarterly meeting for its advisement in the matter;[33] in the meantime individual contributions were urged on all who felt inclined to endow a worthy cause.* The amounts given were frequent though small, many of them being about £5.[34]

Establishment of funds of basic importance

In addition to the local expenses of the meetings, (1) for worship, (2) for the use of schools, (3) for the maintenance of the poor, etc., there were also quotas to be raised for the yearly meeting stock, which added materially to the burden of each

---

[29]Min. Falls Mo. Mtg., 12—5—1787, 444.
[30]*Ibid.*, 11—4—1789, 19.
[31]*Ibid.*, 8—4—1790, 41.
[32]*Ibid.*, 7—6—1791, 68.
*Min. Falls Mo. Mtg., 12—6—1797, 238.
[33]*Ibid.*   [34]*Ibid.*, 10—5—1796, 210.

of the preparative meetings. The quota for the meetings belonging to Falls in 1797 was £500.[35]

If we may look over the Quaker treasurer's shoulder as he runs his accounts at the end of the century, we find him situated financially as follows:

Financial status of Falls at end of century

We the committee appointed to examine and settle the Treasurer's accounts, having attended thereto, find a balance in his hands of £136/8/11 school money; also, £3/10/7 poor money; and £9/00/00 of interest received on John Large's legacy, making the whole £148/19/6, in the treasurer's hands, and the monies upon interest stand as in the following statement, viz.

Bonds for School Money

I	bond for	"	"		£250/
I	" "	"	"		£7/9/4½
I	legacy without a bond "		"		£50
I	bond for	"	"		£50
I	" "	"	"		£50
I	" "	"	"		£130
I	" "	"	"		£100
I	" "	"	"		£50
I	" "	"	"		£40
	Included in a bond of £75				£40
					—————
					£777/9/4½

Interest due on school money	£40/00/11
And one year's rent on house and lot	£12/00/00
And one year's rent on house and lot	£12/00/00[36]

Middletown

The Middletown Meeting began its educational work more promptly than did Falls.[37] Ten years after the first establishment of the meeting a request was brought forward as follows:

School requested in Middletown meeting house

Some Friends have signified the likeliness of having a schoolmaster hereabouts to instruct children and also requested that they might have the privilege to teach in the meeting house, to which this meeting does give their free consent, provided it be no hindrance to Friends Meetings.[38]

It is quite probable that the school established as requested, was a temporary and irregular affair, depending on the will

[35]Min. Falls Mo. Mtg., 2—5—1797, 238.   [36]*Ibid.*, 11—6—1799—288.
[37]References for Middletown are to their transcribed minutes in the Pub. of Gen. Soc. of Pa., H. S. P.
[38]G. S. P. P., No. 66, p. 64.

of the individual patrons. Certainly, it had not any official connection with the meeting, and probably did not have for many years. In 1699, a request similar to that of 1693 was made by Thomas Stackhouse and others, desiring the use of the meeting house for a schoolmaster,[39] which implies they had not advanced much beyond their state of 1693. This request was likewise granted, provided no hindrance be caused to the meetings.

Because of very inadequate records in this regard, much is left to be surmised concerning the continuation of the schools thus early begun. The meeting was in continual touch with the desires and proposals of the yearly meeting,[40] and it does not seem justifiable to suppose that education languished, because scant records of it remain. The general tone of their minutes is one of self-satisfaction, and implies that they themselves were well pleased with their state. The elaborate recommendations of the yearly meeting in 1750[41] did not meet with their approval as they thought it quite impossible for those members living remote in the country districts.[42] That they disagreed with the plan indicates neither a lack of interest in the subject, nor a lack of schools in their locality. Rather, it may indicate the opposite.

In 1755 there was made the first donation to a permanent foundation for a free school.[43] At a meeting in that year an extract of Adam Harker's will was produced, where it appeared he had,

given a sum of money to them with others in trust to be employed toward raising a fund for settling and maintaining a Free School under the care and direction of this meeting . . . shall and will therewith purchase an annuity or yearly ground rent, or in such other manner as they may think most proper employ the said sum (£40) towards raising a fund for settling and maintaining a Free School in Middletown aforesaid, under the direction and control of the monthly Meeting of Friends there.[43]

Whether there was a new school erected as a result of the bequest or whether it was turned to the use of one already

---

[39]J. S. P. P., 1—1—1699, 114.
[40]*Ibid.*, 10—6—1772, 407; 1—7—1733, 578.
[41]Advices of the Burlington and Philadelphia Yearly Meeting, 250.
[42]Min. Middletown Mo. Mtg., 6—1—1751, 679.
[43]*Ibid.*, 8—7—1755, 11.

existing does not appear; the latter suggestion is much the
more probable. The advices of 1777 and 1778 and the years
following aroused the members to the responsibilities which
they must accept. In 1779 they made report as follows:

> Although it appears that the education of the youth has been too
> much neglected, we believe there is an increasing care that Friends may
> be more careful in that weighty concern.[44]

And in 1870:

> We believe a good degree of care is taken by some in regard to the
> education of those under their care, and that an increase in that is
> necessary.[45]

All questions in regard to schools or educational affairs
whatsoever were dismissed summarily, and given to the

All details
under the
care of a
committee
on schools

charge of the committee on schools.[46] A committee reported
in 1782 that nothing had been done more than to visit the
school they already had.[47] The failure to bring forth results
may have been with the committee; at any rate the meeting
decided to try a new one.

> This meeting taking into consideration the several matters recom-
> mended in the extracts . . . . respecting the education of the
> youth and their school tuition, are of the opinion that a reappointment
> on those important subjects is necessary; wherefore, Woolston J.
> Paxson, W. Blakeley, J. Watson and R. Hartshorne are appointed as
> committee to those services, and they are desired to closely attend
> thereto in order that the present and former advices may be carried as
> fully into execution as possible.[48]

New com-
mittee
appointed

In 1785 this committee reported that visits had been made
to families in the interests of education but that little was
effected.[49] The committee was released and the consideration of education left to the next meeting,[50] at which a new
committee of three was appointed. This one, so far as their
record goes, was neither more active nor more successful than
the others. In 1788 they report "nothing much has been done
in respect to schools since last year," which report was sent

Activities
of the com-
mittee not
effective

---

[44]Min. Middletown Mo. Mtg., 8—5—1779, 445.
[45]*Ibid.*, 8—3—1780, 481.
[46]*Ibid.*, 9—7—1780, 484; 8—7—1783, 557.
[47]*Ibid.*, 8—1—1782, 537.
[48]*Ibid.*, 12—4—1783, 562.
[49]*Ibid.*, 1—6—1785, 586.
[50]*Ibid.*

to the yearly meeting.[51] The record is not complete to the
end of the century, but for the period considered does not
offer any evidence of more than passing educational interest
and activity. Nothing unusual is to be noted in the finance
and support of the school at Middletown. Mention was
made of Harker's will, which, it seems, was the first legacy
left to its benefit.[52]

The attention of the meeting was early given to the care
of the orphans and the poor, and especially to their satisfactory placement among people as apprentices. The following
from the records for 1699 will serve for illustration.

Care of poor orphan; apprenticing

> It is agreed and concluded upon by this meeting that the meeting take
> care of all Friends children that are left as orphans and unsettled, to
> inspect and see that all such be taken care of and settled in the best and
> suitablest manner according to their capacity, that thereby they may
> discharge their duty and all such be eased by taking such due care. . . .

The attention of Buckingham Meeting was also turned
toward the education of apprentices, and careful scrutiny
given those who removed to apprentice themselves elsewhere, as also those who removed to Buckingham Meeting.
In 1764 Mahlon Michener, son of John, removed his certificate to Philadelphia, "having been placed as apprentice" in
the vicinity of that meeting.[53] John Parry, minor, an apprentice to Thomas Fell, blacksmith, produced a certificate in
Abington Monthly,[54] which was accepted and also that of
Isaac Gommere from the same place.[55] The poor were provided for by the legacy left for that purpose by John Holcomb
in 1749.[56] Whether this might, a part of it, have been spent
for schooling is not known.

Buckingham

Apprentices; care in their certification

In 1755 there was a minute entered in the records to the
effect that a legacy had been left to Buckingham by their
deceased friend Adam Harker, for the purpose of establishing
a free school in that place.[57] The amount of the bequest was
the same (£40) as that left to the Middletown Meeting by

Harker legacy for a free school

[51]Min. Middletown Mo. Mtg., 8—7—1788, 668.
[52]See page 93.
[53]Min. Buckingham Mo. Mtg. Extracts, 7—2—1764, 114.
[54]*Ibid.*, 5—4—1772, 155.
[55]*Ibid.*, 9—2—1776, 179.
[56]*Ibid.*, 2—3—1749, 61.
[57]*Ibid.*, 5—5—1755, 79.

Harker.[58] This was the first bequest for definite school purposes; the indications are that many followed. In 1778, a
minute gives their financial status as £244/4/11½ and they
entertained a proposition and concluded to raise £500 more.[59]
At the same time, the recommendations from the yearly
meeting being read,[60] a committee of the following persons
was appointed for investigation and assistance on the subject
Committee
appointed
on schools of schools, viz.: Paul Preston, Joseph Watson, Joseph
Preston, John Gillingham, Benjamin Paxson, Benjamin
Kinsey, Thomas Watson, Joseph Eastburn, John Kinsey,
John Balderston, Jonathan Shaw, Benjamin Cutler, Thomas
Good, Jr., John Brown, and Robert Kirkbride.[61] The action
of this committee is not brought out in the minutes of the
meeting.

The quarterly meeting made a new appeal in 1780 for a
more decided action by the various tributary meetings which
was followed by the appointment of a new committee.[62]
They were requested to "visit the school" for the "help and
assistance" of the master and to report their action to a
future meeting. In the twelfth month of the same year they
made these recommendations:

Visiting schools required

> The committee appointed for the proper establishment and regulation
> of schools made report in writing that it is their sense and judgment that
> the monthly meeting should recommend to the particular meetings
> severally, to promote subscriptions toward the setting up and building
> upon their meeting's lands as may be convenient for schoolhouses and
> such conveniences as may accommodate settled persons who live near
> the same, as also to encourage their contributions toward making up
> funds or salaries for the constant support of schools therein which is
> recommended to the preparative meetings.[63]

Committee's recommenda-
tions

A new committee was appointed in 1784.[64] They convened with the committees of the preparatives and discussed
the recommendations and means suggested by the yearly
meeting. Their conclusion was to the effect that one thing
in the recommendations was absolutely necessary, namely,

---

[58]See page 93.
[59]Min. Buckingham Mo. Mtg., 12—7—1778, 194.
[60]Advices, 250.
[61]Min. Buckingham Mo. Mtg., 12—7—1778, 194.
[62]*Ibid.*, 9—4—1780, 206.
[63]*Ibid.*, 12—13—1780, 210.
[64]*Ibid.*, 1—5—1784, 234.

that all funds, legacies, properties, etc., provided for the schools, should be vested in trustees for that purpose.[65] Without taking this step they saw no way to attain even the least success. It was further suggested that the trustees or committee thus appointed should investigate the present houses for schools, their condition and location, in each of the particular meetings, that a wiser plan might be followed in locating the new ones. The meeting considering the report decided to adopt its suggestions and accordingly appointed thirteen men,

Appointment of trustees necessary

> to inspect into the state of such schools as are now kept and where it may be necessary, to promote others,

and make a report as soon as possible.[66] Its report, produced in the first month, 1785, was quite long. Only the essential points of it are given in the following digest.[67]

1. Most of the committee appointed met and decided to confirm the former committee's report.

2. We find that there are many schoolhouses within the bounds that include the members of the meeting.

Summary of committee's report of 1785

    a. These are not well situated for the service of schools.

    b. Some are well situated, however, as (1) one on land granted by Samuel Eastburn and vested in the school trustees, (2) one on land granted by Thomas Goode, vested in members of the meeting, but not in trust for the meeting.

3. They suggest that these two houses be used as previously and that new houses be erected not more than three miles apart.

4. They maintain an uncertain state has prevailed among the schools.

5. The following places are recommended for new schools to be built:

    a. At the schoolhouse near Samuel Eastburn's.

    b. On the work road between William Jitchin's and Thomas Rose's.

    c. On the road from Newtown to Coryell's Ferry.

---

[65]Min. Buckingham Mo. Mtg., 3—1—1784, 236.
[66]*Ibid.*
[67]*Ibid.*, 1—3—1785, 317.

d. At the intersection of the lower work road and the street road.

e. Near the south side of Watson Weldin's land.

f. On Durham Road near Thomas Gilbert's.

g. On Plumstead's Meeting House land.

h. And at the schoolhouse near Thomas Goode's.[68]

It was thought such divisions would as nearly answer the needs as rivers and mountains would permit, and would provide for all of Buckingham territory and a little of Wrightstown. Any variation from this proposed building plan was desired to be brought before the committee for their judgment and acquiescence. In accordance with this suggestion the Friends of Solebury (1785) requested the assistance and advice of the committee in locating their school which they desired in a different place from that previously suggested by the committee. They conferred with the committee and finding their choice of site as good as could be obtained, it was agreed to build the new house on the southeast corner of Hugh Ely's land, of Solebury.[69] In 1786 Solebury Friends requested a committee of the monthly meeting to be named to whom they might give a title for the land.[70] In 1793 Buckingham was permitted to build a school on the meeting house land, the meeting to be in charge of the said school.[71]

New school property of Solebury and Buckingham

Having settled thus satisfactorily a systematic method of getting the schools located, they addressed themselves to the task of raising school funds.[72] A committee of eleven members was appointed, which, four months later, reported a plan of subscription paper to be used in getting funds for purchasing lands and buildings.[73] The plan as reported and approved by the monthly meeting was the following:

Problem of funds attacked

We the subscribers do hereby engage to pay or cause to be paid unto A. B. the several sums annexed to our names to be applied to the use of purchasing a lot of land of C. D. and building a schoolhouse thereon, the property and government to belong entirely to the society of the people called Quakers and under the direction of the Monthly Meeting of

Subscription form presented

---

[68]Min. Buckingham Mo. Mtg., 1—3—1785, 317.
[69]*Ibid.*, 3—7—1785, 244.
[70]*Ibid.*, 2—6—1786, 252.
[71]*Ibid.*, 6—3—1793, 306.
[72]*Ibid.*, 6—6—1785, 247.
[73]*Ibid.*, 10—3—1785, 249.

Buckingham, the title of which is to be wholly vested in the trustees appointed by the said monthly meeting. The rules and orders of the school when erected is to be prescribed by the aforesaid monthly meetings or a committee thereof consistent with our religious principles, and that no tutor shall be permitted to teach in said school until . . . . approved by the monthly meeting or a committee of the aforesaid.

In 1790 the state of schools in the monthly meeting was given as follows:

It appears that preparatory to the plan pointed out by the yearly meeting last year, there are two schoolhouses under the direction of this meeting. Schools in general among us, both as to tutors and to school government, are in a better state than they formerly were; and some property has been vested in the meeting towards a fund for the use of schools.[74]

State of schools in 1790

The form of subscription above mentioned was used for raising funds till 1793 when a committee on schools incorporated it with a few other suggestions in their plans.[75] These may be summarized as follows:

1. Each contributor to subscribe a principal sum.

2. All sums to be lumped together and invested in trustees, accountable to the monthly meeting.

3. All interests to be paid annually and applied each year to the schools in the compass of the monthly meeting.

4. All tutors to be members of Friends.

5. Funds to be first applied to the schooling of poor Friends' children, their necessities to be judged by the monthly meeting.

6. The remainder to be applied equally to the payment for other children, proportionate to the time they attend school.[76]

7. Interest to continue till the principal is paid.

8. All principals paid in are to be invested or "put to use" by the trustees.

Summary of later form used for subscription

The total number of subscriptions listed up to date was 117; the total amount subscribed was £759; the individual subscriptions varied from £1 to £25.[77] The meeting also

Amount of subscriptions

---

[74]Min. Buckingham Mo. Mtg., 8—2—1790, 283.

[75]*Ibid.*, 4—1—1793, 302.

[76]*Ibid.*, 5—5—1794, 315. (It was in 1794 suggested that any surplus be used for the bound apprentices of members, though they were not themselves members of the meeting.)

[77]*Ibid.*, 4—1—1793, 302.

succeeded in getting such former donations, as Harker's legacy, appropriated to this permanent fund.[78]

Special
committee on
school-
masters

In 1796 Jeremiah Praul, Joseph Yerkes, and Benjamin Kite were appointed to have the care of receiving all applications from prospective masters, and in case of vacancies to seek and have ready a list of available and well-qualified members.[79]

Wrightstown

One can hardly attempt to place a date for the beginning of the schools in Wrightstown Meeting. But by a report made late in the eighteenth century (1792) we gather a very good idea of the state of schools in that locality. The cause of the rather halting progress is perhaps found in the latter part of this committee's report, which states that the best plan conceived is for each particular meeting to raise its own subscription for its own school,[80] which in part was right, but more direction on the part of the monthly meeting would doubtless have produced better results. The report of 1792 is here submitted.

Progress
slow; reasons

We the committee appointed to take into consideration the state of schools within the limits of this meeting, after having several times met and attended to our appointment, find the main cause why our schools are so unsettled and so frequently occupied by unqualified teachers is the want of sufficient salaries to make tuition an object of employment worthy the attention of those who are or may be best qualified to discharge that trust; having duly investigated that subject it plainly appears very few amongst us who are interested in schools are of ability to advance money towards raising a fund on any other consideration than that of immediately receiving the benefit thereof; we are, therefore, of opinion nothing affords a fairer prospect of promoting the work than for separate neighborhoods to enter subscriptions for raising funds for the support and establishment of their own particular schools, which was read and referred to the consideration of next meeting.[81]

Want of money
to pay qualified
teachers

In 1793 the extracts from the yearly meeting being read and especially those concerned with the establishment of schools, it was decided to appoint a committee "to endeavor to promote that service as recommended," and make a report that might be sent to the yearly asembly.[82]

---

[78]Min. Buckingham Mo. Mtg., 2—3—1794, 310.
[79]*Ibid.*, 12—5—1796, 332.
[80]Min. Wrightstown Mo. Mtg., 8—7—1792, 88.
[81]*Ibid.*
[82]*Ibid.*, 1—8—1793, 96.

In 1790 a committee was appointed to look after the state of various legacies which had been left from time to time for the "support of a free school."[83] This committee made report shortly thereafter that the amount of the principals and interest at the time was £248/13/10.[84] A question arose as to the proper application of the interest on a legacy left by Jonathan Abbitt and others, and was referred to the school committee. They decided it might be expended for the schooling of Friends' children in straightened circumstances, provided they be taught in a school kept in Wrightstown.[85]

Committee on school legacies, etc., reports £248/13/10

A number of other legacies were granted from time to time for the encouragement of a free school, among them being one by Adam Harker (£40),[86] who had also benefitted Middletown and Buckingham, and that of David Buckman, the text of which is given below.

I give and bequeath to Isaac Wiggins of the township of Northampton, David Buckman and James Briggs of the township of Newtown, and Joseph Hampton and Isaac Chapman of the township of Wrightstown, all in the County of Bucks, and the survivors of them, the sum of £50 in gold or silver currency in trust . . . . place the same at interest on real security or therewith purchase an annuity or ground-rent or such other method as they may think proper for securing the same and apply the interest thereof as the same shall thereafter be received, towards the establishing and maintaining a free school in Wrightstown aforesaid near the meeting house for the instruction of Friends children belonging to the monthly meeting of Friends in Wrightstown, in useful learning, and the said school to be under the care and direction of the monthly meeting aforesaid.[87]

Buckman's will

In 1791 a committee presented a report on the status of legacies, which is given herewith in shortened form.

1. The will of David Twining.

I give to the monthly meeting of Friends at Wrightstown the sum of five pounds to be applied towards a Free School in Wrightstown, near the meeting house, that is under the direction and care of Friends.

Digest of report on legacies at Wrightstown

[83]Min. Wrightstown Mo. Mtg., 10—5—1790, 57.
[84]*Ibid.*, 12—7—1790, 60.
[85]*Ibid.*, 1—4—1791, 62.
[86]The Harker legacy at this time had increased to £183/4/4 (see Wrightstown Minutes, 10—2—1792, 92).
[87]*Ibid.*, 9—6—1791, 71.

2. A committee of six suggested to take the said legacy and apply its interest to the said school.

3. Report of a committee on Adam Harker's will.

All trustees have died without having made any purchase of any groundrent or annuity for the purpose aforementioned.

4. The trustees appointed by David Buckman, deceased, in his last will and testament to have the care of a legacy of £50 given by the said David to this meeting for establishing a Free School in Wrightstown, report that they have received said legacy and put it out to interest on a mortgage bearing date the seventeenth day of the third month last.[88]

In 1799 a legacy of £30 was left to Wrightstown Meeting "to be laid out in the education of poor children in the school house on the meeting house land."[89]   From later records running into the first two decades of the next century, it appears that the state of the donations was never gotten into very good shape.   When they came into the hands of the

Funds in chaotic state

trustees in 1822 they were "indistinguishable one from another," so far as the purposes for which each was intended. At the time when some of the bequests were made there was a large stone schoolhouse standing on the meeting's grounds to which they alluded in their wills.[90]   This building was torn down about 1815 and two schools set up, one two miles above the meeting house, and the other about three-quarters of a mile below it.   The total amount of the legacies had increased by 1822 to about $6,800.[91]

Richland

Richland Monthly Meeting (1742), the latest of all in Bucks County to be established, with which we are now dealing, belonged to the Abington Quarter (whose limits

date of school

were chiefly in Montgomery County).   The school, its date of beginning not known (probably in 1742),* was early endowed with legacies left voluntarily and primarily for the

Endowment for use of poor

education of the poor; the first one of considerable worth was that of Morris Morris.   An extract from the minutes shows that,

[88]Min. Wrightstown Mo. Mtg., 9—5—1791, 83f.
[89]*Ibid.*, 5—7—1799, 233.
[90]*Ibid.*, 254.
[91]*Ibid.*
*Wickersham, 83.

At this meeting were exhibited two bonds for two sums of money amounting in the whole to £100, it being a free and generous donation given by our ancient Friend, Morris Morris, for the use and encouragement of a school to be kept at or near this meeting house, which bonds are legally executed to the Friends heretofore appointed as trustees for this meeting, who are to take care from time to time to lay out the interest arising from the said donation for procuring necessary learning for such poor Friends' children who may be the most proper objects of such charitable help and the said trustees to render yearly account to this meeting of their service in the said distribution.[92]

This beginning was increased in 1796 by £20 granted from the estate of Edward Roberts.[93] The following record from a school account book of legacies, known as the "Jonathan Walton Fund" is cited, which indicates the manner of the school expenditures:

1792—for schooling		
to Jesse Foulke	15/10/00	Items of
to Jonathan Carr	1/10/00	expenditure
to ditto	7/00	for schooling
to Abraham Walton	16/6/00	in Richland
to Jesse Foulke	1/10/7	
to John Nash	5/00	
to Jesse Hicks	1/2/6	
1793—		
to Jonathan Carr	7/6	
to Nathan Walton	5/4	
to Sam Norris	2/12/11	
to Abraham Walton	18/7	
to Jesse Hicks	15/00	
to Samuel Norris	3/6/3½	
Paid to Daniel B. Ayres for teaching children	2/1/8	
	3/2/2	
Paid for teaching and books	2/1/4[94]	

SUMMARY

The establishment of schools of Falls, Middletown, Wrightstown, Buckingham, and Richland meetings is discussed in this chapter. Their first activity was to establish youths' meetings and look after the placing of apprentices. The date of the first school at Falls is not determined, though

The meetings

Falls

---

[92]Min. Richland Mo. Mtg., 1—21—1762.
[93]*Ibid.*, 12—21—1769.
[94]Expenditures, J. Walton Fund, I, 1.

the educational activity appears to have been on a par with other meetings.   In 1759 property was conveyed to trustees for the use of the school, and at various dates thereafter.   A school committee reported three schools, one in each preparative, in 1784.   The usual means of support were employed. The school money amounted in 1799 to £777/9/4½.

Middletown's first school was held in the meeting house, in accord with a permit granted by Friends.   The real progress of schools among them is not determined, though we know that they are supplied with schools.   It is likely, judging from the nature of the committee's reports, that they did *not meet* the standards set by the yearly meeting.   The free school, endowed with £40 in 1755 by Harker, was to be under care of the monthly meeting.

Buckingham meeting assumed a regular care in the apprenticing of children, and, like Middletown, was endowed by Adam Harker.   A school committee was appointed in 1778, and the visiting of schools required.   An unusual plan for building schoolhouses was devised in 1785; and also a scheme for school support in 1785 which was improved in 1793.   A special committee of two men had charge of employing masters   Two schools are reported as under the care of the meetings' committee, in 1790.

The cause for the apparently slow progress of Wrightstown concerning schools lay chiefly in a lack of permanent funds. Back of this, there seems to have been a failure on the part of the monthly meeting to unite and direct the activities of its preparatives, for the individual contributions were considerable.   Though "schools" are mentioned in the minutes, it seems most likely that only the one at Wrightstown was in reality a school of the monthly meeting.

Little is discovered concerning the Richland school save that it was endowed in 1762 by Morris.   The account books of the Walton fund show that the children were schooled at the expense of the meeting.

There were probably eight schools regularly established in the five monthly meetings.

Permanent property acquired

Three schools reported

Middletown

First school in meeting house

Free school endowed

Buckingham

Plan for buildings and support

Wrightstown

One school under monthly meeting

Richland

Total number of schools

CHAPTER VI

SCHOOLS IN MONTGOMERY COUNTY

Following the procedure in the preceding chapter, the establishment of schools in Montgomery County will be treated (1) under the head of the monthly meetings in whose limits they were located and (2) in the order of the time of settlement. The monthly meetings in Montgomery County and their dates of establishment are as follows: (1) Abington, 1683; (2) Gwynedd, set off from Radnor, located in present Delaware County, 1714, and (3) Horsham, set off from Abington in 1782.[1] In connection with the schools established in Montgomery County will also be considered briefly the same activity of Warrington Monthly Meeting (York County), which belongs at present to Baltimore Yearly Meeting. Warrington was established as a monthly meeting in 1747,[2] being set off from that of Sadsbury. Brief mention is made of Westland Meeting.

The meetings

The first records left by Abington Meeting, which relate particularly to any phase of education, are those in reference to the establishment of youths' meetings. It is implied by these minutes that nothing was done in this regard till about 1695, when,

Abington

Youths' meetings

> It was agreed upon . . . that four friends belonging to this monthly meeting be asked to take care of the Youth belonging to each meeting as concerning their orderly walking . . . according to the good advice of Friends, in an epistle from the Yearly Meeting at Burlington 1694, wherefore . . . men appointed.[3]

This apparently resulted in an agreement that the youths' meetings should be established at the home of Richard

---

[1]Bunting, 23, 26, 25, respectively; also, first volumes of the respective records.
[2]See abstracts of Warrington Records, H. S. P. Library; Prowell, *Hist. York County*, I, 112.
[3]Min. Abington Mo. Mtg., 2—29—1695, 25.

Established | Worrall.[4]   It is to be inferred that considerable attention was given to this earliest phase of education. In 1699 the Friends of Abington urged:

> Those Friends that are appointed to inspect into the behavior of the youth and their respective meetings; that they may be stirred to discharge their places, and to give account to the monthly meeting.[5]

Youths' meetings shifted often | The youths' meetings were not of permanent foundation, and their date for meeting was shifted frequently, which gave them characteristic irregularity.[6] The purposes to be secured by the youths' meetings were chiefly moral.[7]

Land deeded for meeting and school | The gift of property for the foundation of Abington Friends' School dates back to 1697.[8] The donor, John Barnes, had purchased 250 acres adjoining the tract possessed by Sarah Fuller, receiving patent for the same on June 1st, 1684.[9] Shortly after this he added to his possessions also the tract formerly possessed by Sarah Fuller.[10] From this total (600 acres) he deeded one hundred and thirty acres on Feb. 5th, 1696, to the use of a meeting house and schoolhouse for the Friends of Abington Meeting.* The tract lies about ten miles north of the city of Philadelphia. The Abington School, thus possessing such a large heritage and firm foundation in a material way, at least is a close rival of the Penn Charter School of Philadelphia, the petition for which was presented to the Council 1697-8,** and whose first charter was granted in 1701.[11]

Meeting house built | The exact date when a school was first held in property on this land cannot be determined. The meeting house on the newly acquired lands was built between the years 1697 and 1700, with assistance from the meeting at Philadelphia. It is probable that a school may have been taught at the meeting house for a time as that custom was followed in many other

---

[4]Min. Abington Mo. Mtg., 1—29—1697, 30.
[5]*Ibid.*, 1—27—1699, 35.
[6]*Ibid.*, 8—25—1703, 48.
[7]See page 172.
[8]Bean, 679; also, *Friends Intelligencer*, 8—15—1896, 539.
[9]*Ibid.*, 679.
[10]*Ibid.*
Friends Intelligencer, 8—15—1896, 539.
**Col. Rec. I, 499.
[11]See pp. 47-52.

meetings,[12] but this is a mere probability. The best evidence of a school at an early date is that relating to Jacob Taylor who, about 1701, was "concerned in a school at Abington," but was to be asked to take the management of a land office.[13] Mr. Bean, writing in the local history of Montgomery County, says that Jacob Taylor was land surveyor from 1706 to 1733.[14] That he was engaged in teaching during the entire period from 1701 to 1706 we do not know, but it is quite probable that he was the first schoolmaster who taught in a regularly established school.

Jacob Taylor concerned in a school

Taylor, land surveyor

In 1722, referring to the bequest of land by John Barnes, the minute of the monthly meeting states:

> Whereas John Barnes deceased, having given a legacy or yearly income towards maintaining of a school at Abington . . . and in the said deed of trust to Friends, he left this meeting in power to choose a trustee when any Friends that were intrusted did remove or decease. Now seeing Thomas Canby being one intrusted is removed into the County of Bucks, this meeting does appoint Richard Martin to act in his room.[15]

Land in care of trustees

In 1726 Thomas Fletcher was chosen to act as one of the trustees of the said donation and the school affairs, in the place of his deceased father, Robert Fletcher.[16] Everard Bolton's place (deceased) was filled by Nicholas Austen as trustee in 1727.[17] In 1742 Abington Friends took a deed of conveyance of Thomas Canby for the land and premises belonging to their school and meeting house.[18] Besides the bequest of Barnes already mentioned, there were several others which deserve mention. In 1749 a committee appointed to investigate the donation left to the meeting by William Carter in his last will and testament, reported they had attended to it, and produced to the meeting an extract from the will before mentioned.[19] Quoting from the Abington records the purpose of the will was given to be as follows:

Carter's donation

---

[12]See pp. 93 and 136.
[13]*2 Pa. Archives*, XIX, 24⁰.
[14]Bean, 680.
[15]Min. Abington Mo. Mtg., 1—26—1722, 124.
[16]*Ibid.*, 8—31—1726, 149.
[17]*Ibid.*, 11—29—1727, 155.
[18]*Ibid.*, 6—30—1742, 249.
[19]*Ibid.*, 1—27—1749, 50.

. . . two certain yearly groundrents one of six, the other of four
pounds, are invested in trustees, in order that the same may be conveyed, and . . . as this meeting shall think fit to appoint to the
intent and purpose that the same shall be annually laid on and expended
in the pay for the schooling and teaching of such whose parents or overseers . . . in the verge of this meeting are not able to pay for them,
or the relief of the poor of this meeting, when and as such poor children
are not to be found. . . [20]

**Expenditure
of funds in
charge of
committees**

The details of the expenditure of money left for such purposes were taken care of usually by the overseers of the poor
and also by the school committee, whose duty it was to
inquire in each of the preparative meetings concerning children who might be in need of help and whether they would be
willing to accept assistance. Their investigations were
reported to the monthly meeting to be considered before any
expenditures were made.[21] If they were satisfactory to the
meeting, disbursements were then ordered to the preparatives
according to their needs as stated.[22] The preparative meeting was also free to make a voluntary request for a part of any
fund for aid to poor children, if they desired to do so. In
1760,

**Funds
requested for
schooling
children**

Horsham Friends requested the sum of four pounds of Carter's legacy
towards the schooling of a poor child; this meeting orders that our
treasurer do pay them that sum.[23] And again, the present treasurer,
Joshua Morris, is ordered to pay to Thomas Lloyd a sum of eight pounds
to defray the charges of dieting Joseph Kirk, a poor Friend's child,
belonging to Horsham Meeting, who is put to school at the charge of
Horsham Meeting.[24]

**How dis-
tributed**

It was not always necessary to bring the cases to the
monthly meeting to be decided whether aid should be given
or withheld. It occurred often that the funds were appor-
tioned to the various preparatives, monthly or quarterly
meetings and their representatives allowed to apply it
according to their judgment.[25] In 1766 those appointed to
view the accounts of the treasurer of Abington Meeting made

[20]Min. Abington Mo. Mtg., 1—27—1749, 50.
[21]*Ibid.*, 1—30—1755, 148.
[22]*Ibid.*, 8—25—1755, 151.
[23]*Ibid.*, 5—26—1760, 260.
[24]*Ibid.*, 6—29—1761, 284.
[25]*Ibid.*, 7—27—1767, 420.

the following report as to the state of the funds which had accrued:

We the subscribers having perused the accounts of Joshua Morris, the meeting's treasurer, do report that the said treasurer credits the meeting with several sums received on the meeting's accounts from the year 1761 . . . . including £28 for the rent of William Carter's legacy to this meeting, the whole being the sum of £157/12/11, and that he paid by order of this meeting in that time (including £40 paid for schools for poor children) the sum of £137/11/8; balance in his hands the 24th of the 11th month, 1766 is £20/1/3.

Report on funds

We likewise report that we find five years' rent of four pounds a year and a year's rent of six pounds on the said Carter's legacy outstanding and not yet collected or received by him.[26]

A minute of 1735 entered in the meeting's records affords us an interesting glimpse into the nature of the books used for the Friends' schools. These books are very frequently mentioned in many of the meeting's records, and many of them were always on sale by booksellers such as Franklin in Philadelphia.[27] There seems to be no doubt that they constituted one of the staples of the mental pabulum. The extract in which they are mentioned illustrates also the initiative taken by the meeting in the direction of affairs relating to schools.

And further to let the quarterly meeting understand that this meeting conceives that reprinting a quantity of George Fox's *Primers* and Stephen Crisp's ditto and of George Fox's *The Youngers* might be advantageous to those children of Friends in school or elsewhere. We, therefore, refer the same to said meeting's consideration.[28]

Books used in schools

The Abington Meeting began at an early date to work for a better organization among its schools, coöperating heartily with the suggestions of the yearly meeting from time to time. The yearly meeting in 1746 and 1750 made several suggestions for the improvement of schools,[29] which were in 1751 followed by Abington with a statement that

This meeting has gone through in the several branches thereof in the service of visiting of families and to general satisfaction, and as to the settling of schools we have had it under consideration and some are

---

[26]Min. Abington Mo. Mtg., 11—24—1766, 406.
[27]*Pa. Gazette*, 1740, No. 582.
[28]Min. Abington Mo. Mtg., 8—27—1735, 207.
[29]Advices, 250.

desirous to promote the same but find many discouragements at the
present, yet are in hopes it may be further considered, and . . .[30]

This report means nothing in terms of accomplishment, but
indicates willingness and an active interest in educational
problems. In reading of their "discouragements" one must
keep in mind the standards set by the yearly meeting, and
that their report was their idea of how they measured up
to them.

Gwynedd

The first mention of any school (or any reference to indicate
there may have been a school in the limits of Gwynedd) is
that of 1721, in a petition for a road, entered by Roland Hugh
and Robert Humphrey.[31]   The mention herein made is of a
schoolhouse located near the property of Robert Humphrey

Schoohouse
mentioned
1721

and Roland Hughes and not far distant from the road to
Philadelphia.   Neither has trace been found of any school
actually established nor of schoolmaster to have charge over
it, yet the presence of a building erected for that purpose
lends credence to the view that there was a school there,
though perhaps irregularly conducted.   Procedure in other
districts was usually that schools were present before the
schoolhouses were built.[32]

The first mention of a schoolmaster is relative to Marmaduke Pardo, who came with the following certificate from

Marmaduke
Pardo
teacher

Pembrokeshire in Wales.

We whose names are hereunto subscribed, being the curate and others
of the inhabitants of the Parish of St. Davids, do hereby certify whom it
may concern, that the bearer hereof, Marmaduke Pardo, of the city of
St. Davids and County of Pembroke, has to the utmost of our knowledge
and all appearances lived a very sober and pious life, demeaning himself
according to the strictest rules of his profession, viz., what we call
Quakerism, and that he has for these several years past took upon himself the keeping of a private school in this city, in which station he
acquitted himself with the common applause and to the general satisfaction of all of us who have committed our children to his care and
tuition, etc.[33]

This certificate was signed by Richard Roberts and several
others.   With such recommendations, the citizens of Gwynedd

[30]Min. Abington Mo. Mtg., 5—29—1751, 78.
[31]Jenkins, *Historical Collections of Gwynedd*.
[32]For example, those in Philadelphia, Middletown and Merion.
[33]Quoted from Jenkins, *Historical Collections of Gwynedd*, pp. 395-6.

were very fortunate if perchance they did secure him as a master. Other writers have, it seems, taken for granted that he actually taught in the school, but there is no exact evidence on the point, only a very great probability.*

The following extract indicates there was an established school at Morristown in 1766.

Plymouth overseers acquaint this meeting that Mordecai Moore on his own and family's account and several neighboring friends request the privilege of holding a meeting at the schoolhouse near his dwelling house in Morristown every first day until the general spring meeting. The which is granted.[34]

School at Morristown Quaker?

As with the schools and school affairs of other meetings, their history becomes more tangible about the last quarter of the century. The recommendations of the yearly meeting being received in 1777 and their attention thus directed consciously to the question of education, a committee was appointed consisting of the following men: David Bacon, John Elliott, Jr., Charles West, David Estaugh, William Brown, Thomas Hollowell, John Gracey, Abraham Liddon, Samuel Lloyd, Abraham Cadwalader, John Heman, David Evans, Samuel Lee, Joseph Penrose, Joseph Lukens and John Evans.[35] The committee reported in 1779 that the establishment of schools had been under consideration, but that no fund had yet been raised or land purchased for the establishment thereof, as the yearly meeting had directed.** Accordingly the same committee was continued. In 1780 a minute of the meeting states that:

Committee on schools appointed

The matter relating to the establishment of schools is continued and it is desired that the several preparative meetings will attend to that matter as recommended by the committee some time past, and that the committee . . . the same under their care and make a report when anything is done toward accomplishing that service.[36]

And again in 1785:

A care remains on the Friends' minds for the right education of the youth, though little progress hath yet been made in establishing schools under proper regulations, although attention hath been paid thereto.

"Little progress" reported

---

*Wickersham, 83.
[34] Min. Gwynedd Mo. Mtg., 10—28—1766, 457.
[35] *Ibid.*, 12—30—1777, 259.
**Ibid.*, 4—27—1779, 296.
[36] *Ibid.*, 1—25—1780, 16.

Those matters respecting the Africans are under the care of a committee, though little progress hath been made in inspecting their particular cases.[37]

The activity of the committee does not appear to have been very great. After a consideration of their obligations on the subject again in 1791 it was decided to appoint a new committee which was to work definitely toward a plan for raising a fund for school purposes, and to make a report on the state of schools in the monthly meeting. Their report which appeared in 1793 showed a considerable number of schools but none established on permanent foundations, and many not in the membership of Friends. The state of all the schools as reported is given in the following extract.[38]

Committee to aid in raising funds

The committee appointed on schools reports that within the limits of Gwynedd Meeting a school in the township of Montgomery is kept in a house, property of Friends, there is a lot on two acres of land and two rooms for a master to live in, adjoining the schoolhouse, and there is remaining of a donation to the inhabitants of said township in common towards the support of a school, about fifty pounds per annum, to be kept in the said schoolhouse, the master a member of our Society; within the compass of Plymouth meeting, there is a schoolhouse built by a subscription on a small lot of land given as a donation with the interest accruing on five hundred pounds, which is free for all the inhabitants within a mile and a half of the donor's land, the master not in membership with Friends.

School in Montgomery Township

Plymouth school

One school, held in a house adjoining the meeting house at Plymouth which hath for several years been continued under the care and direction of that preparative meeting. There are several temporary schools within the limits of our Monthly Meetings, chiefly made up of persons not of our society, and kept by masters of different professions, no funds provided for any of them, into which Friends in such neighborhood send their children, there is a subscription gone into within the compass of one of the preparative meetings towards building a schoolhouse on a lot of land given for that purpose—the raising of funds for the support of schools has been under care, but not much progress has yet been made therein. Signed in behalf of the committee by

Temporary schools

> EVAN JONES,
> JOHN WILSON,
> ISAAC WEEKS.

Education of poor and orphans

The care and education of the poor was an occasion for great concern among the Friends of Gwynedd. This means

[37]Min. Gwynedd Mo. Mtg., 7—26—1785, 221.
[38]*Ibid.*, 1—29—1793, 177.

not only that their education was looked after but that in case father and mother married a second time, the meeting saw to it that the children's (if any by the first marriage) rights should be regarded. The affairs of the children had to be settled before permission for marriage was fully and freely given.[39] They were not always satisfied with their dealing with such children, however. About 1756 they declared that the children are well taken care of physically but that there is too great a neglect in regard to their learning and apprenticeship among Friends.[40]

Later they are able to report, no doubt with considerable satisfaction, that after due inspection, no Friends' children are found placed from among Friends.[41] All cases of necessity in the concern of education were resolutely dealt with, even though, as shown in the following extract, the recipients of the assistance were rather unwilling.

Their education neglected

Some unwilling to receive aid

> The Gwynedd Friends acquaint this meeting that Robert Roberts, Jr., is in very low circumstances and not able to maintain his wife and children reputably and that they have not been able to prevail with him and his wife to bind their children out to lessen their expense, therefore, this meeting appoints John Davies and John Evans to advise them to comply with Friends' direction, otherwise, this meeting must take further notice of them.[42]

For a slight insight into the condition of schools in the latter years of the eighteenth century, we can do no better than present a letter written by Joseph Foulke, which furnishes a personal touch not found elsewhere.

> My earliest recollection of the schools which I attended was at Gwynedd meeting. There was no house for the purpose, but what was called the "little meeting house" was used. An old tottering man by the name of Samuel Evans was the teacher. The reading books were the Bible and the Testament; we had Dilworth's spelling book, and Dilworth's Assistant or arithmetic. Grammar was a thing hardly thought of; there was, however, a small part of the spelling book, called "a new guide to the English tongue," and a few of the older pupils learned portions of this by rote, and would occasionally recite to the master, but the substance appeared to be equally obscure both to master and scholar.

Schools as related by Joseph Foulke

[39]Min. Gwynedd Mo. .Mtg., 4—27—1727, 100.
[40]*Ibid.*, 7—27—1756, 163.
[41]*Ibid.*, 7—26—1768, 40.
[42]*Ibid.*, 9—17—1765, 424.

My next schooling was in 1795, in the house, late the property of William Buzby, on the Bethlehem road, above the spring house. It was a kind of family school taught by Hannah Lukens. Here, Dr. Walton, of Stroudsburg, laid the foundation of his education. I went to Joshua Foulke, my father's elder brother, an old man. He taught in a log schoolhouse near the eighteen-mile stone on the Bethlehem road. My father, with the help of his neighbors, built this house (about 1798) on a lot set apart for the purpose on the southern extremity of his premises. This log schoolhouse stood about thirty years, and beside Joshua Foulke, we had for teachers William Coggins, Hannah Foulke, Benjamin Albertson, Hugh Foulke (my brother), John Chamberlain, Christian Dull, Daniel Price, and Samuel Jones. I have probably not named all or given them in the order in which they came.[43]

Merion

Merion seems to have left no written records of educational activity. There is a possibility that Marmaduke Pardo[44] may have been connected with a school there, soon after his coming from Wales, but this is little better than a conjecture.[*] In the loft of the present building (which, however, does not date back so early as this study) there is a school room in which are rude tables and benches. One of them bears the date, 1711, rudely cut with a jackknife. If, in the early eighteenth century, the meeting house still sufficed for school, it is quite probable that the same was true much earlier; at any rate, no search thus far has revealed anything concerning an early schoolhouse. The Radnor Monthly Meeting Minutes in 1791 state:

School, at least not according to plan of yearly meeting

> At Merion and Valley we have not discovered any progress in laying a foundation for schools in the way proposed by the yearly meeting.[45]

which would favor still further the idea that any school held there at that time was perhaps in the meeting house.

Horsham

The earliest mention made of Horsham Meeting is that in the Abington Minutes of 1777, stating:

> It is agreed that there be two overseers chosen for Horsham Meeting, viz., John Michener and Thomas Iredell.[46]

This was doubtless very near the time of its first establishment as a preparative meeting. The earliest preparative

---

[43] Jenkins, *Hist., Col. of Gwynedd*, 396–7.
[44] See p. 110.
[45] Min. Radnor Mo. Mtg., 7—12—1791, 24.
[*] Wickersham, 83.
[46] Min. Abington Mo. Mtg., 5—30—1717.

minutes accessible are those beginning 1757.[47]   We may feel
certain, however, that there was a school before this time, for
in the *Gazette* for 1753 there appeared an advertisement which
stated:

> Any person well qualified for keeping a school and comes well recom-
> mended by applying to John Lukens, surveyor, Abraham Lukens, or
> Benjamin Cadwalader, living in Horsham township, near the meeting
> house, may meet with proper encouragement.[48]

This may have been the same stone house in which Isaac
Comly of Byberry taught in 1799, we cannot say.   In the
records of the preparative meeting on the first page there is an
account of donations concerning schools, but the page is
so badly mutilated that no straight account can be made of
it.[49]   It will be recalled from the account given of Abington
schools that Horsham members were also benefitted by
Carter's legacy and others.[50]

Assistance
by donations

A committee appointed to investigate the conditions of
schools in Horsham Meeting reported (1779):

> We, the committee appointed, report as follows: That upon inquiry
> we found that the schoolhouse on the meeting house land is wholly
> the property of Friends, and the subscribers generally Friends; we also
> find that there has been a schoolhouse lately built on a piece of land held
> in trust for that purpose between John Parry's and John Walton's
> wholly by the Friends, and generally Friends subscribers; there is also
> one other schoolhouse near the Billet on a piece of land held in trust for
> that purpose by Friends and others, and one other schoolhouse near
> John Jarret's upon sufferance; the two last mentioned schools being
> made up by subscribers of different societies; which, after being con-
> sidered, the same Friends are continued with John Parry, Samuel
> Shoemaker (mason), John Conrad, and John Jarrett added to them as a
> committee, to have the oversight of such schools as may be properly
> under the notice of this meeting.[51]

Report on
Horsham
schools,
1779

Four schools
mentioned

And again in 1783 that,

> The committee on schools report they have several times visited the
> schools of Friends belonging to this meeting since their appointment, and
> that there appears an improvement in them, they having drawn up an

Rules drawn
for the
conduct of
schools

---

[47]At 15th and Race Streets, Philadelphia.
[48]*Pa. Gazette*, No. 1261, 1753.
[49]Min. Horsham Prep. Mtg., Vol. 1.
[50]See pp. 107f; Horsham Prep. Mtg., 1—24—1772.
[51]*Ibid.*, 12—24—1779.

essay of rules for the government of said schools, which were read and approved by this meeting. . .[52]

From 1782 onwards Horsham was a regularly constituted monthly meeting.[53] Almost the first thing performed by this newly constituted body was to order a report on schools which was brought into the monthly meeting in 1784,[54] the text of which is reproduced below.

Report made to Horsham monthly on schools

We, the committee on schools, having met and examined into the situation of such within the compass of this meeting find them as follows, viz.: that within the verge of Byberry meeting there is a school kept in a part of the meeting house under the inspection of part of the same committee, by Christopher Smith, a member of our society, whose number of scholars are about thirty at 10/ a scholar, per quarter, raised by subscription; also another school taught a small distance from said meeting house by Isaac Carver in his own house who formerly was a member among us, to which some Friends send their children, and within the compass of Horsham Particular Meeting there is a school taught on the meeting land near the meeting house by Byran Fitzpatrick, who is not a member, the number of scholars about twenty-five at 10/ a scholar per quarter; there is also one other schoolhouse built by Friends on a piece of land given for a term of years for that purpose in which there is no school kept at present. There are several other schools within the compass of said meeting, the houses of which are the property of Friends and others to which some Friends send their children. There are no funds belonging to any of the aforesaid schools, but there is a donation left to Horsham Particular Meeting, which if it were not for some circumstances attending it, might be of an advantage in establishing schools within the limits of that meeting which we think demands the attention of this meeting.

Signed on behalf of the committee by

DANIEL THOMAS.

Four schools named; others, where the houses belong to Friends

No funds established

Each particular meeting to name its own committee

After this there was no report for nearly two years, when the meeting, taking cognizance of the fact, urged all the preparatives to appoint individual committees of their own to attend to school affairs. In 1787 the committee of the monthly meeting made report that within the compass of the monthly meeting there were three schools under the care of the preparative meetings, in all of which the masters were members of the society of Friends.[55]

Three schools in the preparatives

---

[52]Horsham Prep., Mtg. 1—24—1783; (the rules are quite similar to those proposed for the Philadelphia schools, which are mentioned on pp. 183ff.).
[53]Horsham Mo. Mtg. Vol. I, first page.
[54]*Ibid.*, 4—28—1784.
[55]*Ibid.*, 5—1—1787.

The value of the organization of meetings for getting something accomplished can hardly be overestimated. The directing power of the quarterly meeting must have often been the cause which produced a conscious activity in the lower meetings. The quarterly meetings were at all times feeling the educational pulse of their constituents and making suggestions, requiring reports, etc., which did not fail to keep up the local interest. The quarterly meeting at Abington in 1792 made the following suggestions:

> At a quarterly meeting held at Abington, November 8, 1792, the subject of schools coming under consideration, it is thought expedient that the meetings be earnestly requested to take that matter into solid consideration and send up in their reports next quarter how far the advice of the yearly meeting has been complied with in that respect. The clerk is requested to furnish each member with a copy of this minute extracted from the minutes of the quarterly meeting.
> NATHAN CLEAVER, Clerk.

> The clerk is directed to furnish the preparatives with a copy of the above minute, and they are desired to inform this meeting of their situation in the above respects.[56]

The report of the monthly meeting in 1792 indicates that that meeting's concern for the education of the poor was comparable to others mentioned; they state that all of the children "partake of learning freely" and their and other Friends' children "are placed among Friends" as apprentices.

The earliest Quaker settlements in Warrington were in 1735,[57] and their first meetings for worship were held with the Friends at Newberry. Warrington Preparative Meeting was organized in 1745;[58] while the monthly meeting records date to 1747.[59] For nearly thirty years there is no notice in the records concerned with education, saving those which refer to the settling of youths' meetings. Those were very frequent.[60] The report on the youths' meetings in 1779 was as follows:

> Some of the Friends appointed to attend the Youths' Meeting report that four of them attended it and gave it as their sense that it was a good

[56]Horsham Prep. Mtg., 11—28—1792.
[57]Prowell's *Hist.*, I, 1084.
[58]*Ibid.*
[59]Warrington Mo. Mtg. Min., Vol. I.
[60]*Ibid.*, 4—20—1754, 44; 12—12—1761, 44; 8—7—1779, 45, etc.

meeting, and that if it should be as well attended in the future, it might be of use.[61]

Three years later, 1782, it was considered necessary to leave off holding the youths' meetings, for what reasons it is not known, but on a protest from some members it was concluded that it might be continued for at least another meeting.[62] In 1778 the yearly meeting extract was received, in which the establishment of schools was recommended; committees of both men and women were at once named for the service and desired to report.[63] In the year following, the report was made on the part of Warrington Preparative Meeting:

Committees of men and women named on schools

> Warrington Meeting informs us that they have made choice of William Underwood, Peter Cleaver, Benjamin Walker, and Joseph Elgar for trustees and overseers of a school, with which this meeting concurs.[64]

The trustees thus appointed, it seems, were not so successful as might have been desired, if we may judge by their report made in 1780.

No progress reported 1780

> William Underwood, on behalf of the committee appointed to have under their care and labor to promote the education of the youth, as well as a reformation with that respect to other deficiencies in our society, informed this meeting that they have several times met and conferred together on the occasion, but have not proceeded any further in that service, neither have any prospect at this time of proceeding therein, etc.[65]

The tone of the next report of 1782 is more encouraging.

> The Friends appointed to the care of schools report they have made some progress therein, some of them having attended each of our preparative meetings and endeavored to encourage Friends in setting up of schools agreeable to the intention of the Yearly Meeting and find there is a willingness in the minds of Friends to endeavor to have schools set up amongst us agreeable thereto, as nearly as the circumstances of the several Meetings will admit of. They are continued and desired to assist where there may be occasions and report to this Meeting in the third month next.[66]

[61] Warrington Mo. Mtg. Min., Vol. I, 11—13—1779, 45.
[62] Ibid., 1—12—1782, 46.
[63] Ibid., 1—10—1778, 46.
[64] Ibid., 9—11—1779, 46f.
[65] Ibid., 8—12—1780, 46f.
[66] Ibid., 1—12—1782, 47.

In 1784 it was reported that the committee had attended at York and that there appeared to be a good prospect for a school to be established there according to the desires expressed in the yearly meeting's advices.[67] It was also stated that some provision was made at each particular meeting for the same, and it was expected a particular report would be rendered thereof.[68] This report, however, did not come into the monthly meeting as it appears.

School to be at York

The conditions at York seem to have been the most promising as presented in a committee's report of 1784 which is here submitted:

The committee appointed to promote the establishment of schools report that they have paid some attention to the service; most of them attended a meeting at York, and find that Friends there have a house nearly finished and have entered into some subscriptions to encourage such a school, of which it is agreed that the Quarterly Meeting be informed, as well as of houses being built for that purpose at Newbury and Warrington, and that the committee be released from the service.[69]

Schoolhouse at York; subscriptions started

The statements of the monthly meeting in the above report are corroborated by a later report of the Warrington and Fairfax Quarterly, which was made a few months later, though it appears the schoolhouse at Warrington was not yet completed.[70]

Same statement by quarterly meeting

The progress that had been made by Westland Monthly Meeting[71] is indicated by the following report of that date:

The minutes of the school committee for several seasons past being read, and they have proposed a reappointment, William Wilson, Matthew Heald, Jonas Cattell, William Dixon, Joshua Dixon, and Eleazar Brown are appointed to have the general care of schools and admission of Tutors. And it appears requisite that a few Friends be appointed by each Preparative Meeting to have the immediate oversight of the school or schools within the limits of such meetings; said committee to unite and confer together as they see occasion, and the clerk is desired to notify each preparative meeting by a copy of this Minute.[72]

---

[67]Warrington No. Mtg, Min., 1—10—1784, 47.
[68]*Ibid.*, 3—13—1784, 47.
[69]*Ibid.*, 5—8—1784, 47.
[70]Min. Warrington and Fairfax Q. Mtg., 9—20—1784, 175f.
[71]Records of Westland Mo. Mtg. Washington County are found in the collections of the Genealogical Society of Pennsylvania.
[72]Min. Westland Mo. Mtg., 12—26—1789, 49.

A still later report of 1797 is no more definite than the
former; this is very generally characteristic of the reports,
and even at a late date when other meetings were making
very definite ones, indicates that a very unsatisfactory state
existed in the schools of Westland. Many other reports
examined, which were sent in before the committee, of the
century, made no improvement in regard to definiteness.

*Later
reports
still
indefinite*

SUMMARY

*The
meetings*

The schools in the limits of Abington, Gwynedd, Horsham,
Warrington, and Westland meetings are discussed in this
chapter.

Abington

Probably the first schoolmaster at Abington, who was connected with a regularly established school, was Jacob Taylor.
Land for the meeting and school uses was deeded by John
Barnes in 1696, and a meeting house built by 1700. Assistance was also afforded by a legacy granted by William Carter
for educating poor children. Such funds were in charge of,
and expended by, trustees appointed for that purpose.
Fox's and Crisp's *Primers* are mentioned for use in the schools.

Gwynedd

Mention is made of a schoolhouse near Gwynedd in 1721,
but no records of the school are discovered. Marmaduke
Pardo, an experienced teacher, came to Gwynedd from Wales,
and being well recommended as such, it is likely that he was
employed in school teaching; but nothing explicit to that
effect is found. Late in the century Joseph Foulke states he
attended school in Gwynedd. A schoolhouse at Morristown
is mentioned in 1766. Committees on schools and funds
followed the procedure noticed in other meetings. School
land, schoolhouse funds, and a house for a master were provided in Montgomery township in 1793. Another school in
the compass of Plymouth is mentioned, and another one,
"adjoining the meeting house at Plymouth." Other temporary schools, used under varying circumstances, are said to
be maintained. Merion and the Valley do not appear to
have met the yearly meeting's requirements in any way.

*Morristown
schoolhouse
mentioned*

*Three
regular
schools*

Horsham

No explicit mention is made of a school at Horsham in the
early minutes, but the advertisement for a teacher in 1753
indicates they were supplied with a school. A report of

Horsham Preparative in 1729 mentions four schools, kept "nearly agreeable to direction." In 1783 a list of rules was adopted for their government. Each preparative meeting was directed in 1787 to have its own committee on schools.

Judging from the minutes of their transactions, the schools of Warrington and Westland meetings seem to have been organized and carried on in a very desultory fashion. Those at York and Warrington were the best situated. There were probably as many as twelve regularly established schools in the above meetings by the end of the century.

Warrington
Westland

Probably
twelve
regularly
established
schools

CHAPTER VII

SCHOOLS OF CHESTER COUNTY

The several monthly meetings, which are discussed in this chapter, were, for the period of this study (before 1800) members of Chester (or Concord Quarterly) Meeting, until the establishment of Western Quarterly Meeting in 1758,[1] when a number of them were included in that quarter. In 1800 a new Quarterly Meeting (Caln) was established from those formerly constituting Western Quarterly.[2] The monthly meetings with which we are to deal, the dates of their establishment, and the order of their presentation here, are as

The meetings considered

follows: (1) Kennett, known as Newark till 1760, 1686, or before; (2) New Garden, set off from Kennett in 1718; (3) Goshen, set off from Chester, 1722; (4) Bradford, 1737; (5) Uwchlan, set off from Goshen, 1763; (6) London Grove, set off from New Garden, 1792.[3] Those just named were situated within the limits of present Chester County.[4] The last meeting to be considered in this chapter, (7) Sadsbury, established in 1737, was situated in Lancaster County.[5]

Kennett

In the records of Kennett (Newark) Meeting, the writer has been unable to find any early explicit reference to education. Among the early references to children, are the minutes of 1715 in regard to those of the widow Howard at the time of her remarriage.[6] The meeting appointed a committee to look after the affairs of her children to see that the will of the deceased father was entirely complied with. Again in 1727 the meeting appointed a committee to see that the

Early care for children

---

[1]Min. Western Q. Mtg. I, 1 (Deposited at West Grove); Bunting, 55.
[2]Min. Caln Q. Mtg., I, 1; Bunting, 48.
[3]Bunting, 59, 62, 43, 51, 52, and 61, respectively; also first volume of records for each meeting.
[4]See map.
[5]Bunting, 49.
[6]Min. Kennett Mo. Mtg., 11—7—1715, 28.

provision for the orphan children be fulfilled before allowing the widow to remarry.[7] These two cases serve to point out that an early care and interest in the affairs of children was manifested on the part of the meeting.

Local historians have very little to offer in the way of clews to the education of the Quakers in the last part of the seventeenth and early eighteenth century, though they all agree that the Quakers furnished the foundations of education, and it was begun very early, even from the first establishment in the various counties.[8] Some of the early schools have already been discussed, in cases where it was possible to state the earliest beginnings.[9]

Local history credits Quakers with furnishing the foundation of schools

In 1777 those who had attended the Western Quarterly Meeting reported they had received the recommendations of the yearly meeting requiring the monthly meetings to have particular charge of the education of the children, with especial reference to the employment of schoolmasters who were Friends.[10] The same concern being mentioned a month later, with emphasis on the *school education*, a committee of six Friends was appointed to join with a committee of the quarterly meeting to confer on the matter.[11] In 1779, their action appears to be just a little more definite, but from the records it is difficult to say whether it meant very much or not; the minutes at that time stated:

Yearly recommendations received

School committee appointed

John Way, John Marshall, James Bennett, Caleb Pierce, David Greame, Samuel Nichols, and Thomas Carlton, Jr., are appointed to unit together and endeavor to promote such schools as (are) recommended.[12]

From that date (1779) to 1781, there appears no comment on the subject, save the usual periodic announcements that the Advices of the Yearly Meeting "have been regularly received." In 1781, however,

Union school of Kennett, Bradford, and New Garden

Caleb Pierce on behalf of the committee on schools, reports there is a school made up by some of the members of this, Bradford, and New

[7]Min. Kennett Mo. Mtg., 12—3—1727, 188.
[8]Futhey & Cope, *Hist. Chester Co.*, 302f; Jordan, *Hist. Del. Co.*, II, 423ff.
[9]See page 42, Philadelphia 107, Abington 154, Darby.
[10]Min. Kennett Mo. Mtg., 12—11—1777, 625.
[11]*Ibid.*, 1—15—1778, 626.
[12]*Ibid.*, 1—14—1779, 658.

Garden monthly meetings; John Parker and Caleb Pierce are appointed to join with the Friends of those meetings in the oversight thereof, and report to this meeting when necessary.[13]

The school
discontinued

In the seventh month thereafter, in the same year, John Parker reported that the school which he and Caleb Pierce had been appointed to oversee was discontinued.[14] They were released from their service in the care of schools. The former committee on that subject, appointed in 1779, seems, however, from the minute of the tenth month, 1781, to have been continued as a standing committee on the subject.[15]

New com-
mittee has
more specific
duties

The following extract implies that the committee of 1779 was replaced by another which, by the way, had more specifically named duties. The implication of the minute is that there were at least two schools, perhaps more.

> The concern for the promotion of schools, under the directions of Friends revived, Samuel Harlan, John Way, Aaron Hollingsworth,— John Swain, Amos Harvey, Samuel Pennock, and James Jackson are appointed to have the care and oversight of schools, also promote the establishment of schools where there is yet want of assistance, and report to this meeting when necessary.[16]

In the same year it was also recommended to the preparative meetings that each appoint a committee of their own to represent them and act with the committee of the monthly meeting in the concern of schools.[17] The intervening years, from 1783 to 1785, offer nothing beyond the usual general reports concerning the appointment of committees and the like. In 1785, the committee on schools produced this report:

Several
schools
reported;
some
according to
demand of
yearly
meeting

> We have lately had a conference on the subject, and do find that there are several schools in the compass of our monthly meeting, kept by Friends and under the care of this committee, and may inform that they are kept to a good degree of satisfaction, yet there are some that employ teachers, not members of our society, without the advice of the committee or the monthly meeting. We, likewise, agree to lay before the monthly meeting the reappointment of a committee for this service in future as the members of this committee have been long on the appointment and desire to be released, which we submit to the meeting. Signed —John Way (and five others).[18]

---

[13]Min. Kennett Mo. Mtg., 2—15—1781, 730.
[14]*Ibid.*, 7—12—1781, 741.   [15]*Ibid.*, 10—11—1781, 746.
[16]*Ibid.*, 9—11—1783, 787.   [17]*Ibid.*, 5—13—1783, 795.
[18]*Ibid.*, 5—12—1785, 814.

The answer to the fifth query of the same year likewise informs us that care has been taken in the education of the poor children, and Friends' children "are generally placed among Friends."[19]

The request for the appointment of a new committee on schools, made by the old committee, does not seem to have received consideration till 1788 In the meantime we must assume that the old committee continued to serve, since occasional reports were sent in. The men appointed on the new committee were: Jacob Greave, Samuel Nichols, Amos Harvey, Samuel Harlan, Moses Pennock, Robert Lambourn, Jr., Christopher Hollingsworth, John Way, and William Phillips, Jr.[20] In 1790 the monthly meeting ordered a special committee to recommend a deeper educational concern to the particular meetings.[21]

New school committee appointed

The desired results, in the shape of a more perfected organization and permanent foundation to be provided for schools, did not come until about 1792 and thereafter. In that year, the committee reported its past activity in respect to schools established, and made certain valuable suggestions to guide future action, as the following extract witnesses:

The committee, appointed at last meeting, report: We, the committee appointed by the monthly meeting at the request of Kennett Preparative Meeting, respecting the establishment of schools within the verge thereof, agree to report, we have attended thereto, and find they have purchased a piece of ground, with the approbation of the committee of this meeting, of Abraham Taylor, about two miles and a half westerly from Kennett Meeting House, adjoining the public road, leading to Nottingham, and obtained his conveyance to Jacob Pierce, Samuel Pennock, Townsend Lambourn, Thomas Pierce, William Parker, and David Pierce, trustees for the same, meted and bounded as mentioned in the said conveyance and recorded . . . . and as it appears to us necessary in order for a fixed object whereon to lay a foundation for establishing a fund agreeable to the Yearly Meeting, that the monthly meeting should appoint some Friends as trustees to have the care of the said school, and that it should have a name to be distinguished by; we therefore propose it to be called by the name "Number One," within the verge of Kennett Preparative Meeting. We have likewise agreed on some general rules to be observed by the scholars of the said school.

Ground purchased

Rules adopted for the school

[19]Min. Kennett Mo. Mtg., 8—11—1785, 820.
[20]*Ibid.*, 2—14—1788, 874.
[21]*Ibid.*, 1—14—1790, 914.

Signed by Caleb Pierce, Wm. Lambourn, Caleb Kirk, and Jonathan Greave. 12—24—1790.

The above report, being read, is agreed to be further considered at our next meeting.[22] Unfortunately for the satisfaction of our curiosity about the internal organization of the schools, the rules which they state were drawn up were not incorporated in the minutes of the monthly meeting. They were probably similar, however, to those adopted by the Horsham School Committee at a slightly earlier date.[23]

In consideration of the recommendations made in the above report, the meeting assembled in the seventh month, appointed nine of their members as trustees, to receive all donations for the purpose of schools.[24] About a year thereafter, a report signed by Joshua Pusey and John Jones was submitted by the monthly meeting to the quarterly meeting, which was in substantial accord with all that had already been done.[25] It may be well to summarize briefly their recommendations.

Summary of committee's report

1. We have considered the relative situation of the members in our compass.

2. The affairs of education have not yet received the attention they deserve.

3. We find several school houses have been erected, but

4. The demands made by the yearly meeting are not met, therefore,

5. Friends must subscribe funds, either in monthly or preparative meetings.

6. The funds must be available for application for meetings. Friends are so scattered and few that they cannot support a school alone and have been forced to patronize "mixed schools."

7. Those laboring under difficulties should be taught gratis, or at least, at low rates.

In 1795 the committee on schools produced a plan for subscriptions to a permanent school fund,[26] which was

---

[22]Min. Kennett Mo. Mtg., 1—12—1792, 14.
[23]Horsham School Com. Minutes, 1—27—1783.
[24]Min. Kennett Mo. Mtg., 7—12—1792, 25.
[25]*Ibid.*, 3—14—1793, 39.
[26]*Ibid.*, 2—12—1795, 83.

referred to the next meeting. A report was then made, but it was thought that since all of the committee had not collaborated it should be, and accordingly was, postponed for the time being.[27] In the fifth month a report was made, but still some changes were thought to be necessary.[28]

Not until the twelfth month (1785) was the report finally produced, which is given below. There has been some reference made by local historians of Chester County, stating that Kennett Monthly Meeting had as early as 1787 provided a plan for subscription for the provision of permanent funds.[29] The rule "number 5," which is quoted by them, is exactly the same rule as the fifth one which is mentioned below. The writer has found no such reference to a plan for funds at the earlier date (1787). It seems quite probable that the statement made in Mr. Cope's work is an oversight, perhaps an error in setting up an eight in place of a nine. The entire list of nine rules is given.

Question of a plan for school funds prior to 1795

1. A plan for raising fund for the benefit of schools within the bounds of Kennett Monthly Meeting, whereby Friends may have an opportunity of manifesting their benevolent intentions by subscribing thereto.

1st. That each subscriber to this plan pay at the time of subscription, or give his or her note to the treasurer or clerk of the trustees, or their successors appointed by Kennett Monthly Meeting, to have the care of this fund, for a sum of money payable at any time, not exceeding three years after date, with the interest of five per cent. per annum paid annually for the same.

Scheme for funds reported in 1795

2d. The treasurer shall have a book for that purpose, and keep fair entries of all money due and received; likewise of all money expended and his receipts shall be a sufficient discharge for any money paid to him for the use of schools.

3rd. Whenever the treasurer may receive any new subscription or any money for the benefit of schools, he shall report the same at the next meeting of the trustees of the said schools.

4th. When the trustees receive any money for the use of schools, they shall as soon as they can conveniently put the same to interest upon good security; or they may purchase land or ground rent therewith as shall appear best for the time being.

5th. The trustees shall, as soon as they see occasion, apply the interest arising from this fund to securing the schooling of the children

---

[27]Min Kennett Mo. Mtg., 4—16—1795, 88.
[28]*Ibid.*, 5—14—1795, 91.
[29]Futhey & Cope, *Hist. Chester Co.*, 302.

of such poor people, whether Friends or others, as live within the verge of the aforesaid monthly meeting, provided such children comply with their rules.

6th.   We recommend it to each other as often as we find an increase of property and openness of heart to add something to our subscription whereby it is hoped the monthly meeting may in time be enabled more fully to comply with the advice of the Yearly Meeting in 1778, respecting schools.

7th.   As a variety of circumstances may in future occur which the human eye can not foresee, nor understanding conceive, therefore the trustees shall from time to time manage this fund as shall appear to them best, to promote the welfare of the said schools and the poor thereunto belonging; also if the interest may be to spare, they may assist therewith in keeping the schoolhouse in repair and in paying the salaries of school-masters or mistresses within the verge of said meeting, provided the principal be not thereby lessened.

8th.   If at any time the trustees may not all judge alike how they ought to proceed in such cases, they are to apply to the aforesaid monthly meeting for assistance.

9th.   The trustees shall from time to time be accountable to the monthly meeting of Kennett for their management of this fund, as directed in the minute of their appointment.   Signed by order of Kennett Monthly Meeting, held the 15th of the 12th month, 1796.[30]

The condition of the schools in Kennett Monthly Meeting was made known in 1798 in the report presented by Robert Lambourn for the committee.   A digest of that report is as follows:

State of
schools in
1798

1. They have had the subject "under care."
2. There are two schools "within their compass."
3. The town's schools are taught by Friends' members.[31]
4. They are under the charge of the meeting's committee.

New Garden

The New Garden Meeting in 1773 made record of having placed £4/11/9 in the hands of Jacob Wright, to be applied at the further directions of the meeting to the placing out of poor Friends' children or the relief of indigent Friends.[32]

Care for the
indigent

Between that time and 1778, we learn no more of this educational philanthropic interest.   In that year the usual reminder sent out by the yearly meeting came to them, calling

---

[30]Min. Kennett Mo. Mtg., 12—15—1796, 146.
[31]*Ibid.*, 8—16—1798, 199.
[32]Min. New Garden Mo. Mtg., 3—6—1773, 174.

attention to educational needs.[33]   A committee was appointed
which stated in a report, 1779, "some care is taken therein,
and more appearing necessary, they are continued."[34]   An
extract of a few months later is as follows:

> The committee respecting schools, having the matter under care, two
> schools being under their notice, and another proposed to be established,
> they are continued and desired to report when necessary, and the clerk
> to enter the substance of the case in their report.[35]

Two schools; another proposed

Following the report of 1779, which showed there were
two schools in charge of the meeting, there is furnished no
further information until 1785.   In the third month, 1785, a
large committee of thirteen members was appointed to take
charge of the "weighty affairs" recommended.[36]   This committee produced a report in the eighth month of the same
year, which is gratifying in that it is more substantial than
many others brought in.   It is given herewith.

> The committee in the care of schools report that they have had
> several conferences together since last meeting, and are of the mind that
> concern for the right education of our youth rather increases among
> Friends, and that a new school house has been lately built near Jeremiah
> Barnard's on a small piece of land conveyed by him for that purpose,
> which account is satisfying to this meeting.   The committee is con-
> tinued for further service and desired to report as they may see occasion.[37]

Report of 1785

In 1786, George Gawthrop and Thomas Richards were
added to the committee.[38]   From the first to the fourth
month of that year, the committee reported they had visited
one school,[39] but their report indicates nothing performed,
more than the visit.   Four months later it is reported they
had attended to the subject of schools somewhat, but that it
still required much greater attention; and they were advised
to meet with the monthly meeting's clerk that he might prepare his report on schools for the quarterly meeting.[40]

Though that report and the one of the quarterly meeting
really tell us nothing, we are better rewarded in one produced
just a year later, which points plainly to some of the difficulties the early school trustees had to face.

---

[33]Min. Kennett Mo. Mtg., 6—6—1778, 388.
[34]*Ibid.*, 5—1—1779, 22.   [35]*Ibid.*, 8—7—1779, 34.
[36]*Ibid.*, 3—5—1785, 234.   [37]*Ibid.*, 8—6—1785, 256.
[38]*Ibid.*, 1—7—1786, 275.   [40]*Ibid.*, 8—5—1786, 312.
[39]*Ibid.*, 4—1—1786, 290.

Report of
1787

The committee in the care of schools reported as follows: the substance whereof the clerk is directed to insert in our report of the quarterly meeting.

The care of schools has been under our care and attention and on
conferring together, we agree to report—under the present circumstances
of things amongst us, it is found most convenient to employ mistresses,
as the teachers in our schools most generally in the summer season,
several of which are now under the care of Friends to pretty good satisfaction, and we hope the concern is in a reviving way amongst us, though
there are discouragements by some Friends encouraging or promoting
schools taught by persons not agreeable to the advice of the society.[41]

**Mistresses
employed in
summer;
some schools
not accord-
ing to advice**

In 1794 William Jackson deeded to Joseph Preston and
others a piece of ground for a schoolhouse,[42] which was to be
in trust for the Friends' meeting. This is the first transfer
of ground for school purposes found among the New Garden
Friends. Among the stipulations of the deed are the following:

**Require-
ments for
the school
at New
Garden**

1. The master is to be a member of Friends.

2. The master must teach according to the rules laid down
(presumably by the school trustees) as before mentioned in
the case of the Horsham School Rules.[43]

3. The purpose stated is for the "promotion of piety and
good order" and to "propagate useful learning."

Goshen

On 12—2—1701, some Friends at Goshen applied to their
quarterly meeting for the privilege of establishing a meeting
for worship,[44] but this request was not approved until the
meeting of the quarter in 1703.[45] In 1707 they proposed
building a house for worship which was granted by the
quarterly meeting in the twelfth month.[46] Their monthly
meeting, as stated before, was not established until 1722.[47]
The preparative meetings in its compass were Goshen, Newtown, and Uwchlan.[48]

Though starting at a much later date as a monthly meeting
the records of Goshen are in some ways far superior to many

[41]Min. Kennett Mo. Mtg., 8—4—1787, 355.
[42]Deed No. 88, Chester Co. (the deed is deposited in a fireproof at
Orthodox Meeting House, custody of Edgar Haines, West Grove, Pa.).
[43]Min. Horsham Sch. Com., 1—27—1783.
[44]Min. Chester Q. Mtg., 12—2—1701.
[45]*Ibid.*, 9—1—1703.
[46]*Ibid.*, 12—2—1707.
[47]See page 122.
[48]See first book of Goshen Mo. Mtg. Records.

other meetings. In the first place, they devoted considerable attention to the yearly meetings' proposals of 1746 and 1750,[49] which by many meetings received very scant attention. The concrete results of this attention, however, do not stand forth, as reports on the subjects are not plentiful till the "1778 era." In that year of all years, they received the urgent accounts from the yearly meeting.[50] They appear to have gone to work at once, or perhaps had already begun, as a committee in the care of schools reported in the sixth month, 1779, that "a piece of ground is agreed for and a schoolhouse is now building in East Bradford."[51] This school was to be made up from the Friends of Goshen, Bradford, and Birmingham,[52] and to be established in accord with the stipulations of the yearly meeting aforesaid.[53] Goshen Monthly Meeting was requested to name some Friend to receive the land in trust, and Thomas Hoopes, Jr., was accordingly appointed for the purpose.[54]

A school in East Bradford for Goshen, Bradford and Birmingham

In 1782, the present school committee, deciding that something should be done concerning the regulation of schools, desired an addition to their number, those added being Abraham Pratt, William Lewis, John Mailin, and Josiah Hibberd.[55] Two months later this committee brought forth the following proposals, which are self-explanatory.

Increased committee reported 1782

We have met sundry times since the last meeting on the subject and are unanimous in judgment that it will be convenient for Friends to have a school house built near Jesse Garrett's smith shop on the east side of the road leading from the valley where about five acres may be purchased of William Garrett and William Garrett, Jr., in order to erect a school house on, and also a house for a school master, which we request the monthly meeting to take under consideration; and if they approve thereof, that it may be encouraged by a subscription amongst Friends only, and to be established on the plan proposed by the Yearly Meeting and subject to the direction of the monthly meeting from time to time, to remove or alter as they may see cause, or time may show to be necessary. We propose the house to be twenty-seven feet square from out to

Land to be purchased for school and master's accommodations

---

[49]Advices of the Yr. Mtg., 250.
[50]Min. Goshen Mo. Mtg., 1—8—1779.
[51]*Ibid.*, 6—11—1779.
[52]Futhey and Cope mention a school at Birmingham as early as 1753, *Hist. Chester Co.*, 302.
[53]Min. Goshen Mo. Mtg., 6—11—1779.
[54]*Ibid.*
[55]*Ibid.*, 1—11—1782.

The building
and cost

out, and compute the expense of building to be £150 exclusive of the land which will be £25, which we submit to the monthly meeting.   Signed in behalf of the committee—Thomas Hoopes, Jr.[56]

Their report was left for further consideration.

In 1784 a drive was organized on the preparative meetings. The monthly meeting received a visit from the committee of the quarterly meeting, which suggested the appointment of a large committee and the distribution of the printed advices of the yearly meeting of 1778, to be read before each of the preparative meetings.[57]   In conformity with this suggestion, the former school committee was released and a new one of ten members appointed as a standing committee, directed to follow out the previously made suggestions.[58]   In their report issued shortly thereafter, there is an account of the beginning of a school in Willistown, which is as the following:

Attempt to
bestir the
preparatives

School at
Willistown;
master's
house, etc.,
proposed

The committee in the care of schools report that a school is kept in the new house built in Willistown by a Friend, and endeavors are used to have it conducted as near as may be to the directions of the Yearly Meeting, and the building of a house for the master is proposed and a considerable sum of money is subscribed towards the same, provided a sufficiency can in like manner be raised.[59]

Another report for 1785 gives the state of schools for that date.

One school
the property
of the
monthly
meeting

There are several schools in the verge of our monthly meeting, kept by members of our society, one of which belongs to the monthly meeting, with several acres of land, whereon Friends are now building a house for a master, which when completed there will be a small fund towards schooling poor children.[60]

The chief concern to which the committee now addressed itself was the problem as to how they might establish a permanent fund for the schooling of poor children in their limits. For this problem they seem to have found a satisfactory solution for the time being, in 1786, which they reported to the monthly meeting for its approval.   It appears to have been satisfactory to the meeting in the following form, the

---

[56]Min. Goshen Mo. Mtg., 3—8—1782.
[57]*Ibid.*, 1—9—1784.
[58]*Ibid.*
[59]*Ibid.*, 8—6—1784.
[60]*Ibid.*, 8—5—1785.

essential features being the same as those incorporated in the plans of meetings already mentioned.

We, the subscribers, do hereby promise to pay unto . . . . treasurer for Friends' schools, within the compass of Goshen Monthly Meeting, or to other Friends as may be from time to time appointed by said committee to that service, the sum of money severally written against our names, which sums are so subscribed to be and remain a permanent fund under the care of and direction of the monthly meeting's committee of the people called Quakers, held at Goshen for the time being, appointed for this and other such purposes relative to schools, to be by them laid out in such manner as they shall from time to time judge most conducive to securing an income to the said schools, which income or annuity so arising therefrom to be applied to the education of such children as live within the compass of Goshen Monthly Meeting, whose parents, whether Friends or others, are not of ability to pay for the same and other such purposes as a majority of said committee shall from time to time direct, consistent with the object of the institution. Witness our hands—etc.[61]

Goshen plan for establishing funds

similar to others

For the next six years there are but two reports worthy of attention, which may be briefly summarized in this manner:

1787

1. One school, under the monthly meeting,
    a. has a large school house, and
    b. a dwelling house and garden for a master, who
    c. is a member of Friends
    d. The school is in charge of a standing committee
2. Another school house, whose
    a. master is a member of Friends, but
    b. the house is not Friends' property.[62]

The state of schools in 1787

1792

1. There is a school in Williston
    a. kept by a member of Friends,
    b. cared for by a standing committee of the monthly meeting,
    c. much in accord with yearly meeting's demands.
    d. There has been no increase in the permanent fund since last year.[63]

1792

The report of the standing monthly meeting's committee in 1795 notes these further advances. The reference to the

---

[61]Min. Goshen Mo. Mtg., 8—11—1786.
[62]*Ibid.*, 8—10—1787.   [63]*Ibid.*, 7—6—1792.

purchase of ground in Willistown would lead to the belief that
the school of Willistown mentioned in the report of 1792 was
not located on the meeting's property; but the tenor of the
report of 1784 leaves the impression that the "new house"
might have been the meeting's property.[64]   The report of
1795 is as follows:

1795

> The meeting's committee in the care of schools report that they have
> for some time had in contemplation the establishment of another school
> within the verge of the monthly meeting to be conducted agreeable to
> the advice of the Yearly Meeting, and have so far proceeded as to have
> purchased 4⅓ acres of land of Samuel Thomas in Willistown, which is
> deeded to some Friends in trust for the use and benefit of Goshen
> Monthly Meeting, to improve, alter, sell, or otherwise as the meeting
> may think proper, or time show to be necessary; therefore, if the
> monthly meeting unites with our proceedings, we desire they may take
> the same under their patronage.[65]

One school
closed tem-
porarily

In 1796 the school at Goshen was apparently closed for
several months, though the reference made to this fact may
have been to one at Willistown;[66] exactly which one can not
be deciphered from the minutes.   In 1797 the committee
reported a house had been built on the ground lately purchased (presumably that mentioned in the report of 1795)[67]
and a school was being kept therein, according to the advices
in all respects, save the membership of the master being outside of Friends.[68] "The other school" was taught by a
member, and was very much as might be desired in all
respects.[69]   One of the schools (not clear which one) became
vacant again for a short time in 1798.[70]

Union school
of 1779

What became of the school established about 1779 by
Bradford, Goshen, and Birmingham[71] is not made clear by
Goshen records.   It is probable that when the two schools
at Willistown and Goshen came under their direction, they
ceased to have any further connection with the earlier one in
East Bradford.   Further mention will be made of the East

[64]See page 132.
[65]Min. Goshen Mo. Mtg., 4—10—1795.
[66]*Ibid.*, 8—5—1796.
[67]See page 132.
[68]Min. Goshen Mo. Mtg., 8—11—1797.
[69]*Ibid.*
[70]*Ibid.*, 8—10—1798.
[71]See page 131.

Bradford school in the material presented for that monthly meeting, in the pages just following. It may be only briefly mentioned in this connection that in 1797 the Goshen meeting appointed a committee to secure subscriptions for the yearly meeting's boarding school which had been proposed in 1794,[72] and was opened for students in 1799.[73]

Some meetings for worship by the Friends in the district, later to be known as Bradford Meeting, were held as early as 1719,[74] and regular meetings for worship were established in 1725.[75] Not until 1737, however, had they become of sufficient importance to warrant the establishment of a monthly meeting.[76]

Bradford meeting established

In 1762 Bradford's minutes refer to settling the affairs and providing for the support and the education of the children.[77] It was proposed that application be made to the next court that those under indenture to —— might be bound out so as to have a Christian education, and to enable them "to acquire a livelihood with reputation."[78] It is implied that the Mr. —— had not provided for them properly in those respects.   In 1765 fourteen epistles were received and directed to be read in each of the preparative meetings (Bradford and Caln).[79] Though no school is mentioned at these early dates, there seems to be no doubt that schools were in operation, perhaps a sort of family school. This brief extract would indicate that the above assumption is not without foundation:

Two of the Friends appointed report they had an opportunity with Benjamin Faris respecting schooling of Isaac Few, and that he informed them that he would undertake to school him for the term of one year, for the sum of £25, which proposal the meeting complies with and agrees to pay the half.[80]

The cost of this schooling was paid by the two preparative meetings which produced their quotas four months later.[81]

---

[72]See page 73f.
[73]Min. Goshen Mo. Mtg., 1—6—1797.
[74]Min. Chester Q. Mtg., 9—9—1719.
[75]*Ibid.*, 3—10—1725.
[76]See page 122; also Bunting, 51.
[77]Min. Bradford Mo. Mtg., 6—18—1762.
[78]*Ibid.*
[79]*Ibid.*, 12—13—1765.
[80]*Ibid.*, 4—7—1767.
[81]*Ibid.*, 8—14—1767.

Thenceforward, till 1778, nothing of note is recorded, save occasional notices of the education of the youth.

The year 1778 produced the following minute:

The extracts of last Yearly Meeting were produced here and read, containing much seasonable advice and instruction which is recommended to the solid consideration and observation of individuals; in particular, that of encouragement of proper schools for the instruction of youth in useful learning.[82]

Like an electric current suddenly shunted into the circuit, these extracts of 1777 and 1778 seemed to increase the voltage in the wires of the organization, producing a general hum of activity. A committee, immediately appointed, reported in 1779 they had considered the situation,[83] and in 1780 produced the report which is given below. As will be noted, their report mentions the "Union School" of Goshen, East Bradford and Birmingham, which has already received some consideration in the case of Goshen.[84]

We, the committee appointed in the care of schools, report that most of us attended to the appointment and have several times met and conferred together and have given our assistance toward the settling of a school between Goshen, Bradford, and Birmingham Preparative Meeting in a new schoolhouse built by Friends; one at East Bradford in the old schoolhouse near the meeting house; one at East Caln kept at the meeting house at present, agreed to be under the direction of Friends nearly agreeable to the Advices of the Yearly Meeting; and we think it expedient to appoint Friends to take the necessary care of said schools; but there appear to be many Friends that are not yet accommodated with suitable schools, and we think a committee of a few Friends to be continued to assist therein will be necessary, all of which we submit to the meeting. (Signed by the committee). . . .

Which being read and considered, the meeting appoints William England, William Cooper, Humphrey Marshall, and Thomas Baldwin to have the care of the school near Bradford Meeting House, and Thomas Fisher, Griffith Mendenhall, Isaac Coates and Isaac Pim to have the care of the school now kept in the meeting house at East Caln, who are desired to take the necessary care therein and the former committee is still continued.[85]

Three schools established; a committee to assist in establishing others

A subsequent report of 1781 points out that an additional school has been established, presumably through the coöpera-

[82]Min. Bradford Mo. Mtg., 12—15—1778.
[83]*Ibid.*, 2—12—1779.
[84]See page 133f.
[85]Min. Bradford Mo. Mtg., 5—12—1780.

tion of the meetings of Bradford, Kennett, and New Garden.[86] The records of Kennett and New Garden do not seem to recognize this coöperative school, however. To the writer, it seems that the probable state of affairs was that the one school was so located that it was patronized by the three communities though its direction lay in the hands of Bradford Meeting. The contiguous situation of the townships makes this a plausible and a probable solution. The school was soon to be discontinued for a time.[87] The report of 1781 is herewith submitted.

The Friends in the care of schools report that they attended the school set between this meeting, New Garden, and Kennett Monthly Meetings, and purpose taking further care therein; and those to have the care of the school at Bradford report that a school is held there in pretty regular order, considering the situation of the master in regard to his sight, and they that had the care of the school at East Caln informed that they had divers opportunities with the master and scholars, and are of the mind that further care in that respect is necessary; which being considered, this meeting continues the said Friends and desires that they may attend to the service for which they are appointed.[88]

A school between Bradford, Kennett and New Garden

The conditions presented in the report of the second month remained the same, save that the school between Kennett, New Garden, and Bradford was reported "discontinued" in the sixth month, 1781.[89] Later in that year, the old committee was released and a new list of men, Thomas Baldwin, Joel Harlan, Thomas Sugar, Nathan Cooper, Benjamin Hanley, John Hoopes, Thomas Fisher, Griffith Mendenhall, Samuel Fisher, and George Harrison constituted a "standing committee."[90] In 1782 four schools were reported;[91] in 1783, several schools not entirely agreeable to the desires expressed in the Yearly Meeting's Advices;[92] in 1784, three are reported in the verge of Bradford Particular Meeting, mostly under the direction of Friends, but "none at either of the Calns" (East or West).[93] Subsequent reports show that the cessation of the schools at Caln was only temporary. The presentation of this very brief span of their history may be

Four schools reported by committee

[86]Min. Bradford Mo. Mtg., 2—16—1781.
[87]*Ibid.*, 6—16—1781.
[88]*Ibid.*, 2—16—1781.
[89]*Ibid.*, 6—16—1781.
[90]*Ibid.*, 9—14—1781.
[91]*Ibid.*, 2—15—1782.
[92]*Ibid.*, 8—15—1783.
[93]*Ibid.*, 2—13—1784.

closed with an abbreviated statement of a committee report
made in 1792.[94]

1. We visited four schools in our verge, one more left, making five.
2. The fifth is likely to be discontinued soon.
3. Number
    one near Bradford Meeting House (in care of Friends).
    one in East Bradford (part Friends and part not).
    one in East Caln (the masters not members of Friends, but will-
    ing to be under their direction).
4. The committee was released on request.

In the same year that Uwchlan became a monthly meeting,
the Friends entered a protest, saying that the making of wills

was too much neglected, but that such as were made were not
misapplied.[95]   It is quite probable that the first statement is
an indication of a philanthropic spirit in the meeting, between
which and educational activity there has been noted a high
correlation.   Moreover, their explicit statement in 1765
concerning the education of the negroes would indicate the

education of their own children was already taken care of.[96]
The usual transformation in the kind of reports, noted in
other meetings about 1778 and following, is likewise apparent
in the meeting at present under discussion.

Though a school committee was appointed much earlier
(1779) there was a very definite report made before 1782.
Two reports made then in successive months are worthy of
our attention.

The committee respecting schools report that they have attended to
the service, having visited one school, the master whereof is a member
of this meeting, to a good degree of satisfaction, some of the employers

and scholars being present.   They are continued to proceed in that
service as way may open and report to next meeting[97].   . . .

And a month later

The Friends appointed report that they have visited two other schools,
the masters whereof and many of the employers are members of this
meeting, and   . . . .   being enabled to communicate some advice,
which appeared to be well received, they are continued.[98]

In 1783 a new committee was commissioned to procure a
particular statement of the schools wherein Friends were con-

[94]Min. Bradford Mo. Mtg., 9—14—1792.
[95]Min. Uwchlan Mo. Mtg., 8—3—1763, 22.
[96]*Ibid.*, 3—1—1765, 66.
[97]*Ibid.*, 11—7—1782, 132.   [98]*Ibid.*, 12—5—1782, 106.

cerned either as masters or as employers, viz.: Thomas
Richards, Jesse Jones, Joshua Baldwin, Reuben John, William
Millhouse, Griffith John, Simon Meredith, William Cooper,
Elihu Evans, Aaron Duncan, and Joseph Starr.[99] This committee is not to be confused with the trustees of the school
funds, who were entirely distinct, and whose sole function was
to receive and apply the funds for the education of the indigent children. The trustees' report stated in 1784 that the
amount of the legacies and donations up to that date
amounted to £ 120 /10 /oo.[100]

New
committee
appointed

The state
of funds

Near this time, very probably in 1784, a new school was
established by Friends at Nantmeal, for which Uwchlan
Meeting appointed a special committee which was to make a
report; the report made in 1785 stated that they had visited
the school and found it well conducted.[101] In 1787, the school
committee produced a report on all schools, which was to be
sent to the quarterly meeting. It embodied some statement
of the results achieved, difficulties to be faced, and further
gave an insight into the coöperation of Friends in the "mixed
schools" of their communities. As sent to the quarterly
meeting, the report was as follows:

School set
up at
Nantmeal

We of the committee appointed to essay a report to the quarterly
meeting of the situation of our members in regard to schools and the
progress of our monthly meeting in that important concern, having had
several conferences and opportunities of enquiring into that subject,
report as follows: that some have been appointed and continued from
time to time by our monthly meeting for several years past, who have
used many endeavors to promote the establishment of schools agreeable
to the advices of the Yearly Meeting; but our number generally living
so remote from each other, has prevented much progress being made
therein, save one house being built by Friends at Nantmeal nearly on
the plan proposed, in which a school has been kept some time, but now
dropped for want of a salary for the master, there not being a sufficient
number of Friends settled contiguous thereto nor to each other, in any
other part of our meeting to support a school; and the boarding out of
our children appears an expense too heavy for many of us, so that we are
generally in the practice of schooling our children in a mixed manner,
though mostly under the tutorage of Friends, or persons friendly disposed, to whom some care has been extended and their schools frequently

Report of
1787

Nantmeal
school
discontinued

---

[99]Min. Uwchlan Mo. Mtg., 12—4—1783, 158.
[100]*Ibid.*, 2–5–1784, 162.   [101]*Ibid.*, 2–10–1785, 184.

visited by our committee some time back.   Signed by order of the school
committee by William Millhouse, clerk.[102]

London
Grove

In 1794, the London Grove Monthly Meeting, just created,
began its educational work by appointing a committee to
take subscriptions for a fund to support a "regular school."[103]
In 1795, the preparative meeting proposing that a standing
committee be appointed to inspect the necessities of the poor
and the school education of their children, the following were
named to unite with a committee of women on that concern,
viz.:   Samuel Swayne, Josiah Hoopes, John Man, and

Committee
of men and
women
appointed
for schools

Jonathan Buslow.[104] Four months later the committee
appointed to raise the funds by subscription (see above)
reported that a sum of "more than fifty pounds" was already
subscribed.[105] No statement of the number of schools
established in the limits of the London Grove Meeting is
given between the time of its establishment and the end of the
century; nor are any other details vouchsafed.   It will
suffice for a voucher of their intentions and the work actually
begun in that period, to insert the following statement of
their plan for founding their schools.

Plan pro-
duced for
settling
schools

Pursuant to the advice and recommendations of the Yearly Meeting
of Friends for many years, and excited by consideration in our own
minds for an improvement of the school education of the youth, especially those in low circumstances, we, the subscribers hereto, have agreed
to promote the raising of a fund or stock, the increase whereof to be for
the benefit of the several schools which are or may be under the care of
London Grove Monthly Meeting, and to be distributed amongst them
at the direction of a committee of the said meeting, appointed from time
to time in the care of schools.   The sum annexed to each of our names
we hereby engage each for himself or heirs, executors and administrators
respectively, to pay or to cause to be paid to such Friend or Friends as
the abovesaid monthly meeting shall appoint as treasurer for the same,
and that at any time, when demanded, after the whole subscription
amounts to the sum of fifty pounds.   The treasurer, so appointed, we
enjoin to be subject to the inspection and control of the said monthly
meeting and to render a fair and true account thereto of his proceedings
therein once a year, and if the said meeting shall at any time see cause
to release the treasurer, then he shall give up his accounts and pay the

[102]Min. Bradford Mo. Mtg., 8—9—1787, 235.
[103]Min. London Grove Mtg., 12—3—1794, 56.
[104]*Ibid.*, 3—4—1795, 62.
[105]*Ibid.*, 7—1—1795, 73.

money or transfer such other property as may be under his care, appertaining to the said fund unto such other Friends as the monthly meeting
may appoint to succeed him in the said trust. Our subscriptions, until
they amount to fifty pounds or upwards, we direct to be kept in stock
and be deposited in some safe way so as to produce increase either by a
loan upon land at the discretion and direction of the said monthly
meeting or committee thereof. The interest, rent, or increase whereof
we direct to be applied for the benefit of the aforesaid schools in such a
manner and at such times as the school committee of the said monthly
meeting for the time being, or a majority of them shall direct. And
although our present endeavor may appear feeble and small, yet we trust
and hope it may gradually increase so as to become more useful in time.[106]

There remains to be presented in this chapter the activities
of Sadsbury Meeting, which, though outside the limits of
Chester County, was made up very largely of members
residing in Chester County.[107] The most distinctly educational work of any sort was the youths' meeting, which was
very frequently mentioned as early as 1739, only two years
after they became a monthly meeting.[108] Numerous statements of these meetings occur throughout the first thirty
years and more. Attention was also directed to a care for
the children of the poor.

Sadsbury

Youths'
meetings
established
in 1739

One of the Friends appointed in the case of John Marsh's child report
they attended the service and met with some encouragement concerning
the education of the child, the person with whom it resides being its
grandmother; the meeting concludes to leave it under the care and
notice of Henry Marsh, the child's uncle.[109]

In 1779 the first committee to carry out the instruction of
1777 and 1778 was appointed, consisting of the following
members: James Miller, Andrew Moore, and Samuel
Simons.[110] They were to afford assistance to each of the
preparative meetings (Sadsbury and Leacock). This they
reported in the second month they had done; James Moore,
Isaac Taylor, John Moore, James Smith, Abraham Gibbons,
and James Webb were then appointed to do the work.[111] In
1782 a visit was made to Sadsbury Meeting by the committee

Committee
appointed
on schools

[106]Min. London Grove Mtg., 11—4—1795, 78.
[107]Futhey and Cope, *Hist. Chester Co.*, 239.
[108]Min. Sadsbury Mo. Mtg., 3—6—1739, 7.
[109]*Ibid.*, 6—21—1769, 180.
[110]*Ibid.*, 1—20—1779, 297.
[111]*Ibid.*, 2—20—1779, 298.

appointed by the quarterly meeting.[112] They reported further at that time:

School at Sadsbury mentioned

> The Monthly Meeting committee has it under care and there is a school set up at Sadsbury, and it is closely recommended to Friends for a further progress and to the committee of this meeting in particular, to which George Cooper, Andrew Moore, and Joseph Dickinson are added.[113]

The conditions remain substantially the same for the five subsequent years, with frequently interspersed reports, made to the monthly meetings and to be sent to the quarterly meeting. In that year, as the following report shows, the school at Sadsbury was discontinued, and the old committee removed to make place for a new one.

Discontinued, but not long

> Several Friends of the committee respecting schools report they have conferred together since the last meeting, and it doth not appear that there is any school at this time within the verge of this meeting under the care and direction of Friends, and the said committee expressing their desire to be released, the meeting consents thereto, yet in order to keep alive the concern and promote a matter so interesting, concludes to appoint a fresh committee, and James Miller, John Moore, son of James, Isaac Taylor, and Joseph Williams, Joseph Brinton, Moses Brinton, William Downing, and Gaius Dickinson are appointed for the service.[114]

It is not ascertainable from the minutes just how long this school remained closed, but a minute of 1789, directing that Barclay's *Catechism* be distributed for the use of the schools, indicates that it was not discontinued for a long time.[115] Isaac Taylor, R. Moore, William Gibbons, and William Webb were appointed to distribute the said books.[116]

Barclay's *Catechism* for use in schools

In 1792, Lampeter Preparative Meeting (called Leacock in 1732, but changed to Lampeter in 1749)[117] laid before the monthly meeting a request to be permitted to build a school house on or near their meeting house land for the purpose of a boarding school to be under the care of the monthly meeting.[118] Their request was not acted upon until the next meeting when it was referred to a committee of eleven men, who were

Lampeter requests to build schoolhouse, 1792

---

[112]Min. Sadsbury Mo. Mtg., 6—19—1782, 337.   [113]*Ibid.*
[114]*Ibid.*, 3—21—1787, 39f.
[115]*Ibid.*, 6—17—1789, 70.
[116]*Ibid.*
[117]Futhey and Cope, *Hist. Chester Co.*, 239.
[118]Min. Sadsbury Mo. Mtg., 2—22—1792, 106.

to consider the proposals and report their judgment to the monthly meeting when convenient.[119] It appears from the following extract of the monthly meeting that they were somewhat critical.

The committee appointed to consider the proposals of Lampeter Preparative Meeting for building a school house made a report in writing, which not meeting the approbation of this meeting, is returned and Joseph Brinton, Abraham Gibbons, William Brinton, James Smith, John Ferris, James Cooper, and Levi Powell are added to the former committee and William Webb is requested to consider the matter and report to the next meeting.[120]

Committee's suggestions for Lampeter school not accepted

At the session of the monthly meeting held two months later, the newly appointed committee was successful in getting a satisfactory hearing for their decision in regard to the Lampeter Boarding School.

The proposal of Lampeter Preparative Meeting comes again under consideration and the following report being produced and divers times read, is concurred with.

To Sadsbury Monthly Meeting—

We, the committee appointed to consider Lampeter's proposals for building a school house and having again met and had a solid conference together unite in judgment that the proposals are nearly agreeable to the advices of the Yearly Meeting and under the present circumstances are of the mind the monthly meeting may be safe in leaving that meeting at liberty to erect a building proportioned in size to their Friends and the probabilities of what may be obtained by subscription (which is submitted to the meeting by James Miller and signed by fourteen others). 6—25—1792.[121]

The accepted report

In 1793, the school committee recommended in the following report that more definite steps be taken to meet the demand of the yearly meeting in regard to (1) the accommodations for a master and (2) the establishment of a permanent school fund.

The committee in the care of schools made the following report in writing which, after being solidly considered, is adopted and the clerk is directed to furnish each preparative meeting with a copy of this minute together with the report of the committee (which follows). Most of the committee appointed in the care of establishing well regulated schools for the instruction of our youth report they met twice on

---

[119]Min. Sadsbury Mo. Mtg., 3—21—1792, 107.
[120]*Ibid.*, 5—23—1792, 109.
[121]*Ibid.*, 7—10—1792, 112.

the subject and solidly considering the same, believe it would be right
for the monthly meeting to recommend to Sadsbury Preparative Meeting the making of such suitable provisions for the accommodation of a
school master as is recommended by the Yearly Meeting Minute of

**Funds to be
raised**

1778—That Sadsbury and Lampeter Preparative Meetings be stirred up
to use their endeavors to raise such funds for their respective meetings
by subscription as is recommended—as well as in a minute of our last
quarterly meeting, by William Webb (and five others).[122]

By a later minute we are informed that an instrument of
writing (subscription plan) has been drawn up for the purpose
of raising funds,[123] which, however, did not prove wholly
satisfactory,[124] and was postponed for further consideration.
As presented finally and accepted on twelfth month, 10th,
1793, the plan for raising permanent funds was as follows:

Whereas the Yearly Meeting is impressed with a sense of the advantages that would arise from a religious education of our youth, has frequently recommended the establishment of schools under the care of a
standing committee of monthly or particular meetings and especially in
1778, recommended the promoting a subscription towards a fund, the
increase whereof might be employed in paying the master's salary, if

**Plans for
raising funds
adopted**

necessary, and promoting the education of poor Friends' children. This
provision may be made to take in poor children of Friends or others
taught gratis or at such moderate rates as their parents or guardians can
afford to pay at the discretion of the trustees, etc.

And we, the subscribers, writing with the above recommendations and
willing to part with a portion of the substance, we as stewards are blessed
with, in order to carry the same into effect (provided always, nevertheless, that no part of the fund shall ever be applied towards paying the
master's salary so as to reduce the schooling of children who are in
affluent circumstances, lower than 40 shillings per annum, and may be
raised at the discretion of the trustees), do hereby promise for ourselves,
our heirs, and executors, or administrators to pay, or cause to be paid,
the several sums to our names annexed, to the trustees for . . . .
school.   Otherwise, five per cent. interest from the dates respectively to
our names prefixed until paid or till such other persons as may be
appointed by the monthly meeting to receive the same. In witness
whereof, ...[125]

The situation of schools near the close of the century is
shown in a report of 1797 to be as stated below.   Though this
report states no fund is established, a later report of 1798
states that some progress has been made in that respect.[126]

---

[122]Min. Sadsbury Mo. Mtg., 4—17—1793, 120.
[123]*Ibid.*, 5—13—1793, 121.   [125]*Ibid.*, 12—10—1793, 128.
[124]*Ibid.*, 9—18—1793, 125.   [126]*Ibid.*, 1—7—1798, 175.

The report for 1797 is as follows:

The committee in the care of schools report that there is no fund established for this purpose, yet there are three schools within the compass of our monthly meeting taught by masters who are Friends and are under the especial care of a committee of this meeting.[127]

At the very close of the century Sadsbury Friends were interested in raising a fund to help in the establishment of the Yearly Meeting's boarding school at Westtown, Pennsylvania.[128]

SUMMARY

This chapter considers the establishment of schools in Kennett, New Garden, Goshen, Bradford, Uwchlan, London Grove and Sadsbury monthly meetings.

No early definite reference is made to education, though the careful interest in children's welfare is at all times evident. Not until the "1777 era" do the reports give any considerable information concerning schools. Committees were thereafter always in attendance upon the problems of the schools. In 1781 a "union school" was reported between Kennett, Bradford and New Garden, which was afterwards discontinued. In 1785 they report "several schools," in partial accord with demands of the yearly meeting. Land for Kennett school "number one" was purchased in 1792, and rules drawn up for its control. Their scheme for raising permanent funds was not completed until 1795. Two schools, taught by members of the society, were under the care of the meeting's committee in 1798.

Two schools were reported at New Garden in 1779 and another was at that time proposed. Some land was conveyed to the meeting in 1785 for the use of a school, and a house built upon it. Another piece of land was deeded by William Jackson in 1794 for a similar purpose. Certain stipulations were made concerning the school to be established there. It was found more consistent in summer to employ mistresses rather than masters.

Though established at a late date, Goshen was very active educationally. Land was purchased and a house was being

---

[127]Min. Sadsbury Mo. Mtg., 7—19—1797, 168.
[128]*Ibid.*, 4—24—1799, 187.

built for a union school between Goshen, Bradford and Birmingham, in 1779. Committees were appointed, which

Two schools gave reports better than those usually returned. A plan for funds was adopted in 1786. No further mention is found in regard to the union schools after the establishment of the schools at Goshen and Willistown.

Bradford's first educational activity was in connection

Bradford with the apprenticing of children. A single case in which a boy was put to school by the meeting occurred in 1767; the expense therefore was defrayed by the preparative meetings. Educational activity increased in 1778; three schools were

Three school reported in 1780 and a committee appointed to assist in
1780 establishing others. They appear to have been successful; five schools were reported in 1792, though one was about to

Five schools be discontinued. Not all of the masters were Friends.
1792

The statement that Negroes were being educated in 1765, induces one to believe that Friends' children were provided

Uwchlan for. Three schools were mentioned in 1779, in which the masters and many of the employers were Friends. In 1789

Nantmeal a school was established at Nantmeal under a special com-
School, 1789 mittee of Uwchlan Meeting; it was reported discontinued in 1787. The meeting at London Grove, established (1792),

London reported no schools in its compass before the end of the
Grove century; although an elaborate plan was drawn up for the establishment of school funds.

Youths' meetings were established by Sadsbury as early as

Sadsbury 1739 and instances in which poor children were educated are cited for 1769. The first committee seems to have been appointed for schools in 1779. A school was reported for

Lampeter Sadsbury in 1782, but was later discontinued for a brief time,
boarding which cannot be definitely determined. In 1792 it was
school agreed that Lampeter Preparative might have permission to establish a boarding school. A plan for funds was drawn up,

Three but no success reported in raising them until 1798. Three
schools schools are reported established, and under the care of Quaker masters in 1797.

Total, The entire number of schools set up by the above named
18 or 19 meetings was eighteen or nineteen.
schools

CHAPTER VIII

SCHOOLS OF DELAWARE COUNTY

The activity of the several monthly meetings in Delaware County in the establishment of schools will be considered under the heads of the respective meetings in the following order, Chester, Darby, Radnor, and Concord. These are four of the earliest monthly meetings established in Pennsylvania, the dates of their establishment being: Chester, 1681; and Darby, Radnor, and Concord in 1684.[1] The aim of this chapter, as of the others dealing with the several counties, is to present, first the source material which has been found to have any bearing on the establishment of schools and the attitude of the monthly meetings toward them.

The meetings

Penn having come to New Castle on October 27, 1682, and performed the ceremonies of taking possession of the province,[2] appears to have gone thence to Upland, from whence he sent a letter to Ephriam Harman (dated October 29, 1682) regarding summoning a court to be held at New Castle (November 2, 1682).[3] But Upland was not destined to remain the name of the city, as Penn's biographers tell us. It is stated that Penn, having arrived and being filled with emotion at having had a successful journey, turned to a friend and said, "What wilt thou that I should call this place?" He replied, "Chester."[4]

Naming of Chester

In passing it should be mentioned that an interest in education does not date entirely from the coming of the Quakers and the establishment of Penn's colony. The records of the court of Upland inform us (1679) that, without a doubt, some children received the advantages of an education. It may

Education before coming of Quakers

---

[1]Bunting, 40, 39, 19 and 42, respectively; also first vols. of each respective meeting's records.
[2]Smith, *Hist. Del. Co.*, 138; see also page 41, chapter on Philadelphia.
[3]*Ibid.*, 139.
[4]Clarkson's *Penn*, I, 259; Hazard's *Annals*, 695.

have been very restricted, we cannot determine that. The
records of that date state, however, that: "The Plt demands
of this Deft 200 Gilders for teaching this Defts children to
read one yeare."[5]   There is no doubt that Friends were not
concerned with education in this case.[6]

The first meetings of Chester Monthly Meeting were held
in the Court House[7] at Chester, and meetings for worship
usually among the members at their homes, previously
designated.[8]   In March, 1686, Urin Keen conveyed in trust
to John Simcock, Thomas Brassey, John Brinton, Caleb
Pusey, Randall Vernon, Thomas Vernon, Joshua Hastings,
Mordecai Maddock, Thomas Martin, Richard Few, Walter
Faucet and Edward Carter, a piece of ground in Chester

**Property
granted the
meeting and
house built**

beginning at said Urin's lot or Garding, and so running, 60 feet along
and fronting the street towards the prison house, thence down the lower
edge in Chester Creek—thence along the Creek 60 feet—thence to the
place of beginning . . . . to the use and behoof of the said Chester—the people of God called Quakers and their successors forever.[9]

In the year following, it was urged by the monthly meeting
that Friends agree with workmen to build a meeting house at
Chester 24 feet square by 16 feet in height.[10]   The first meeting house, built on the ground above mentioned, was completed about 1793.[11]

**First land
devised for
schools in
1769**

The earliest record of schools established by Friends dates
back to about 1770.   Though this is the first record of a
device of property for the purpose, and the minutes of the
meeting are also negligent of educational affairs, it does not
seem probable to the writer that the locality was without
schools.   There were probably neighborhood schools, not

**Hoskins wills
ground for
schools**

subject to any organization on the part of the meeting.   On
December 31, 1769, Joseph Hoskins, a Friend, willed a lot
of ground for the use of schools,[12] and though his death did

---

[5]Rec. Upland Court, 121; Smith, *Hist. Del. Co.*, 121; Hazard,
Annals, 462.
[6]Would not likely take the case to court.
[7]It appears from a record of sale that the court house was sold to
Robert Wade, 1686. (Record of sale quoted in Jordan, *Hist. Del.
Co.*, I, 112.)
[8]Jordan, *Hist. Del. Co.*, I, 104; Smith, *Hist. Del. Co.*, 137.
[9]Smith, *Hist. Del. Co.*, 166.
[10]Rec. of Chester Mo. Mtg., 1687, I.; Smith, 166.
[11]Smith, 188.   [12]Jordan, II, 441.

not occur till some years later, the meeting appears to have known of the intended bequest and to have built a school house in 1770.[13] It was further ordered by the will that the sum of thirty pounds be paid to John Eyre and James Barton for the schooling and education of such poor children of the inhabitants of the borough of said Chester as the preparative meeting shall for the time being think fit to order and direct.[14] Mr. Jordan in his history of the county, describes the schoolhouse:

Poor to be schooled

> The schoolhouse was built of bricks, laid in Flemish bond, the ends of the headers being burnt black, a style much in vogue at that time. In the south gable large numerals, 1770, were inserted in the wall, the figures being formed by the black ends of the headers.[15]

The school mentioned in the committee's report on schools situated at Middletown,[16] was established by Friends in 1783, but an earlier school existed (1740), according to Mr. Jordan,[17] the buildings for the same having been donated by Thomas Yarnall and Thomas Minshall, whose names are very prominently mentioned in Quaker records. The meeting minutes make no mention of such a school being established, however, and it must be understood to have been entirely on individual initiative. In 1791, Enock Taylor and wife, Quakers, conveyed a quarter acre of land to the use of Chester Monthly Meeting of Friends for the use of a school.[18] Judging, however, from the later reports of the monthly meeting we would be led to believe that no school was established at that time.[19] On December 20, 1791, David Hall conveyed adjoining property for the same use.[20]

School at Middletown probably in 1740

Land donated by Taylor and wife

About 1778 the monthly meeting became more active in regard to its interest in schools, appointing committees to investigate conditions and report the state to its sessions.[21] In 1779 and 1781, there appeared two reports on the condition

Committees appointed on education

---

[13]Jordan, II, 441.
[14]*Ibid.*
[15]*Ibid.*
[16]Min. Chester Mo. Mtg., 1—27—1800.
[17]Jordan, II, 43—45.
[18]*Ibid.*
[19]The absence of any mention of it in the meeting records.
[20]The writer was unable to find a record of this deed.
[21]No committee reports were noted before that date.

of the Negroes and their education which are presented in another chapter.[22] In 1782 there likewise appeared a report of the committee on schools in general.[23] This committee, appointed in accord with the suggestions of the yearly meeting, agreed substantially that the best way to the establishment of schools systematically, was to arrange for a subscription which might be applied to that use at the discretion of

Subscriptions to be started for funds

the monthly meeting. This was to be used for paying the master's salary, and to educate poor Friends' children, where it mght appear to be of advantage to do so.[24] These suggestions were directed to be copied and put into the hands of the members in each of the preparative meetings.[25] Three months thereafter, the meeting appointed a treasurer for funds and a committee for the oversight of schools, who were to act in general accord with the suggestions made in the first report.[26] The minute of the meeting of that date runs as follows:

A form of subscription was proposed which might be entered into by those who desired, and was approved by the meeting and all urged to forward the signing of it.[27]

The work thus started was not entirely satisfactory to the committee, however. They report that "the work goes very slowly" and name, as one cause, the great difficulty of getting

Qualified teachers scarce

suitable teachers.[28] Provision seems to have been made for the schooling of poor children, "such as can conveniently be sent."[29] This reference may mean that all such were schooled who were within reach of a school, or that they sent all for whom they had a sufficient fund. In 1783 they acknowledged the receipt of the most recent advices of the yearly meeting which again recommended the serious subject of schools to their attention. Again in 1792 we find this minute:

The subject of schools being now resumed and the several paragraphs contained in the extracts of 1778, 1779 and 1789 being read relative thereto, Friends, of the several preparative meetings are desired to pay

---

[22]See chapter on Negroes, page 228.
[23]Min. Chester Mo. Mtg., 1—28—1782, 87.
[24]*Ibid.*   [25]*Ibid.*
[26]*Ibid.*, 4—29—1782.   [27]*Ibid.*
[28]*Ibid.*, 7—28—1783, 130.   [29]*Ibid.*

close attention to the several repeated advises of the yearly meeting no this important subject.[30]

In 1796 the concern of a boarding school, which we have found was also interesting all of the other monthly meetings, in the Philadelphia Yearly Meeting, came also to the attention of Chester. They indicated their willingness to coöperate in the scheme by the appointment of a committee, which appears from a minute made in the meeting in 1793.

William Worrall, Daniel Sharpless, Josiah Rhoads, Edward Fell, Mahlon Parsons, Roger Dirks, Thomas Sharpless and Jacob Minshall are appointed to prepare a subscription paper and promote Friends' subscriptions towards the establishment and support of the boarding school agreeable to the recommendations of our last Yearly Meeting, and report of their care to next or a future meeting.[31]

Subscriptions promoted for boarding school

The general state of schools under the meeting's jurisdiction is made known by the following report sent in by the school committee to the monthly meeting held on 1–27–1800.

The committee appointed to the care of schools report there are three kept within the verge of this meeting under Friends care, viz.:

1. One at Springfield taught by a Friend.
1. One at Middletown, taught by a person not in membership.
3. One at Blue Hill under similar circumstances, all of which we trust are conducted in a good degree orderly, but that there has been little or no addition to our fund since last year, except what it has increased by use. The school committee also informs that the Friends who were by the last will of our Friend George Miller and James Turner, left trustees to the lots at Blue Hill have conveyed the same by instruments of writing duly executed as follows, to wit: the dwelling house and lot to Jacob Minshall, Edward Fell, Ambrose Smedley, Isaac Sharpless, John Hill, Jr., and Joseph Pennell, Jr., and the schoolhouse and lot to George Miller, Edward Fell, Ambrose Smedley, James Smedley, Isaac Sharpless, John Hill, Jr., and Joseph Jonnell, Jr., which said conveyances have since been recorded and are lodged with the other writings relating thereto, in the hands of the treasurer of the school fund which is satisfactory to the meeting.[32]

Three schools under Chester Meeting

The Blue Hill School, mentioned in the above report of the committee, no doubt dated back to a few years following 1791, in which James Turner bequeathed his "Blue Hill Estate" to George Miller for the use of schools established at the direction of Chester Monthly Meeting.[33]

---

[30]Min. Chester Mo. Mtg., 4—30—1792, 347.
[31]*Ibid.*, 12—26—1796, 447.
[32]*Ibid.*, 1—27—1800, 508.   [33]*Ibid.*, 5—30—1791, 319.

I give, devise and bequeath to George Miller, the son of my cousin George Miller, my house and lot of Ground situated in the Province aforesaid (commonly called Blue Hill) with the appurtenances to hold by him and his heirs and assigns forever.

"Blue Hill" estate bequeathed by James Turner

Upon special trust and confidence, nevertheless and to and for the use, intent and purpose hereinafter expressed, mentioned and declared, and moreover for the use of the society of Protestants, commonly called Quakers, of and belonging to the Monthly Meeting of Chester for the erecting one or more houses for the teaching and instructing youth therein, and all necessary conveniences thereto belonging under and subject to the rules and regulations and orders of the said meeting for the time being forever.

Item, I give and bequeath to my Friend Jacob Minshall, all the rest and residue of my estate in trust for the use of a school which may at times be kept at or near my lot of ground above mentioned, subject to the direction of the Chester Monthly Meeting.[34]

The meeting's schools also received a considerable assistance through a legacy of £50 left by Thomas Evans for the establishment and support of a school within the verge of Chester Monthly.[35] He makes it clear in his bequest that he has been influenced to do this by the recommendations of the yearly meeting, the influence of which has been instanced in many cases before this one.

Legacy from Thomas Evans

Not only to the advancement of education and enlightenment by means of schools alone did Friends of the Chester Meeting lend their encouragement.   In a minute of 1689 we find an interesting reference to assistance proposed for the encouragement of printing in Philadelphia.

The business proposed to the Friends of Philadelphia concerning allowing William Bradford, the printer, £40 by the year to encourage him to continue in the art and practise of Printing. This meeting approving the said proposal, orders for Darby Monthly Meeting John Blunston and Joshua Fearne and for Chester Monthly Meeting Caleb Pusey, Randall Vernon and for Chichester Monthly Jacob Chandler and John Mendenhall to take subscription according to proposal.[36]

Printing encouraged by the meeting

We have noticed that there appeared to be very little in the records of the monthly meeting until about 1770 and that they contained little of educational interest before that time.   The records of the Quarterly Meeting of Chester (later known as

---

[34]Min. Chester Mo. Mtg.
[35]*Ibid.*, 9—23—1785, 177.
[36]Min. Chester Q. Meeting, 12—3—1689, 7.

Concord) are, however, full of suggestions which indicate that educational interests had their attention much before that date, though they were not under a perfected organization. As early as 1732 advances were made for the care and instruction of poor children which would fit them to earn a living. We may mention the financial assistance promised by Joseph Mead in that year.

An early attention to education reported by the quarterly meeting

Our ancient Friend Joseph Mead having by letter communicated to this meeting his mind, signifying his willingness to do something that might be conducive towards a public good, and in order thereto offers to give £50 toward a stock to be kept in this meeting for the putting of poor Friends' children to trades or for relieving of poor or indigent Friends which this meeting very kindly accepts of at the hand of said Friend.[37] . . . and this meeting being informed that our Friend Joseph Mead continues steadfast in his mind respecting his donation towards pious uses, and desires he may know to whom he may deliver the said gift. After some consideration thereon this meeting do nominate . . . Jacob Howell and John Davis to be receivers and are by this meeting empowered to receive the above and all such bequests . . . , in behalf of and for the use of this meeting, and to put out upon interest as soon as they conveniently can all such money into good and responsible hands and to render to this meeting when required thereto or to whom the said meeting shall appoint a true and just account of what may be delivered hereafter by any person or persons into their hands for the uses aforesaid.[38]

In 1739 the interest arising from this gift was withdrawn at his request and paid to the Springfield Friends to help them build their meeting house.[39]

In response to the yearly meeting's urgent request of 1746 and 1750,[40] we have their action recorded in this minute of the year 1754.

According to a minute of the advice of the Last Yearly Meeting concerning the settling of schools in the country, it is agreed for the encouragement thereof that the several and respective clerks of the monthly meetings belonging to this quarterly meeting do inquire and bring in a true report of all legacies, donations or estates which have been heretofore given to their respective meetings and of the uses to which the moneys arising therefrom are applied, and bring the account thereof to our next meeting.[41]

Report required on state of legacies

[37]Min. Chester Q. Mtg., 6—14—1732, 128.
[38]*Ibid.*, 9—13—1732, 129.
[39]*Ibid.*, 6—13—1739, 154.
[40]Advices, 250.
[41]Min. Chester Q. Mtg., 5—13—1754, 218.

Darby

The meetings at Darby were at first usually held at the home of John Blunston, who in 1687 deeded one acre of ground in Darby aforesaid for the use of building a meeting house,[42] on which the meeting house was begun in the following year,[43] and finished in 1689.[44] Happily, in the case of Darby Meeting we can point out a definite statement concerning a school established by the meeting, and which, quite probably, was the first school at that place. In 1692 the minutes note that,

Land deeded for meeting

B. Clift's school

> Agreed at this meeting that Benjamin Clift teach school, beginning the twelfth day of the 7th month, and to continue one whole year except two weeks.[45]

His salary for the first year is not known, but the minutes a year later give some clue as to the amount paid.

> Agreed at this meeting that Benjamin Clift teach school a year, beginning this 20th day of this 9th month; and to have £12/00/00.[46]

Slight activity before 1778

As has occurred in all other monthly meetings thus far considered, there was always little done in the way of organization and supervision of school affairs till after 1770.[47] There were however various committees appointed from time to time, especially in the case of legacies and donations which were quite common even at early dates.[48] The movement towards better organization, however, began more earnestly in 1778, with the receipt of a number of letters from the yearly meeting, in regard to which the following minute was made:

Cooperation of monthly and quarterly committees

> This meeting received a number of the general epistles from the last Yearly Meeting held in London and also the same number of copies of an epistle from the same meeting to our last Yearly Meeting, one of each were read at the close of the meeting for worship, to satisfaction, and the clerk is directed to read one of each the forepart of a first day meeting. The remainder were distributed amongst Friends.[49]

In the twelfth month Darby Friends received a committee appointed by the quarterly meeting (Concord) to investigate

---

[42]Smith, *Hist. of Del. Co.*, 166.
[43]*Ibid.*
[44]*Ibid.*
[45]Min. Darby Mo. Mtg., 7—7—1692, 54.
[46]*Ibid.*, 9—20—1693, 56.
[47]See Falls p. 87f; Abington, p. 105ff; and Buckingham, p. 96f.
[48]Min. Darby Mo. Mtg. 7—5—1758, 441; 7—5—1750, 322.
[49]*Ibid.*, 12—3—1778, 263.

conditions and promote schools among the monthly meetings.[50] John Howe, Aaron Oakford, Isaac Lloyd, Benjamin Lobb, and Josiah Bunting were appointed by Darby to join with the quarterly meeting's committee in its work.[51] The next year the question of building a schoolhouse occupied their attention.[52] It was proposed to deal with persons holding some land adjoining that of the meeting, that it might be purchased as school property and a suitable building erected thereon. Finding, however, that those holding the adjacent property were not at the time disposed to sell, it was decided to begin a subscription for erecting a schoolhouse on the meeting's land, which has been mentioned as having been left to the meeting's use by John Blunston.[53] The work on this building was evidently begun between 1779 and 1781, as we may infer from the minute of the latter year.

Building for a school proposed

This meeting resuming the consideration of building a house to accommodate a school were informed by one of the committee that it appeared to be necessary the subscriptions should be enlarged before the work could be completed; therefore Abraham Bonsall, John Humphreys, and Phillip Price are appointed with the former committee in order to forward the work and to report what progress they have made therein to next meeting; Benjamin Lobb requesting to be released from the above service, Morris Truman is appointed in his room.[54]

The tenor of a minute of the meeting next following was to the effect that enough money had been secured for the completion of the work.[55]

In 1784 another visit was received from the committee of the quarterly meeting, whose purpose was "the establishing and keeping up suitable schools," as recommended in the several years past.[56] The reports of the committee of the school at this date indicate that the status was nearly what was expected by the yearly meeting, respecting (1) foundation, (2) masters, (3) supervision by committees, (4) accommodations for the master, etc.[57] In 1787, Nathaniel Newlin

State of school satisfactory 1784

---

[50]Min. Darby Mo. Mtg.
[51]*Ibid.*
[52]*Ibid.*, 2—25—1779, 259.
[53]See page 154.
[54]*Ibid.*, 3—1—1781, 319.
[55]*Ibid.*, 3—29—1781, 320.
[56]*Ibid.*, 1—1—1784, 10.
[57]*Ibid.*, 7—29—1784, 22.

one of the meeting's representatives to the quarterly meeting brought back a request from that body for "a circumstantial account" of the state of schools, to be transmitted to the quarterly meeting the next eighth month.[58] The said Nathaniel was placed on the school committee in the eleventh month following,[59] and later, John Bull and Benjamin Bartram were appointed in the places of Aaron Oakford and Phillip Price who requested to be released.[60] In the first month of the year following there was produced a report by the committee, which in fact became the governing document for the schools established and to be established in Darby.[61] There is presented here a digest of the report; a complete statement of it may be found in Chapter II.

A digest
of report
of 1790

1. Recalling the advices of the yearly meeting, they recognize:

a. the advantages arising from established schools, and

b. the losses sustained from a want thereof.

2. Therefore it is agreed that in the future five Friends should be appointed and called the Overseers of Darby School, three of them to be sufficient number to transact business.

3. Their duties:

a. Visit the school.

b. Examine the progress of the scholars.

c. Inspect the teacher's conduct.

d. Employ teachers, with the approbation of the meeting.

e. Discharge them in similar manner, if cause therefor arise.

f. Discharge unruly pupils, who will not submit to the rules of the school.

g. Settle all differences arising between the master and any employers.

h. Devise some plan for raising permanent funds for the school; also to receive interest from the trustees of donations given for education of the poor, and apply the same as intended.

[58]Min. Darby Mo. Mtg.., 3—29—1787, 68.
[59]*Ibid.*, 11—1—1787, 79.
[60]*Ibid.*, 4—2—1789, 99f.

i. Aid the trustees in getting better securities for the same.

j. Minutes of their proceedings are to be kept and reports made to the monthly meeting once a year, and at other times if called for.[61]

In 1792 the new overseers reported they had continued to visit the school and inspect the learning of the children, which they did with satisfaction, implying that all conditions were as desired.[62]   In the eleventh month four new members were appointed to the school overseers;[63] as it is not stated that any had been released, we are uncertain as to whether the number required had been increased or not; quite likely they were appointed only for temporary assistance.   In 1793 it was reported from the school overseers that Benjamin Lobb had agreed to grant a lot of ground on the upper part of his plantation, to build a schoolhouse upon; the overseers proposed that the expenses be defrayed by subscription.[64]   A subscription was started for the same, and Friends desired to forward it, that the school might be begun.[65]   The cost of this school was estimated at £110.[66]   It is not known just when this school under Friends' care was begun in Upper Darby but at various stages these things are known about it. (1) On the 28th of the third month, 1793, it was reported that Lobb had offered the ground, (2) the cost of the building was estimated, fifth month, second, 1793, at £110, (3) eighth month, twelfth, 1793, the Chester Quarterly Meeting received the report that Darby was going to establish a school for Friends, (4) in 1796 the committee of overseers reported, "our school has been kept in good degree accordingly as desired by the yearly meeting,"[67] (5) the committee of overseers still mention but one *school* under their care and (6) eighth month, second, 1798, the school overseers report that the *schools* are kept as recommended by the yearly meeting.   It would

Margin notes:
New overseers added temporarily

Schoolhouse to be built on Lobb lot by subscription

Not begun until 1797 or 1798

[61]Min. Darby Mo. Mtg., 1—28—1790, 114.   (For entire report see page 23).   [62]*Ibid.*, 8—2—1792, 157.
[63]*Ibid.*, 11—29—1792, 160.
[64]*Ibid.*, 3—28—1793, 165.
[65]*Ibid.*, 5—2—1793, 166.
[66]*Ibid.*
[67]*Ibid.*, 7—26—1796, 207.

appear then that the school did not actually begin until some time between 1797 and 1798,[68] since all prior reports had recognized but one *school*.

Mr. Jordan states that in 1779 a deed set aside 24 perches of ground in upper Darby on the Darby-Haverford Road for the use of schools.[69]   This seems to have no connection with the schools established by the meeting; it was the first official deed for ground for schools, but many bequests of great value had been made previously.[70]   The text of the

The state
of education
in 1797 and

minutes recording these bequests follows on a later page.

The state of schools as reported by the committee in 1797 was as follows:

> Our school has been kept since last accounts . . . . as recommended by the Yearly Meeting; visited by the overseers and the scholars learning inspected to a good degree of satisfaction.   There has been expended for schooling children of Friends and others the sum of £12/10 and on settlement there appears a balance in the treasurer's hands of £6/15/5; the stock remains the same as at last year.   Signed . . . . Morris Truman, Isaac Oakford, and John Hunt.[71]

1798

As mentioned above, the second school in Upper Darby seems to have been put into operation by 1798.   The committee's report, summarized, is as the following.[72]

1. Schools kept as recommended by the yearly meeting since last year.

2. Scholars' learning has been inspected.

3. Schools have been visited.

4. Children of the poor and of others have been schooled.

5. Stock remains at £14/00/00 as last year.

Signed Truman Morris, John Hunt and Isaac Oakford.

Support of
schools by
legacies

As has been previously suggested the financial assistance to Darby schools came in a very considerable measure from legacies, left from time to time, but it was also neccessary to use subscription and rate plans for school support.   The text of one of these bequests, as recorded in the Darby records, is given below.

---

[68]Min. Darby Mo. Mtg., 8—2—1798, 243.
[69]Jordan, II, 432.
[70]Min. Darby Mo. Mtg. 1739, 258; 7—5—1750, 322.
[71]*Ibid.*, 8—3—1797, 226.
[72]*Ibid.*, 8—2—1798, 243.

Likewise I give and bequeath to my friend John Griffith, Thomas Pearson, and Samuel Bunting, all of Darby aforesaid, the sum of £50, nevertheless my aforesaid gift and bequest to them is only in trust, that they the said John Griffith, Thomas Pearson and Samuel Bunting shall reconvey and receive from the hands of my executors aforesaid the sum of £50 and when so received, put out the said monies to interest on good securities with the approbation of the monthly meeting of the people called Quakers in Darby aforesaid, and at the risk of those benefitted thereby and so from time to time forever, with the approbation of the said meeting for the time being. To the intent and purpose that by and out of the interests and profits thereof, they the said John Griffiths . . . . pay for the learning to read and write of such and so many poor Friends children in unity and church fellowship with the said people and belonging to the said meeting, as the said meeting shall order and appoint from time to time forever, and when any of my said trustees shall die, it is my will and mind that the said meeting shall appoint another to succeed and so from time to time forever.[73]

Smith's *History of Delaware County* states that as early as 1788 there was a school established at Radnor.[74] The first reference to a school found in the Radnor Monthly Meeting's records was in 1731.[75] At that date Richard Harrison and some Friends

Radnor

A school mentioned in 1731

signified to this meeting in writing that the meeting appointed last 7th month to be kept at the said Richard's schoolhouse was duly and religiously kept and further requested to be permitted to keep an afternoon meeting . . . . which is allowed of and to be at four o'clock.

The school had doubtless been in existence for at least a short time before that. Their answers to the fifth query in 1757 state that they are careful of the education of the poor and find themselves clear of placing children from among Friends.[76] They also, at that date, report themselves free of

The poor educated

---

[73]Min Darby Mo., Mtg., 1739, 258. (Other bequests were made by Blunston and . . . the value of which in 1791, amounted to £97 15/6; the committee reporting thereon, add: "we are united in opinion it will be best to lay out the money in a building on the meeting lot and in order thereto have had an estimate made for a house 16 ft. by 26 ft. from out to out, two stories high with a cellar under the whole, which amounts to £160 or thereabouts." (A Committee was appointed to see whether this would be according to the wish of the donor, Darby Minutes 12—29—1791, 145. In 1792 the committee reported it would be best to build the house for the master's accommodation with the money of the legacies, and use the rents arising therefrom for the schooling of poor children, Darby Minutes, 2—2—1792, 147.)

[74]Smith, *Hist. of Del. County*, 347.

[75]Min. Radnor Mo. Mtg., 1—11—1731, 189.

[76]*Ibid.*, 1—11—1757, 300.

holding slaves;[77] likewise in 1759, in regard to both.[78]   In 1768, in regard to a case of apprenticing children, this minute is recorded by the meeting:

> The meeting taking the request to reimburse them the expense accruing on account of Jane Atkinson, deceased, into consideration, came to a result of paying them as soon as we can, and as there is one of her children not put out yet, it is desired Samuel Humphreys and William Lawrence would take some care in putting them out. . . .[79]

In 1759 we find that Friends are reminded by the monthly meeting of the "necessary duty" of making their wills in time of health, and that endeavors are used to apply public gifts to the uses intended.[80]   The only "uses intended" must have been for some of these purposes: The support of the poor, their education, for negro support and education, or for purely religious purposes, all of which, the last one excepted, were, in a way, if we may judge from other meetings' practices, educational.   The suggestion of leaving bequests for public purposes, taken in connection with the answers to the fifth and seventh queries, and the known fact that there was a school in 1731, lead us to believe that the Radnor Meeting was pretty well awake to educational problems.   However true that may be, it is just as certain that any exact data on her schools are very rare for the early period before 1778.   In that year the usual declaration of the yearly meeting at Philadelphia was received concerning the question of schools.[81]

A committee of the quarterly meeting in 1778 produced a report embodying certain conclusions arrived at, both as to causes of existing evils and the proposed solutions.   Only a digest of this report can be given here.[82]

1.   We believe it a subject of much importance.

2.   Corruptions have been introduced by mingling in outside schools.

3.   It is necessary to have schools under masters and mistresses who take care of religious education.

---

[77]Min. Radnor Mo. Mtg., see also page 228, chapter on Negro education.
[78]Min. Radnor Mo. Mtg., 4—10—1759, 28.
[79]*Ibid.*, 12—8—1768, 220.
[80]*Ibid.*, 1—7—1759, 18.
[81]Advices, 250.
[82]Min. Radnor Mo. Mtg., 8—14—1778, 133.

4. We believe it our duty to spread the work through the yearly meeting.

The effect of the yearly and quarterly meetings' suggestions was the appointment of Samuel Briggs, William Lawrence, Jacob Jones, John Robeson, Samuel Richards, and Daniel Maule to attend to the affairs of education, "as may be opened in the wisdom of truth."[83] This last may, to our modern way of thinking, suggest rather a blind guidance, but not so to the old time Friends. The report to the quarterly meeting in 1779 does not suggest that any progress has been made, as was desired, save in respect to the masters employed in the schools.

Committee appointed on education

. . . . to attend the ensuing quarterly meeting at Philadelphia, and report, that the . . . . answers are to be transmitted as nearly our state. That some care has been taken to advise such negroes who have been restored to freedom. That the proposals respecting schools have been under consideration and some essays made by employing masters who are Friends. That small progress has been made as yet in laboring for the pious education of the youth.[84]

The next step, as reported in 1781, was the appointment of Friends to attend each of the preparative meetings and to do all possible "to spread the concern" of schools and excite an attention thereunto. No visits were as yet made to individual families, and the general feeling of the meeting appeared to be that not much progress had been made.[85] When reading these reports of the monthly meetings it is well to keep in mind the chief things which the yearly meeting had desired, (1) the *establishment of permanent school funds*, (2) *employment of Friends as teachers*, (3) *houses and permanent lands, gardens and so forth to be provided for the accommodation of the masters*, etc. With this in mind it is easy to see that the report of the meetings might be rather faltering even though they were in some manner supplied with the benefits of education. In 1781 the quarterly meeting advised those still unsuccessful in their attempts to meet the set standards "should be animated and encouraged to give weighty atten-

Preparatives visited

The demands of the yearly meeting

---

[83]Min. Radnor Mo. Mtg., 10—13—1778, 139.
[84]*Ibid.*, 7—13—1779, 169.
[85]*Ibid.*, 7—10—1781, 233.

tion to this important matter."[86]   The only success achieved
by Radnor, according to their own report, was in the employment of Friends for school masters.[87]   In 1786,

> The important subjects . . . . relative to schools engages in
> some degree the minds of Friends here but have little further to mention
> at present saving that the teachers employed in several schools appear to
> be those in religious profession with Friends.[88]

Purchase of ground proposed

In 1790 it was reported that one of the preparative meetings
was considering the purchase of a lot of ground for the purpose
of schools,[89] probably that of Haverford.   In July 1791 the
committee on school affairs gave a pretty full report, at any
rate the best we can get, on the condition of Radnor's schools
situated in each of the preparative meetings.   The statement
issued by the committee was the following:

Report of 1791

Two schools under Friends' meeting

Haverford and Radnor

> The committee on schools also produced their report thereon in writing
> as follows—We . . . . take the interesting subject of schools into
> consideration, and to visit those wherein either our preparatives are con-
> cerned, have given unction thereto, and find that although there are
> divers schools kept in the compass of the monthly meeting, two only
> appear subject to the rule and direction of Friends, the one being at
> Haverford, kept in a house erected in a small lot of ground belonging to
> that meeting: This school we visited in company with a committee of
> that preparative, which to us seems under its present circumstances
> tolerably well conducted; but it does not appear there are funds estab-
> lished, the salary of the master being made up by the neighborhood sub-
> scription. . . . some poor children principally are taught, the
> expense whereof is defrayed out of a small annual income arising from a
> sum left by a friend for such uses.—The other school is at Radnor, the
> house being Friends' property also; on a visit made to this school in com-
> pany of a committee of that preparative meeting, we found it large at the
> time and under rules which appeared pretty well adapted for the govern-
> ment thereof, but the salary there, as in the aforementioned school,
> depends on the transient subscription, and therefore uncertain.   At
> Merion and the Valley we have not discovered any progress made in
> laying a foundation for schools in the way proposed by the Yearly
> Meeting.   After considering this weighty subject with attention we are
> of the mind the several preparatives (notwithstanding difficulties may
> occur) should be encouraged to a continuance of care and exertion
> herein as strength may be afforded; in order to carry into effect this

[86]Min. Phila. Q. Mtg., 8—6—1781, 235.
[87]Min. Radnor Mo. Mtg., 9—7—1782, 260.
[88]*Ibid.*, 7—11—1786, 4.
[89]*Ibid.*, 7—13—1790, 8.

desirable object among us.—Signed on behalf of the said committee by James Jones.[90]

The definition of the time when Concord established its first schools under the meeting's care, is only possible within rather extended limits. We can only say that at such a time certain schools were in existence; earlier than that we have no authentic source of information. Jordan, in his *History of Delaware County*, places the date of Birmingham's first school as 1806,[91] it being built on a lot conveyed for that purpose by John Burgess. From the report of the Concord Monthly Meeting in 1779, which will be presented later, it appears that Birmingham had a school at that date which was established "in some measure agreeable to the demands of the yearly meeting."[92] It is spoken of as a regularly established school, which the writer has found in most meetings to mean that a house, master, funds, and sometimes a permanent lot were provided. This is merely suggestive. It certainly does not prove that there was a lot and building provided, but the indications are in favor of that, rather than against it. The same author, in reference to Upper Chichester, states,

Concord

Birmingham School at least as early as 1779

School at Chichester

In 1793 the Society of Friends established a school in Upper Chichester which was maintained by the Society until the public school system was introduced.[93]

The source for the statement is not given, but it appears it must be subject to the like inaccuracy suggested above in reference to Birmingham.

The report of the school committee which seems to contravert the time of the establishment of schools, given by Jordan, is herewith included.

We of the committee appointed to the care of schools and education of the youth, report we have in some degree attended to the importance of the service, have lately visited two schools, which are now established in some measure agreeable to the concern of the Yearly Meeting as recommended in the extracts for that purpose. . . .

Report of 1779

One of which in the verge of Chichester, the other Birmingham particular meeting; which visits, on observing the economy and regularity of said schools, have afforded us much satisfaction. With increasing desires

Two schools

---

[90]Min. Radnor Mo. Mtg., 7—12—1791, 24.
[91]Jordan, II, 429.
[92]Min. Concord Mo. Mtg., 8—4—1779, 94.
[93]Jordan, II, 430.

for the establishment of another in the verge of Concord which unitedly appears to be much wanting as divers Friends now labor under very considerable inconvenience for want thereof. Signed by nine of the committee.[94]

In 1780 the minutes of the meeting state that another full report on schools was brought in, but such a report is not found in the minutes. In 1781, the question being revived by the receipt of the yearly meeting's extracts, a committee of Joshua Sharpe, Richard Strode, Hugh Judge, Samuel Trimble, George Martin, and Caleb Pierce were appointed to take the

Committee visits preparatives

extracts and visit each of the preparative meetings, at which they were to be read.[95] They further directed the time for Birmingham to hold their meeting, so that the visit of the committee might be arranged.[96] It is known that these visits were performed, and others following that date.[97]

It was noted in the committee's report presented in 1779, that Concord did not yet have a school under its care,[98] though one was desired. The report of 1786 indicates that all of the preparatives were at that time supplied. A

Report of 1786 and

digest of the said report is produced here, also that of 1787.

The committee informed this meeting that they have appointed John Pierce Treasurer for Chichester, Joseph Trimble for Concord, and William Townsend for Birmingham. We also agree to report, agreeable to the request of the quarterly meeting. . . .[99]

1787 Three schools

Digest of their report.

1.   We have a school and house at each preparative meeting—agreeable to the plan of the yearly meeting.

2.   They are under the care of a steady committee of our monthly meeting.

3.   Schools are conducted to the good satisfaction of Friends.

4.   One of them at present is vacant.

5.   We have also agreed upon a plan to establish a fund for the education of poor children; also for the support of the said schools.

---

[94]Min. Concord Mo. Mtg., 8—4—1779, 94.
[95]*Ibid.*, 12—5—1781, 193.
[96]*Ibid.*   [97]*Ibid.*, 3—3—1784, 275.   [98]*Ibid.*, 8—4—1779, 94.
[99]*Ibid.*, 8—9—1786, 370.

6. There is a treasurer for each particular meeting.

7. Not much progress made in securing funds, up to date.

The report of the next year, 1787, was:[100]

1. The three schools visited.

2. Are conducted to a good degree of satisfaction.

3. Chichester is at present vacant.

4. Request a future urging and some advice of the yearly meeting.

The encouragement given to the school of Concord through individual philanthropy is to be noted in the will of Nathan Yarnall, an extract from which appeared in the Concord minutes.

> I give and bequeath the sum of £50 to be appropriated for the use of Friends School at Concord, if established agreeable to the plan recommended by the Yearly Meeting last year, to be paid into the hands of the committee appointed for the establishment of the said school. . . . It appears that Samuel Trimble, Morris Jones, William Trimble, and Caleb Pierce are a committee appointed by the Concord Preparative meeting to take the immediate care and oversight of that school. They . . . . and to make report to next meeting.[101]

Schools encouraged by individual philanthropy

Such aid as this doubtless hastened the coming of the first school which was reported by the committee in 1786.[102]

SUMMARY

The establishment of schools in Chester, Radnor, Darby and Concord meetings is discussed in this chapter.

The meetings

There is evidence that education was provided for some children in Chester before the Quakers came to the colony. The first meetings at Chester were held in the Court House, but land for a meeting house was devised in 1688. The first property devised for school purposes was that of Hoskins in 1769. A schoolhouse was built on the land in 1770. A school is said to have been at Middletown in 1740, in a building donated by Thomas Yarnall and Thomas Minshall. Land was also given for schools in 1791 by Enock Taylor and his wife. About 1778 the usual committees were appointed and

Chester

Land devised for schools

---

[100]Min. Concord Mo. Mtg., 8—8—1787, 397.
[101]*Ibid.*, 6—5—1782, 213.   [102]*Ibid.*, 8—9—1786, 370; see page 164.

subscription plans formulated. At the end of the century three schools were reported under Friends' care.

The first school at Darby was taught by Benjamin Clift in 1692, 1693 and perhaps longer, though no further record is found. Not much progress is noticed until about 1778, when the quarterly and monthly meetings' committees united on the subject of schools. A schoolhouse was erected be-

tween 1779 and 1781. According to reports of 1784 and 1790 the Darby School was satisfactorily situated. A new school in Upper Darby on Benjamin Lobb's lot was proposed in

1793, but not built before 1798. Two schools, kept as recommended, are reported in 1798.

Smith says that as early as 1788 there was a school at Radnor. The meeting records mention one as early as 1731. The meeting was active in educating and apprenticing the poor.

The reports, however, do not indicate that they were very successful in meeting the standards set by the yearly meeting for the schools. In 1791 one of the preparatives, probably

Haverford, considered the purchase of grounds for a school. A full report of the same year shows two schools (Radnor and Haverford) which are subject to the control of the monthly meeting. Merion and the Valley had no schools established *according to the plan proposed.*

The very early state of Concord's schools has not been

determined, though one was at Birmingham in 1779. Mr. Jordan is inclined to place the date of Birmingham's first school about 1806. The date stated by him for Chichester (1793) also seems to be too late. The minutes recognize the

Birmingham school in 1779 and also one at Chichester at the same date. In 1787 one school is reported for each preparative meeting, Concord, Chichester, and Birmingham.

CHAPTER IX

SCHOOL SUPPORT, ORGANIZATION, AND CURRICULUM

SUPPORT

At various times in the course of this study, it has been mentioned that the activities of the lower branches of the meeting organization were directed by means of advices sent out from the yearly meetings. These advices, particularly at the earlier dates, were of a very general nature, and, as one would judge from the name, were only recommendations as to what should be done, with occasional expressions of appro- bation or reproof as the action of the constituent meetings merited. As years went on, however, the advices became of more consequence, sometimes mapping out plans of action in considerable detail.[1] One of the questions which came to demand a great deal of attention was that of supporting teachers in the schools. Great trouble had always been experienced in getting masters, properly qualified mentally and morally, who would continue long in the same place of service. The suggestions of the yearly meeting in 1750 sought to remedy that serious condition. The opinion then expressed was that,

Problem of support

the most likely means to induce such persons to undertake the business will be to have some certain income fixed, in consideration of which, they should be obliged to teach so many children on behalf of each monthly meeting, as said monthly meeting might judge adequate to the salary and that no person should receive the benefit of the salary, without the appointment of the said meeting.[2]

A fixed salary necessary to secure better teachers and retain them

It was directed that the meeting's clerk send copies of the above recommendation to all quarterly meetings, which were

---

[1] For example, the plan suggested in 1746 and elaborated in the years following.
[2] Advices, 250.

in turn to supply each of their monthly meetings and direct them to send in a report to the next yearly meeting.[3]

The above is cited as one of many similar recommendations; and, without the presentation of any more of them, it may be well to point out one of the great weaknesses of the system—that weakness being the lack of a strong central control in the organization which could formulate plans and compel them to be carried into execution. A financial plan based on that idea would no doubt have resulted quite differently than did the one pursued, which left it wholly to the determination of the locality whether they would settle regular funds for the schools. Since this study is historical we shall limit ourselves to that point of view exclusively. Let us notice then the reception of the recommendations in the case of a few meetings, tracing it to the lowest meeting whence, in the last analysis, the funds usually came.

What became of the recommendation when it had been sent out from the yearly meeting? In some cases committees were appointed in the quarterly meetings to which it came. An instance of this is the case of Concord Quarterly Meeting which in 1754 appointed a committee to inspect and examine the accounts and all moneys which were given to charitable and educational purposes.[4] At another time Concord appointed a committee to visit the monthly and preparative meetings to ascertain the state of schools among them; this committee reported soon after that they had visited the meetings but that not much had been done in regard to schools.[5] The appointment of these committees was quite a common practice and, no doubt, they had considerable influence. They often worked with the committees of the monthly meetings,[6] and in some instances produced very full reports of their activity, which they, of course, forwarded to the yearly meeting.[7] The duties in general performed by the quarterly meetings, as doers of the yearly meeting's will, were as follows:

---

[3]Advices, 250.
[4]Min. Concord Q. Mtg., 8—12—1754, 218.
[5]*Ibid.*, 8—10—1778, 358.   [6]*Ibid.*, 8—9—1784, 413.
[7]*Ibid.*, 8—12—1793, 477; Min. Warrington and Fairfax Q. Mtg., 9—20—1784, 175 ff.

1. To transmit the advices through the representatives to the various monthly meetings.

2. To appoint committees (*a*) for investigation and (*b*) for coöperation with those in the monthly meetings.

3. To collect reports and make final report for their locality to the yearly meeting.

4. At some stages of development the quarterly performed some duties later performed by the monthly meeting.[8]

Duties of the quarterly meeting summarized

What became of the recommendation when sent on from quarterly meeting? After arriving at and being perused by the monthly, they were always sent by the representatives back to the various particulars, or preparatives, there to be considered also.[9] The preparative meeting was not primarily a "record-meeting" and little can be found of their organization, if they had any, for raising funds, save from the reports of the monthly meetings. This does not mean, however, that the preparatives did not share in raising the funds; it means only that the organization for so doing was in the monthly meeting.[10] The plans adopted by that body were drawn up in the most part by a committee which was representative of each particular meeting. Let us examine briefly the general nature of the plans proposed by some of the meetings for establishing permanent funds. Only those of two or three will be mentioned, as there was great similarity in all of them. The text of the plan for some of the meetings may be found in the chapter in which those meetings are considered.[11]

Procedure in the monthly meeting

In 1796 the minutes of Kennett recorded a plan their committee had devised for the establishment of a permanent fund. As has already been suggested, one of the greatest weaknesses of the whole system was that everything was done upon individual choice.[12] That is probably the first thing to

---

[8]Phila. Q. Mtg. in the earliest years transacted considerable detail business, which, years later, it did not touch.

[9]Several definite references are: Min. Middletown Mo. Mtg., 6—6—1778, 409 and 12—4—1783, 562; Min. Horsham Mo. Mtg., II, 12—28—1796.

[10]Min. London Grove Mo. Mtg., 11—4—1795—78; Min. Darby Mo. Mtg., 2—3—1791, 133.

[11]To turn to the text of a plan of subscription, see "school support" in index.

[12]See page 168.

strike the reader's attention as he looks over the plans devised. We will state as concisely as possible the chief points.

Kennett plans for raising funds summarized

(*a*) Subscriptions were voluntary, and if a note were given it bore interest at 5%;

(*b*) There was a regularly constituted board of trustees for the funds;

(*c*) Record was to be kept of receipts and expenditures and reported to the monthly meeting;

(*d*) All money paid in was to be vested in real property as soon as possible;

(*e*) Disagreement among the trustees must be settled before the monthly meeting;

(*f*) Funds were to be used for paying salaries or keeping buildings in repair provided the amount of the principal fund be not lessened.[13] From reports of the success in establishing schools in Kennett meeting,[14] one must believe that their trustees managed the funds wisely and that subscriptions were generously made, but their exact financial state is not given.

Similar plans by Darby, London Grove, Buckingham Sadsbury, and others

Similar plans were devised by many other meetings, such as London Grove,[15] Darby,[16] Sadsbury,[17] and Buckingham.[18] In all the outstanding characteristics are the same as those mentioned in the Kennett plan. One very interesting characteristic which frequently recurs, is that in the fifth rule of Kennett which allows that the funds may be used also for the poor, who are not members of Friends.[19]

Other forms of support besides the subscription just mentioned were, (1) *legacies,* given on terms determined at the will of the donors, (2) *fees,* and, occasionally, (3) *issue of bonds* for rather small sums, which were needed in case of emergency, such as completing a school house which had been begun. An instance of the third method occurred in 1701 when Philadelphia Monthly Meeting agreed that £100 be raised in that

---

[13]Min. Kennett Mo. Mtg., 12—15—1796, 146.
[14]*Ibid.,* 8—16—1798, 199.
[15]Min. London Grove Mo. Mtg., 11—4—1795, 78.
[16]Min. Darby Mo. Mtg., 2—3—1791, 133.
[17]Min. Sadsbury Mo. Mtg., 12—10—1793, 128.
[18]Min. Buckingham Mo. Mtg., 4—1—1793, 302.
[19]Min. Kennett Mo. Mtg., 12—15—1796, 146.

manner for completing the work on the school house.[20] Many similar instances were found in records of other meetings. The rate system was so commonly used as a means of support in the early schools that it needs no special attention here. Some of the rates paid for teaching will be noted in a later presentation of masters' salaries. Legacies have been very frequently mentioned in previous chapters and it is here necessary only to call attention to the chief characteristics of the bequests and refer the reader to previous chapters if he wishes to examine the text of them.[21] The common characteristics are:

(1) Entirely voluntary, though the making of them was frequently urged by the meeting[22] and was in fact the concern of the queries which were regularly sent out. By this means the yearly meeting was informed of the interest taken in making donations.

Main characteristics of the bequests made

(2) Almost universally consisted of (*a*) sums of money or (*b*) land.

(3) The donor chose trustees in the meeting to be subject to its direction.

(4) The purpose was generally definitely stated; also how the money should be invested.

An entire chapter might be devoted to this interesting and very important means of support of the Quaker schools, but much less space must suffice. The value of it may be indicated by a few figures given in statements of a few meetings and school records. The table gives the yearly value of the legacies or other permanent endowments at the year stated. The list is not complete, due to inadequate records, but may be taken as indicative of the extent of this form of support.*

The value of legacies in a few meetings

---

[20]Min. Phila. Mo. Mtg., 10—26—1701, 316.
[21]To find the text of legacies granted, turn to legacies, in the index.
[22]Min. Uwchlan Mo. Mtg., 8—3—1763, 22.
*Attention is called to the fact that during the years mentioned in the following table currency greatly depreciated. This depreciation was most marked in 1779, when, in January, the ratio was 8 to 1; and in November of the same year 38½ to 1. (See Dewey, D. R., *Financial History of U. S.*, 39; also page 212.

VALUE OF LEGACIES FOR SCHOOL SUPPORT

For whose use	Year	Amount
Overseers of Penn Charter School[23]	1776	£574/00/11 1–2
Buckingham Monthly Meeting[24]	1778	244/ 4/11 1–2
Buckingham Monthly Meeting[25]	1793	767/10/00
Wrightstown Monthly Meeting[26]	1790	248/13/10
Falls Monthly Meeting[27]	1799	777/ 9/ 4 1–2
Uwchlan Monthly Meeting[28]	1784	120/10/00
Horsham School Committee*	1793	351/ 2/11

ORGANIZATION

The machinery of organization which had any connection with the direction of the school system has already been frequently referred to.   It is the same organization which was discussed in Chapter II.[29]   It has further been pointed out that one of the functions of the head of this organization, the yearly or general assembly, was to issue advices for the direction of the lower units.   These advices began very early, so far as they are concerned with education.   In 1692 London Yearly Meeting warned all others to be careful of a "Christian care in the education of their children,"[30] and followed it successively each year with more suggestions.[31]   These advices all found their way to the Yearly Meeting of Philadelphia and Burlington, and the similarity between the advices of the two meetings is striking but not surprising.

It may be convenient for the reader if some of the chief recommendations of the London Advices are stated briefly, that the likeness of the two may be noted later when we examine those of Philadelphia.   They are:

1.   Education is to be useful and practical.[32]

London advices on education

London advices summarized

---

[23]Min. Penn Charter School Overseers, I, 301.
[24]Buckingham Mo. Mtg., 12—7—1778, 194.
[25]*Ibid.*, 4—1—1793, 302.
[26]Min. Wrightstown Mo. Mtg., 12—7—1790, 60.
[27]Min. Falls Mo. Mtg., 11—6—1799, 288.
[28]Min. Uwchlan Mo. Mtg., 2—5—1784, 162.
*Min. Horsham School Committee, 3—18—1793.
[29]See page 14ff.
[30]Min. London Yr. Mtg., 3—16—1692, 68.
[31]The yearly meetings also established schools; such was the case in London Yearly, and Philadelphia followed in 1799 with the establishment of Westtown Boarding School in Chester County.   Justice cannot be done to that institution in this work.   The reader is referred to Dewes, *A History of Westtown Boarding School.*
[32]Min. London Yr. Mtg., 3—17 to 24—1703, 114; 5—26 to 31—1760, 339.

2. The major emphasis is placed on Christian and moral instruction.[33]

3. The teachers must be capable of good moral influence.[34]

4. Teachers must be members of Friends.[35]

5. Free education is to be provided for the poor[36] (first it was only mentioned for the children of Friends, later others).

6. The coöperation of teachers is urged for the betterment of methods of teaching.[37]

7. The weaker communities are to be aided by the stronger.[38]

8. Both parents and teachers must realize the force of example.[39]

9. Close censorship of all reading material for the youth.[40]

From this very brief statement of London Advices and with little attention paid to their manner of getting into and influencing those of Philadelphia, save to state that the chief means were: (1) *epistles sent*, (2) *travelling ministers*, and (3) *through representatives sent from the lower meetings*, let us turn to consider those of the last named meeting. As early as 1694 we find that that body approved certain "proposals about the education of youth," the initiative for which seems to have come from Philadelphia Quarterly Meeting.[41] So far as the minute of the meeting goes, one would hardly dignify this statement so much as to say that it suggested a plan of education. If such a plan were submitted, it was carefully kept out of the minutes of that date. The very nature of the advice continues as with those of London until near the middle of the century, but as one reads the records they are seen to grow gradually in definiteness until beginning (to name a definite date) about 1746 and on through the period of 1777 and 1778, there are elaborated certain ideas for the establishment of schools in town and country. It is not

Means of exercising influence: epistles, ministers, and representatives

Philadelphia advices also general for first half century

---

[33]Min. London Yr. Mtg., 3—16 to 19—1692, 68.
[34]*Ibid.*, 4—2 to 7—1745, 268.
[35]*Ibid.*, 4—9 to 11—1690, 52; 4—1 to 4—1691, 60.
[36]*Ibid.*, 3—13 to 17—1695, 89.
[37]*Ibid.*
[38]*Ibid.*, 4—2 to 10—1718, 160.
[39]*Ibid.*, 5-31 to 6—5—1773, 399.
[40]*Ibid.*, 3—29 to 4—3—1732, 210; 4—9 to 11—1690, 52.
[41]Min. Phila. Yr. Mtg., 7—16 and 17—1694, 39.

until those later years that anything like strong central control is felt, and certainly there were earlier no visible results of such centralizing influence.   Even then it took the form of urgent suggestions which, though producing very considerable results, cannot be regarded candidly as the best that might have been done.   It is with these suggestions of the latter part of the century that we are chiefly concerned.   The most important are here stated in brief manner.[42]

Summary of Philadelphia advices

1.   Education is to be useful in nature.

2.   The minima to be attained are moral and Christian training and an ability to read and write.

3.   The meetings are to assist each other in settling schools.

4.   Members of Friends are to be employed as teachers in the schools; good moral influence of the teachers is of first importance.

5.   A fixed income, house, and garden are necessary for securing a better and more permanent teaching body.

6.   All teachers, employed, are to be approved by the monthly meeting.

7.   Quarterly meetings are to appoint visiting committees.

8.   Permanent funds recommended to be put in care of trustees.

9.   Schools to be under the care of monthly meetings' committees and reports are to be made thereon.

10.   The poor children to be educated free of charge, and also the Negroes, where they are not able to pay.   Children not Friends were not omitted,[42] as we find in the plans actually followed by the monthly meetings.

The functions of the quarterly meeting

The chief functions of the quarterly meeting were: (1) to transmit these advices; (2) to gather and return reports of the accomplishments within its limits; and (3) to keep in touch with the work by means of committees.   Sufficient material has in the writer's opinion been presented in the way of reports in previous chapters relating to schools established in the various counties, to make it unnecessary here.[43]   To characterize

---

[42]Advices from Burlington and Philadelphia Yr. Mtg., 1746. 1750, 1753, 1755, 1777, and so forth, page 250 ff.   Also the yearly meeting minutes records for those years, deposited at 304 Arch Street, Phila. (The first reference is the more accessible.)

[43]The reader is referred to the account of establishing schools in Bucks, Montgomery, Delaware Counties, etc.

it as an intermediary agent and its functions as supervisory and directive seems to be adequate.

The monthly meeting was above all others the organizing business unit and the welfare of schools appears to have depended much on its activity.   It is to the monthly meeting that we are indebted for almost all of the reports on schools, and it has been noticed that not until raised to the dignity of being a monthly meeting, did many meetings assume any important part in directing education.   A few preparatives, which might be considered as a little exceptional, were Byberry, Falls, and Horsham.   They appear to have handled their schools a little more independently than did others. Duties which were as a general rule performed by each of the monthly meetings were these:[44] Monthly meeting the business unit

1.   To investigate the state of schools in their preparatives.

2.   To appoint committees to visit, assist and report on schools established, and recommend the establishment of others where necessary. Duties summarized

3.   To approve masters, retire them, and fill vacancies.

4.   Through trustees or committees on funds, (*a*) to finance the education of poor children, (*b*) to pay salaries, (*c*) to build school houses, and (*d*) to establish permanent endowments.

5.   To take final reports to be sent to the yearly meeting.

These functions have all been brought to the reader's attention by reports and minutes quoted in chapters on the schools in various counties.   This brief presentation of the organization and direction on the part of the meetings should be sufficient to point out: (1) that the general nature of the organization is a hierarchy of units;   (2) that the direction of school activities comes from the higher to the lower, and is of a general and suggestive rather than specific and mandatory nature;   (3) that the monthly meeting formed the real working unit, and that on its diligence probably depended the Three points indicated concerning the organization

---

[44]These references are, respectively, to the five points stated below:
> *a.*   Min. Westland Mo. Mtg., 11—11—1786, 12;   3—10—1787, 19.
> *b.*   Min. Horsham Mo. Mtg., 4—28—1784.
> *c.*   Min. Phila. Mo. Mtg., 11—29—1719, 57.
> *d.*   Min. Kennett Mo. Mtg., 12—15—1796, 146.
> *e.*   Min. Chester Mo. Mtg., 1—27—1800, 508; Min. Concord Mo. Mtg., 8—9—1786, 370.

welfare of the preparatives' schools. We shall now attend
for a moment to a few of the details of the school in so far as
we may judge them from the records at our disposal.

THE SCHOOL

It has already been mentioned that one of the yearly
meeting's earnest recommendations was that a lot of ground
be provided where schools might be necessary, sufficient for a

**Permanent
properties
recom-
mended
for schools**

garden, orchard, grass for a cow, etc., and that a suitable
house and stables and other necessary things be arranged for
the securing of more permanent and better qualified teachers.[45]
There were certainly several of the meetings where land for the
purposes of schools was possessed before these recommendations were made. Notable instances, which may be mentioned, were Philadelphia and Abington, and many others,
who early secured permanent lands for the meeting which
were also used for the erection of schools. Some of the early
acquisitions of school property in Philadelphia were: (1)

**Property
acquired by
Philadelphia
schools and
meeting**

that purchased in 1698 of Lionell Brittain;[46] (2) another
deeded by John Goodson and Thomas Lightfoot to the overseers;[47] and (3) that devised by William Forrest, upon which
the overseers erected a school in 1744.[48] There was also the
piece of ground left to the monthly meeting of that place by
George Fox, upon which the meeting gave permission for the
building of a school, free from ground rent.[49] The property

**and
Abington**

gained by Abington in 1696 was for the support of a school.[50]
A meeting house was erected on the land between 1696 and
1700. These cases of endowment directly for schools were
very limited as to locality at the early part of the eighteenth
century. Their number increased in later years, and the
increase may have been due partly to the influence of the
yearly meeting's urgent advices.

---

[45]See the Advices, 250; or the Book of Discipline which has, under the
head of schools, a statement of the various recommendations of the
yearly meetings. See also Yearly Meeting Minute Books at 4th and
Arch Streets, Phila., for years 1746, 1753, 1755, 1777, and 1778.
[46]Min. Phila. Mo. Mtg., 2—29—1698, 229; P. C. S. M., I, 13.
[47]Deed No. 33, mentioned in P. C. S. M., I, 13.
[48]*Ibid.*, 40.   [49]*Ibid.*, 147.
[50]*Friends' Intelligencer*, 8—15—1896, 539; Min. Abington Mo. Mtg.,
1—26—1722, 124.

A few instances of the tendency toward the policy of purchasing permanent lands may be mentioned. In 1779, Warrington and Fairfax Quarterly reported two of their monthly meetings had purchased grounds and erected houses for the said purpose.[51]   Another meeting had purchased sixteen acres, built a house, but had difficulty in securing a suitable master.[52]   All other accommodations recommended for masters had been provided.   Near the close of the century (1794) William Jackson of New Garden deeded a lot of ground to Friends of that meeting for the use of a school.[53]   New Garden also reported a school house built about 1795 on land given for the purpose by Jeremiah Barnard.[54]   In 1792 Kennett reported that their preparative meeting had purchased of Abraham Taylor a piece of ground for a school and were preparing to build a house on it.   It was situated about 2½ miles from Kennett.[55]   Other instances of like procedure were: Goshen, 1795[56] and 1782;[57] Darby, 1793;[58] and Buckingham in 1794.[59]   Similar cases might be cited for almost every monthly meeting in the southeastern part of Pennsylvania, and it doubtless extended elsewhere.   It is to be noted that this general purchasing of school property did not come until late in the eighteenth century, when the great advancement in Quaker education had its beginning.   It may be fairly stated that by the end of the century most of the schools were established on school property held by the meeting for that purpose.   As pointed out above, this had been a slow development, beginning with a few in the seventeenth century that started with land endowments.

The earliest schoolhouses would doubtless present an interesting picture if we could see them inside and out. Unfortunately there is little information extant, which throws light upon the earliest.   In fact, at the very earliest

Warrington and Fairfax Quarterly

New Garden

Goshen, Darby, Buckingham

---

[51]Min. Warrington and Fairfax Q. Mtg., 9—20—1779, 73.
[52]*Ibid.*, 77;   Warrington Mo. Mtg., 8—7—1779, 46.
[53]Deed No. 88 New Garden Township, Chester County. (The original is in Orthodox Friends Meeting House, West Grove, Pa.)
[54]Min. New Garden Mo. Mtg., 8—6—1785, 256.
[55]Min. Kennett Mo. Mtg., 1—12—1792, 14.
[56]Min. Goshen Mo. Mtg., 4—10—1795.
[57]*Ibid.*, 3—8—1782.
[58]Min. Darby Mo. Mtg., 3—28—1793, 165.
[59]Min. Buckingham Mo. Mtg., 4—10—1794, 314.

**Early
schools held
in meeting
houses**

**Family
school**

establishment of schools, there were no special houses built
for them. For many of them this condition prevailed till
fairly near the close of the century. Joseph Foulke, writing
in 1859, concerning his first school days, stated that he first
attended school at Gwynedd, which was held in the meeting
house, there being none other for that purpose.[60] His next
schooling, in 1795, was at a *family school* taught by Hannah
Lukens, who lived in a little house on the Bethlehem Road.
He then attended school in a log schoolhouse, built about
1798 by his father.[61] Other instances may be cited in connection with the use of the meeting house for schoolhouse.
In 1693–4 Middletown Friends allowed a school to be held in
the meeting house, provided it should cause no disturbance,[62]
and again in 1699 a similar request was granted.[63] As late
as 1740 Philadelphia Meeting proposed to erect a meeting
house with chambers over it sufficiently large for the accommodation of a school,[64] though, as mentioned before, they
already had some of their schools in regularly constructed
schoolhouses.[65]

**An old
schoolroom
at Merion,
Pa.**

The writer has had the opportunity to visit one of these
little schoolrooms established in the meeting house. Not
much is known of the school at Merion, though the oldest of
Friends meetings, but it is quite certain that whenever their
school began and however pretentious it may have been, it
must have been held in the upper part of the meeting house.
The schoolroom in the present building is quite hidden away
under the eaves. The walls are bare and the rafters low
overhead. Ample light is furnished. Rude wooden benches
and tables, the latter with sloping tops, constitute the furni-
ture of the room as it now stands. One of the table tops
bears the date 1711, doubtless the telltale of some vandal
outcropping, which might tempt one to place a school at that

[60]Jenkins, *Historical Col. of Gwynedd*, 396.
[61]*Ibid.*
[62]Min. Middletown Mo. Mtg., 12—1—1693—4, 64.
[63]*Ibid.*, 1—1—1699, 114.
[64]Min. Phila. Mo. Mtg., 5—25—1740, 318.
[65]In 1701 they had begun a school house which was to be 60 by 24 feet.
Min. Phila. Mo. Mtg., 4—27—1701, 298.

early date.   It is however too meagre and uncertain evidence to justify such a conclusion.[66]

From a few sources of information we gather some clews as to the size of the schoolhouse generally.   The house proposed by the Goshen Meeting in 1782 was to be 27 feet square from out to out and to cost about £150.[67]   The new one proposed at Falls some twelve years later was to be somewhat more pretentious being twenty-two feet by thirty and having two stories.   Its cost was estimated at £200.[68]   We infer from the minutes that a building was badly needed at Falls, the old roof being "very leaky and the ceiling about to fall."   In spite of this fact it does not appear that the house was erected until about 1799; the final dimensions decided upon were twenty-six feet by twenty-four, one story, and a cellar of the same dimensions.[69]   It is not certain how much space was actually devoted to the use of the school room, since the building doubtless accommodated the master and his family at the same time.   The schoolhouse begun in Philadelphia about 1701,[70] was to be twenty-four by sixty feet.   Another one in 1744, built on the Forrest property, was to be about sixty by thirty-five feet, two stories high, with a basement underneath raised three feet above the surface of the ground.[71]   The cost of the last building when completed in 1746 was £794.[72]   Anthony Benezet, who apparently was teaching in an old building, made complaint in 1744 that it was "too hot in summer and too dark in winter" and therefore urged that a window be put in the south side.[73]   The writer has found a single instance to indicate how the school building was heated.   Judging from such meager data we would say that the first schools probably up to 1715 or 1720 were heated

Size and cost of school houses; Goshen, Falls

Philadelphia

Manner of heating

---

[66]The schoolroom described is in Merion Meeting House, which may be reached from Philadelphia via P.R.R. to Narberth, Pa.; from thence a ten-minute walk.

[67]Min. Goshen Mo. Mtg., 3—8—1782.

[68]Min. Falls Mo. Mtg., 12–3–1794, 169; for value of money see page 212.

[69]*Ibid.*, 9—4—1799, 283.

[70]Min. Phila. Mo. Mtg., 4—27—1701, 298.

[71]*Ibid.*, 11–25–1744, 379; P. C. S. M., I, 40.   Parts of the school buildings were at times used as tenant property thus affording a supporting income, P. C. S. M., I, 22.

[72]P. C. S. M., I, 56.

[73]*Ibid.*, I, 39.

by the old-fashioned brick stoves. They were at any rate employed in some, but were beginning to lose their popularity in that period. One was removed in 1715 and an iron stove substituted for it.[74]

The size of the schools, measured by the number of pupils, must be judged mostly from material found relating to Philadelphia. It was doubtless true that in the country regions there were fewer children within reach of the school and it was not necessary to state limits beyond which they might not go. The yearly meeting certainly recommended that the number of children be specified, which the master was to teach, but this was often taken to mean that they should promise to teach a certain number of children for the use of the school. The schools were always composed of these two classes, the independent or *pay scholar* and the poor or *free scholar*. Some of the Philadelphia reports state the number attending, of each of these classes. In that system the teachers were required to keep a roll, especially of the poor children, and turn it over for the inspection of the overseers.[75] In country districts the school committee usually kept account of the poor scholars, seeing that they were supplied with all things necessary.[76] It may prove interesting to examine the Philadelphia system a little more fully.

First, let it be noted that cases of both boys and girls were investigated by the overseers, and if capable and in need of assistance, they were put under the tutorage of masters or mistresses free of any charge.[77] Not only were the children of Friends admitted, but an effort was made to find out the needy, of other denominations, and put them to school also.[78] All articles necessary were furnished free to the poor scholars by the Board, the master was required to keep an account of each item and present the bill therefor in his reports to that body.[79] The number of poor in Anthony Benezet's school in 1743–4, about a year after he entered it, was 14.[80] There

Marginal notes:

Number of children attending schools

Two classes: the "pay" and the "free" scholar

Both boys and girls assisted

Everything furnished to the "free" scholar

---

[74]Min. Phila. Mo. Mtg., 9—25—1715, 10 ff.
[75]P. C. S. M., I, 95 and 37.
[76]Min. Bradford Mo. Mtg., 6—18—1762; 4—7—1767; 8—14—1767.
[77]P. C. S. M., I, 29 and 25.
[78]*Ibid.*, 31.
[79]*Ibid.*, 95.
[80]*Ibid.*, 37.

was very little fluctuation as to the number for many years; in 1749 there were 17.[81] Below are given the reports of some of the schools in 1757.[82] It seldom or never occurred that a report for all schools was made at one time.

Master	Year	Items	Pay Scholars	Free Scholars	Amount
CHARLES THOMPSON (*Latin*)	1757	Books and firing for poor scholars	31	7	£150/00/00
ALEXANDER SEATON (*English*)	1757	Teaching poor scholars	30	41	58/15/ 4
		Premiums			3/00/00
		Books and firewood			15/ 4/ 9½
		Clothing for poor			6/17/ 8½
JOSEPH STILES	1757	Teaching poor scholars		14	28/18/ 1
		Books and firewood			3/14/ 7
REBECKAH BURCHALL	1757	Teaching poor children		23	36/ 9/10
		Firewood			3/ 4/ 6
ANN THORNTON	1757	Teaching poor children			3/ 2/ 9

Immediately following the above report, another stated there were 38 in the Latin School, 37 free scholars under Alexander Seaton, 17 (free) under Joseph Stiles, 30 under Ann Thornton, and 30 (free) under Rebeckah Burchall.[83] The slight discrepancy in the figures is not explained. A later report of 1784 shows the following schools and the enrollment of each. (1) Proud, (*Latin*), number not given; Todd, (*English*), 88 on the list; Isaac Weaver, 28; William Brown, 29 girls; Sarah Lancaster, 64; Mary Harry, 15 or 16; Joseph Clarke, about 30; Mrs. Clarke, 15 or 16 boys and girls; Ann Marsh, about 50 boys and girls; Mary McDonnell, 15 young children.[84] From this it seems that the only two schools which have increased considerably in number are the Latin and English, both of which employed ushers or assistants.[85] The chief indication of the system's growth is the increase from five or six schools to at least ten. The approximate

Number of poor and pay scholars stated

Indication of the system's growth in the number of schools

[81]P. C. S. M., 72.
[82]*Ibid.*, 151 ff.
[83]*Ibid.*
[84]Min. Phila. Mo. Mtg., 1—30—1784, 123 ff.
[85]P. C. S. M., I, 76 and 79; also I, 198.

number of children recorded as having attended the schools under the overseers from 1712 to 1770 was 720.[86]

Children were frequently sent away from home to attend school, due to a lack of adequate facilities near at hand.   The following letter, from an anxious mother, is a very interesting commentary on the attitude taken by the less educated toward the propriety of spending time for education. Though impolite to read private letters, it may be pardoned in this case.

The 20 of December, 1702.

Dear Brother:

The few liens comes to salute thee and fore prisila which I hope are in helth as blessed be the God of all our mersies I am at this writing.   I long to hear from you both and how prisila likes being at scool and how the like her and whether she thinks that shee will lern anything worth her while to be kept at cool here.   I have sent her some thred to knit me too pares of golves and herself on if there be anough for to mak so much if not one for me and one for her.   bid her be a good gerl and larn well and then I shall love her.   if Abraham Antone have brought . . . . purchas me twenty pound and send it me if thou can by some opportunity in so doing thou wilt much oblige thy most affectionate sister

Abigail ———.[87]

A fairly good mental picture of the school, and the atmosphere pervading it, is obtained from a perusal of the list of rules which were adopted both for the guidance of the masters and the observance of the pupils. We cannot gain much from a discussion since they are self-explanatory, hence there is submitted a concise digest of those issued for the masters and mistresses in the several schools.

1.   All pupils must be at school promptly.

2.   No one shall be absent without a permit from parents.

3.   Strict obedience to the monitor is demanded, but if there is a real grievance, complaint may be made to the master.

4.   Be orderly in coming to and leaving school.

5.   Use the plain language to all persons; be civil to all.

6.   To avoid, in hours of leisure, all "ranting games" and quarrelling with one another.

---

[86]P. C. S. M., see list of scholars; number is approximate.
[87]*Pemberton Mss.*, Vol. 3, p. 2.

7. Shall not play or keep company with rude boys of the town, but play with own school fellows.

8. They shall come to school on 5th day prepared to go to the regular meeting.[88]

The rules above, which, if all followed, one must admit would have made an almost model school so far as behavior was concerned, were shortly thereafter expanded a little to meet the needs of the Latin and English schools. Those rules, however, were more concerned with the curriculum and part of method, and were doubtless a guide for the instructors more than to be followed by the pupils. They will receive attention in the next few pages in the discussion of the curriculum. We shall however be interested at this juncture to read the rules adopted by Robert Proud, schoolmaster and historian, for the government of the Latin School, in which he was the head master for many years. They are very similar to those already noted, though drawn up by Proud for his school alone.

Orders and Directions
In the School

Reverentia Jehovae Caput Scientiae
The fear of the Lord is the beginning of wisdom.

1. Duty in attending.
Fail not to be present in school precisely at or before the time appointed for learning, being clean and decent; except sufficient reason require thy absense; in which case, on thy first returning . . . . before the master, immediately inform him thereof to his satisfaction.

2. On entering, remaining in and departing from school, having taken thy appointed seat, with as little noise and disturbance as may be, move not therefrom, to that of another during the time of learning without absolute necessity and then, very seldom; nor go out of the school without the master's leave or knowledge. And observe the same silently and orderly behavior, in thy departing from the school, as in thy entering it.

3. How to behave and study in the School.
Be always silent, in School or during the time of thy studies, so as to be heard, neither in voice, nor otherwise, as little as possible; except in writing or speaking to the Master or Teacher; and discourse not with

Rules adopted by Robert Proud while master of the Latin School

---

[88]P. C. S. M., I, 102 f. (Rules adopted in 1748.)

thy Schoolfellows during the hours of study, without the Master's permission; unless in asking, or giving information relating to thine or their
learning; and even then observe to whisper, or speak as low as possible
to be heard by him, who is next thee.

4.   Behavior to the Master, and during the presence of visitants, etc.
Make all thy speeches to the master with due respect; and observe
cheerfully to perform all his directions and commands, with readiness
according to thy ability.   And, if a stranger or visitant speak to thee in
the school, stand up, turn thy face towards him respectfully and give a
modest and ready answer, if any answer be required or necessary;
resuming thy seat again, with a silent application to thy study; which
order and silence are more particularly and especially to be strictly
observed and kept during the presence of any stranger, or visitant, in
the School.

5.   Behavior to one another.
Behave thyself always in a submissive and kind manner to thy School
fellows, never provoking, quarreling, nor complaining, especially about
frivolous matters; but use the word *please*, etc., or expressions of similar
signification when asking anything of them; and observe a proper grati-
tude for every kindness received, be it ever so small; using thy utmost
to cultivate a special Friendship with them; not returning injuries, but
learning to forgive; and shew them, by thy exemplary Deportment, how
they ought to behave.

6.   Not to take Another's Property, etc.
Neither take nor use anything which is the property of another or in
his custody, without first having his permission and as much as possible,
avoid borrowing, at any time, but provide thyself with all books, instruments and things necessary for thy learning and studies according to the
Master's direction; always keeping them clean and in good order.

7.   The Language.
Let the common language, used in School, be Latin, as much as conveniently may be, according to the speaker's knowledge and ability
therein, but in all places let every one speak with as much propriety and
grammatical accuracy as he is capable in whatever language he makes
use of.

8.   School transactions not to be divulged.
Be not forward to divulge any transaction, passed in school, more
especially, to the disreputation of any in it; nor mock, nor jeer any of
thy school fellows, for being reproved or corrected, lest it may sometime
happen to be thy own case; but rather be assisting, than troublesome,
to the masters or teachers by rendering thyself as agreeable, both to him
and them, as possible, in all laudable and good order and discipline, as
well as in the advancement and increase of learning and all real improvement in the respective branches thereof: that, instead of introducing

any cause of punishing, severe reproof, or servile fear, the place of thy learning may be a place of pleasure and delight.[89]

Rule 9 deals with the proper attitude and behavior.

Rule 10 deals with the behavior in the religious meetings.

In spite of the most excellent rules, which, we have seen, were drawn,* it appears the attendance problem was one which caused some masters no little worry. Proud's manuscripts again inform us that on one occasion, after continuous aggravation due to absences, he felt called upon to send a note to the overseers concerning that serious affair. He first mentions the ends desired to be gained by such a school, and points out that they are being fallen short of, because of the laxity in attendance. Moreover, the worst offenders are the sons of the overseers. He says in particular:

Pupils remiss in attendance

The attention of board called to the fact

> But the occasion of this present observation to the Board is more particularly that of the present day, viz.—the 4th instant, when out of six of these, who attend the said school (the Latin School) and ought more particularly to have been present at that time, for the example of others and their own benefit, only one of the smallest was at the school and two at the meeting. The rest, being grown and advanced in years, and learning, etc., and consequently more regarded for examples, were at that particular and important time, all absent with about the same proportion of the rest of the school.[90]

There were, it seems, the usual causes at work which produced such havoc in the attendance record, and such distress in the minds of masters. A letter written by James Logan to his friend John Dickinson, in 1704, strengthens our belief that such was the case. He wrote in part:

Dear Friend:

I shall acquaint thee that thy two rugged boys are very lusty, love the river much better this hot weather than their masters' countenances, and the fields and boats far before schools or books. . . .

Thy affectionate Friend,

JAMES LOGAN.[91]

---

[89]*Robert Proud Mss. Collection*, No. 20, pp. 3–7. The rules, he states, were drawn up for his use in the school in 1780.

*The rules presented, taken from records of the Overseers of the Schools in Philadelphia, are quite like those later drawn up by Horsham School Committee. There is nothing additional in the later ones and they were doubtless patterned after them. (Horsham Sch. Com. Min., 1—27—1783).

[90]*Robert Proud Mss.*, No. 156, 45.

[91]*Logan Mss.* Letter for 4th month, 12th, 1704. Vol. I, 49. (J. Dickinson was away on a voyage of some length.)

We have not much information from which to judge the discipline of the school. From the rules already considered one would expect that strict discipline was observed, but of the master's methods of enforcing it we know but little. There were doubtless two extremes. On the one hand, we might take Anthony Benezet as the very personification of mildness, and who ruled by love.[92] On the other hand, there was John Todd who would thrash a boy very severely, and who took great delight in getting his victim to admit the pain that he knew he felt.[93]

Two extremes in discipline

To secure better discipline, attendance, and also to induce striving for scholarship, it was customary to give rewards. We noted in the items sent in to the overseers in masters' reports that certain amounts were for "premiums."[94] This policy of rewards was early agreed upon by the overseers who sought in various ways to establish little funds for that purpose. In 1755 it was proposed that each one pay two shillings for missing a board meeting and one shilling for being late; the accruing amount to be paid out in premiums to encourage industry among the boys.[95] The fines were collected and then turned over to the masters who applied them as they saw fit.[96] The extent of the practice of giving rewards is not exactly known, but it seems to have been general throughout all the schools of the Board in Philadelphia, if we may judge from the regularity with which the bills for "premiums" were presented. It was also true that the school committees in other monthly meetings arranged to give rewards on visiting day to the scholars having the best records.[97]

Premium given to most satisfactory pupils

The early school days seem to have been long and tedious. Attention has already been called to the letter of Pastorius' children to their grandfather, in which they complained of the long eight hour school day.[98] The school continued, according to their account, six days in the week excepting Saturday

Length of school day

[92]Vaux, *Memoirs of Benezet*, 15 f.
[93]Watson, *Annals*, I, 291–2.
[94]See page 181.
[95]P. C. S. M., I, 137.
[96]*Ibid.*, 150.
[97]Min. Horsham Sch. Com., 3—16—1792.
[98]See page 78.

afternoon.[99]   Besides this it was customary in all places to attend meeting on fifth day (Thursday),[100] save in places where it may have been too far distant, an exception was made possible.[101] Evening schools were quite common, as has been stated before in the case of Germantown,[102] and increased in number toward the latter part of the century. In 1750 John Wilson, usher to Robert Willian, expressed his intention of opening an evening school which appears to have been acceptable to the Board.[103] The prevalence of the evening school among people not Friends is at once apparent when one glances at the advertisements in the colonial newspapers. A few of those private evening schools were: one kept by William Dawson and John Gladson, teaching writing, arithmetic, and navigation;[104] others by John Shuppy,[105] Mr. Lyonet,[106] and Messrs. Barthelemy and Besayde.[107]

Evening schools customary

The length of the school day is better indicated, and perhaps the source of information is more reliable, near the end of the century. The rules issued by the Board in 1795 state that the hours are to be from 8 to 12 in the morning, and from 2 to 5 in the afternoon, these hours to be observed from third month, first to eleventh month, first; in the remaining months the hours were 9 to 12 and 2 to 5.[108] Vacations were very scarce and very brief.* In the main, according to the rules issued at least, they were to be: (1) at the periods of the quarterly and yearly meetings; and (2) a vacation of three weeks, commencing on seventh day preceding the last sixth day of the week of the seventh month.[109] The other

Length of school day in 1795: seven hours

---

[99]Page 78.
[100]See list of printed rules for the school in custody of P.C.S.
[101]Min. Horsham Sch. Com., 1—27—1783 (also mentioned in the monthly meeting minutes very frequently).
[102]See page 78f.
[103]P. C. S. M., I, 84.
[104]*Pa. Gazette*, No. 1449, 1756.
[105]*Ibid.*, No. 824, 1744.
[106]*Pa. Packet and Daily Advertiser*, No. 2385, 1786.
[107]*Ibid.*, No. 2386, 1786.
[108]A list of printed rules issued by the Board, found in the depository for the P. C. S. M., in the Provident Life and Trust Building, Phila.
*Darby Meeting employed B. Clift to teach a whole year with the exception of two weeks. (Darby Min., 7—7—1692, 54).
[109]*Ibid.*

rules issued at this date besides these mentioned relating to holidays and length of the school day were the same as were previously stated.[110]   The hours named above appear to us rather long for the small children; arrangement seems to have been made for them, though no statement of it is made in the school regulations.   There were, however, the schools of (1) William Brown and (2) Sarah Lancaster, who taught children for half days,[111] and also the Girls' School, in which Anthony Benezet taught (1754), was mentioned as though it were to be conducted only in the morning.[112]   It is not to be understood that the half day arrangement was always followed in the case of younger children, for Sarah Lancaster taught thirty-five children whole days "at 15/ per quarter."[113]   It seems that the amount of time for them to attend was probably determined by the desires of their parents.

An interesting and instructive light is cast upon the inner life of the school in Philadelphia, by some of the manuscript collections of the very old Philadelphia families.   For instance, we learn that in the public school there were published certain magazines, gazettes, chronicles, and so forth, a few of them named as follows: *The Examiner, The Universal Magazine,* 1774, *Students' Gazette* (about 1774 to 1777), *The P. S. Gazette, Latonia,* 1777 to 1778, the *Public School Gazetteer,* containing the freshest advices, foreign and domestic (a palpable imitation of the newspapers in the city of that date), and *The Students' Magazine.*[114]   The contents of all of them were no doubt very interesting to the boys and girls at the time of their publication, and are so even now, and at times give light on topics of importance.   It may perhaps interest the reader to see some of the entries.   We find the following which gives a clew to the book used for instruction in grammar.

Student papers, and magazines, etc.

---

[110]See page 183 f.
[111]Min. Phila. Mo. Mtg., 1—30—1784, 123 ff.
[112]P. C. S. M., I, 117.
[113]Min. Phila. Mo. Mtg., 1—30—1784, 123 ff.
[114]Some copies and volumes of these illustrious news sheets are found in the *Norris Ms. Collection.*

Was lost on Wednesday in The Public School Rudiman's Grammar newly bound—Whoever has found the same and will bring it to me . . . . shall receive 1 sheet of paper reward.

S. FISHER.[115]

Another of interest bewails the departure of Thomas Lloyd from school to go into Lancaster County.

This worthy Gentleman, was admitted about a 12 month ago into the society of freeholders, since which time he has been a very distinguished member of our community and a firm supporter of our institutions. He has been twice elected Clerk of the Supreme Court and twice raised to the dignity of President of the Honorable House of Assembly, which offices together with Treasurer he filled with most unblemished reputation and unshaked fidelity. His character in the literary world is sufficiently established by many genuine productions of judgment and humor. His affable disposition, his engaging address and behavior endear him to all that had the happiness of his acquaintance and render his departure a cause of great regret.[116]

Another brief notice indicates that the Quaker preferment for plain dress was also made to prevail in the schoolroom.

From a certain expression which lately drop'd from one of the overseers, we would have the greatest reason to believe that Mr. Webster's gay appearance is rather disagreeable.[117]

Some supervision of the work on the part of overseers and school committees seems to have been at all times expected, though attention hardly needs be called to it after the presentation of so many reports made by committees, in the chapters relating to the establishment of schools in the several counties. From the irregularity in the reports we judge, however, that the visitation must have likewise been irregular in many places. In 1755 the Board in Philadelphia decided that for the encouragement of masters and scholars there should be visits made each month, preceding the usual monthly meetings. Also if "play days" were thought necessary they were to be arranged for between the masters and the committee of visitors.[118] The minutes indicate that these monthly visits were regularly performed. The

Supervision

Somewhat
irregular

Monthly
visits
decided
upon

---

[115]*Norris Ms. Collection—The Student's Magazine.*   The little volumes are unpaged; page references are impossible.
[116]*Norris Ms. Collection.*   [117]*Ibid.*
[118]P. C. S. M., I, 135.

Negro School, established in 1770, was also in charge of a committee to visit, superintend, and advise regarding its affairs.[119]

THE CURRICULUM

If we go back to our references on the advices of the yearly meetings of London and Philadelphia we shall find there the basic reasons for the subjects which are to be mentioned as taught regularly in the schools. We recall that there was an emphasis placed on the *moral*, the *useful* and *practical*, and the subjects first to be mentioned were: writing, reading, and arithmetic, which constituted the necessities.[121] Furthermore, the Frame of Government of 1696, the product of Quaker minds and hands, recommended to erect and order all public houses and encourage and reward the authors of useful sciences and laudable inventions.[122] It is seen also from later advices of the yearly meeting that the *useful* was not limited necessarily to the four R's, religion, arithmetic, writing, and reading. In 1737, they recommended that as opportunity could be found, children should be permitted to learn "French, High and Low Dutch, Danish, etc."[123] The use of Latin, Greek, and Hebrew is also justified by Crouch,[124] and it is well known and evident in all their writings that Penn, Barclay, Fothergill, Lloyd, Proud, Pastorius, and innumerable others were classically educated men.

The curriculum of the first school (Enoch Flower's) consisted of reading, writing, and casting accounts,[125] and it seems entirely probable that these were the chief constituents, along with moral instruction, for many years, in all save the Latin School. At any rate there occur no disproving factors in that early period. In 1742, when Anthony Benezet came from the Germantown school to Philadelphia, he was employed to teach arithmetic, writing, accounts, and French.[126]

The curricula are in general in harmony with the recommendations of the yearly meetings; and the Frame of Government

Studies pursued in Flower's school

In Benezet's

Walby's

---

[119]Phila. Mo. Min., I—25—1771, 430.

[121]London Yr. Mtg. Min., 4—2 to 10—1718, 160. Phila. Advices XXX, page 250 (for years from 1746–1778). Also a copy of the Discipline containing the digested recommendations on schools, p. 386 ff. (In first National Bank, Newtown, Pa.).

[122]*Col. Rec.*, I, LXVI.

[123]Extracts from London Yr. Mtg. Min., pub. 1802, 124.

[124]Crouch, *Collection of His Papers*, 183.

[125]*Col. Rec.*, I, 36.

[126]P. C. S. M., I, 33.

John Walby, employed about ten years before him (Benezet) was to teach reading, writing, and arithmetic.[127] Alexander Seaton was employed in 1751 to teach a school "in the upper part of the City," the subjects being writing, arithmetic, and parts of the mathematics.[128] In 1754, when Benezet first began in the Girls' School (mornings), he was required to instruct in reading, writing, arithmetic, and English grammar.[129] Then, besides what we may term the English School, in which Seaton and Benezet taught for some time, there were others which we might term "petty schools," for example, one kept by Debby Godfrey,[130] who taught some poor children to learn to sew and read, and another, taught by Ann Redman (1761), previously occupied by Rebeckah Burchall, where were taught reading, writing, and plain sewing.[131]

Since writing letters was an art much used and cultivated in the Colonial Period, and writing was greatly emphasized in the schools, it may be of interest to insert a letter written by a school boy in 1735. The letter is written in a fairly regular boyish hand, and is probably the production of a youngster about 12 years of age.

margin notes: Seaton's / Girls' School / Godfrey's / Letter writing

Nov. 21, 1735.

Dear Uncle,

I think in duty, I ought to wait on you with my first letter, which I hope will plead excuse for all faults. I remember what you told me, and write or go to school every day—I am much obliged to you for your kind present of tickets, and hope I shall have good success.—Pray give my duty to Uncle and Aunt Penn and all my Cousins. My love to Mr. Philaps, Mr. Jervice and Farmer Dill. With all my Friends.—So conclude.

Dear Uncle
Your Affct. Nep.
THOMAS FREAME.*

Phil. d. Novbr. 21, 1735.

At later dates than those above mentioned the records of the overseers, reports made in the monthly meetings of

---

[127]P. C. S. M., 14.
[128]*Ibid.*, 90.
[129]*Ibid.*, 117.
[130]*Ibid.*, 145.
[131]*Ibid.*, 221.
*A letter written to John Penn, *Penn Ms. Collections*, I, 233.

Curriculum
of later dates

Philadelphia, Horsham School Minutes, Darby, and others, indicate that the curriculum consisted of reading, English, writing, arithmetic, branches of the mathematics, sewing, spelling, needlework, and other things suitable for girls.[132] The only one which is mentioned at this latter date, and not

Spelling

at the former, is spelling. This of course does not mean, necessarily, that spelling had just been introduced. In 1756 the visiting committee reported that spelling books and Bibles were needed in the schools for the poor children,[133] and since Benezet's spelling book came to a second edition in 1779,[134] and Fox's *Instructions for Right Spelling* was published in Philadelphia in 1702,[135] we may be certain that spelling as a regular study began at a very early date. If we

Quaker
school
curricula
compared
with others

compare this curriculum with those mentioned by private tutors at the same time, we find them essentially the same. There was, however, frequent mention of such subjects as navigation, calk guaging, mensuration, bookkeeping,[136] surveying,[137] dialling,[138] astronomy, and fortification,[139] which are not mentioned definitely in the curriculum of the Friends' schools. It is quite probable that those above, dealing with higher mathematics, were included in the higher mathematics taught in the Classical School. But one cannot imagine that "fortification" was granted a place. Those studies of the mathematics may be mentioned again in studying the curriculum of the Latin School.

Studies pursued in the Negro School

The curriculum in the Negro School (1770) consisted approximately of the same subjects, though they may have been modified to some extent in presentation, and restricted more or less to the rudiments. The subjects of instruction mentioned when the school first began were reading, writing, and arithmetic, and were to be taught under "prudent" and "competent" direction.[140]

---

[132]Min. Phila. Mo. Mtg., 7—30, 1779, 151; 1—30—1784, 123 ff. Also, Min. Horsham Sch. Com., 1—27—1783; Min. Horsham Prep. Mtg., 1—24—1783, and Min. Darby Mo. Mtg., 2—28—1793, 165, give some of the books which were used in the schools.

[133]P. C. S. M., I, 138.   [134]Hildeburn, II, 332.
[135]*Ibid.*, I, 39.   [136]*Pa. Gaz.*, No. 1245, 1752.
[137]*Ibid.*, No. 1499, 1757.   [138]*Ibid.*, No. 1861, 1764.
[139]*Ibid.*, No. 1556, 1758.
[140]Min. Phila. Mo. Mtg., 3—30—1770, 370.

What books were used for the instruction in this curriculum of the English and Lower schools? We cannot state absolutely in the case of all studies, but we can judge with comparative certainty what books were most available for their use.

In the case of those used for religious instruction, the meeting records usually mentioned the name, which enables one to state with absolute certainty that certain books were used. Bibles for the use of schools were requested by the visiting committees of the overseers in Philadelphia, for the use of poor scholars.[141] Other books of religious and denominational character such as Penn's *Reflections, Maxims,* and *Advice to His Children,* are mentioned definitely by Darby,[142] Horsham School Committee,[143] Sadsbury,[144] and Byberry Preparative meetings[145] as being received for use in connection with the schools. Byberry Preparative,[146] Radnor[147] and Sadsbury[148] monthly meetings mention further the receipt of Barclay's *Apologies* for school use. Besides these, which were undoubtedly used for school instruction, there was a long list of journals, essays, letters, epistles, histories of Friends, etc., which always were in the possession of each meeting and may have been used indirectly at least. They will be mentioned more at length in pages following.

The spelling book prepared by Fox and published in Philadelphia in 1702,[149] must have claimed a place in the Friends' schools, though the books are nowhere mentioned by name. The title of this book includes reading, writing, spelling, and other things useful and necessary, and may easily have served for other purposes than use in spelling instruction. Other spellers, which became available from time to time, were Benezet's *Pennsylvania Spelling Book* and *The Alphabet* printed by Henry Miller, 1770.[150] Among

Books prominent for religious instruction in the schools

Bible

Apology of Barclay, and Penn's Reflections, Maxims, and Advice to His Children

Books probably used in spelling

---

[141]P. C. S. M., I, 138.
[142]Min. Darby Mo. Mtg., 2—28—1793, 165.
[143]Min. Horsham Sch. Com., 1—11—1793.
[144]Min. Sadsbury Mo. Mtg., 2—20—1793, 118.
[145]Min. Byberry Prep. Mtg., 12—26—1792.
[146]*Ibid.,* 8—26—1789.
[147]Min. Radnor Mo. Mtg., 5—8—1789, 55.
[148]Min. Sadsbury Mo. Mtg., 6—17—1789, II, 70.
[149]Hildeburn, I, 39 (published in London 1697).
[150]*Ibid.,* II, 100.

those which were used later in the century, Prowell, in speaking of the schools in York County, notes Comly's, Cobb's, and Webster's.[151] From this array, which is no doubt incomplete, we may judge the schools were well supplied.

Of the primers available, and likely to be used, there were

Primers likely to be used

a host. The first which should be mentioned was that published by Fox in 1659; it is not known whether this primer was used in Philadelphia. It seems that it was not printed there.[152] In 1677-8, the monthly meeting authorized the purchase of "primmers,"[153] however, and the choice must have been either Fox's or Pastorius'. No student of early printing in Philadelphia has yet been able to determine when the latter's was published. Hildeburn is in doubt,[154] while Smith thinks the "primmers" ordered by the meeting 1697-8 must have been those of Pastorius.[155] The minute, however, does not state which. In 1696 Pastorius indicated his willingness to take charge of a printing press for Friends,[156] but, since it had to be brought from England, it is not likely, though possible, that he himself could have printed the book, before the time of the "primmer" purchase was mentioned. Since Pastorius lists a Fox's *Primmer* among the books in his possession,[157] that book must have been known in the monthly meeting too, and may have been the one used.* The data are inadequate and uncertain for reaching a decision in the matter.

Other primers available for use during the century

Other primers published and available in Philadelphia and which may well have gotten into Friends' schools were Franklin's, 1764; *The New England Primmer Improved*, 1770; *The Newest American Primer*, 1779; *The New England Primmer Improved*, 1779; and *A Primmer*, 1779.[158] The minutes

---

[151]Prowell, I, 540.

[152]In 1689 Phila. Mo. Mtg. authorized W. Bradford to print certain of G. Fox's papers. These are not named and it hardly seems probable that Fox's *Primmer* was in the list. Bradford's request for permission (Geneological Publications, II, 139), H. S. P.

[153]Min. Phila. Mo. Mtg., 12—25—1697-8, p. 227 (G. S. P. P.)

[154]Hildeburn, I, 38.

[155]Smith, *Supplement to Catalogue of Friends Books*, 262.

[156]Min. Phila. Mo. Mtg., 11—29—1696-7, 211. (G. S. P. P., Vol. 4).

[157]Pastorius's *Common Place Book* (Mss.) H. S. P.

[158]Hildeburn, II, 21, 114, 341, 340, and 343, respectively.

*The *Primer* of Stephen Crisp is also mentioned frequently with that of Fox, as being used in the schools. (Min. Abington Mo. Mtg., 8—27—1735, 207.

of the meetings give little guidance as to which were or were not used. We know only they had this list (and perhaps more) from which to select. Still other books which were probably used in the English work were Dilworth's *A New Guide to the English Tongue* and *The Child's New Plaything or Best Amusement, intended to make the Learning to Read a Diversion instead of a Task*, both of which were published in 1757.[159]

For use in the writing school, we find one definite reference made to Bickam's *Universal Penman*, which was purchased for use in Alexander Seaton's School in 1762.[160] The various primers and spellers already mentioned dealt largely with writing also, giving models which were to be set before the pupil in the books or to be written out for him by the master. Some of the mottoes called to mind were: "Command you may your mind from Play" and "A man of words and not of deeds, is like a garden full of weeds."[161] The first exercises in writing were the making of elements such as straight lines, curves, and then single letters, and words. The various samples which the writer has noticed in the boy's letter quoted,[162] and the student manuscript papers,[163] were of very good quality, the median grade of them being about "eleven" on the Thorndike Handwriting Scale.*

In the writing schools

Quality of some samples noted

Various arithmetics may be mentioned. There were Gough's *A Treatise of Arithmetic, Theory*, etc., 1770, and *Practical Arithmetic*, 1767, neither of which appears to have been published in Philadelphia, but may have been better recommended than others, since gotten up by a Friend. Dilworth's *Schoolmaster's Assistant* published in Philadelphia, 1773,[164] was no doubt a close competitor with Pike's, Park's, and Daboll's arithmetics, which Prowell mentions as being common in the latter part of the century.[165] He also describes

Arithmetics used in some of the schools

---

[159]Hildeburn, I, 318.
[160]P. C. S. M., I, 240.
[161]Prowell, I, 541.
[162]See page 191.
[163]Chiefly in the *Norris Mss. Collections.*
*A scale, having units of known value, which is used in measuring accomplishment in handwriting.
[164]Hildeburn, II, 164.
[165]Prowell, I, 540.

a book gotten up by Elihu Underwood, schoolmaster at
Warrington, in which he copied very orderly all the exercises
of the arithmetic,[166] The *Norris Collection* likewise contains a
few pupils' copy books filled with neatly arranged exercises in
addition, multiplication, division, both decimal and vulgar
fractions, and another one which would correspond to our
present-day commercial arithmetic, but which Isaac Norris
probably called his merchants' accounts.[167]   The books vary
in dates from 1729 to 1779.

Ms. collec-
tion indi-
cates the
nature of the
arithmetic
work

The curriculum of the classical school is best indicated by
statements made on employing teachers for that place, which,
though they indicate the *subjects*, do not state *what materials*
were used for study.   Whether the materials used in the
study of the Greek and Latin tongues included the so-called
"profane authors" is a matter for speculation.   Robert
Willian in 1748 was brought from England to teach Latin
and Greek and other parts of learning.[168]   The "other parts"
may have included some English grammar, writing, and
mathematics, as these are frequently mentioned elsewhere as
being a part of the Latin school course.[169]   Several masters
employed from time to time for instruction in these subjects
were (after Willian): Alexander Buller,* writing, mathematics, and the Latin tongue; John Wilson, as usher[170] to the
master in the same school, and later as master;[171] King;[172]
William Johnson;[173]   Charles Thompson;[174] and Robert
Proud.[175]   Others might be named, all of whom seem to have
been employed for teaching substantially the same curriculum.   Arithmetic and reading are at times mentioned as
being taught in the Latin school, usually by the ushers.[176]

Classical
school
curriculum

------

[166]Elihu Underwood was teacher at Warrington in York County in
1784 (See Warrington Mo. Mtg. Min., 1—10—1784, 47.
[167]*Norris Ms. Collection*, H. S. P.
[168]P. C. S. M., I, 64.
[169]*Ibid.*, 26; also Min. Phila. Mo. Mtg., 7–30–1779, 151.
*In 1741 Buller advertised the teaching of writing, arithmetic, mer-
chants' accounts, navigation, algebra, and other parts of the mathematics to be taught at the "Public School." (*Pa. Gaz.* No. 673, 1741).
[170]*Ibid.*, 84.
[171]*Ibid.*, 101.
[172]*Ibid.*, 122.
[173]*Ibid.*, 131.   [174]*Ibid.*, 133.
[175]Min. Phila. Mo. Mtg., 1—30—1784, 123 ff.
[176]*Ibid.*, 7—30—1779, 151.

The curriculum of what was known as the English School overlapped in some respects that of the Latin. Among the subjects usually taught there may be mentioned: arithmetic, writing, accounts, French,[177] reading,[178] and probably some mathematics.[179] The Girls School's curriculum, taught by Benezet in 1754, consisted of reading, writing, arithmetic, and English grammar.[180]

Curriculum in the English school

Some light is cast on the method of instruction in the English and Latin schools by instructions given by the Board for the use of the master. Latin scholars were to be accustomed to analyze and parse their several lessons; and the English scholars to learn it grammatically. Moreover the double translation method for Latin and Greek was required for instruction in those subjects; and practice in handwriting and spelling.[181] The reader is also referred to page 183 to the rules of Robert Proud, in which he states that Latin, as far as the pupils are able, must be used in the school. The reading of the Scriptures was required three times a week,[182] and in later rules (1795), they name also the works of Penn and Barclay as being required. They are placed in the same category with the Scriptures.[183]

Methods used in language instruction

Latin to be used in school as much as possible; Scriptures, Penn, and Barclay required

Of the grammars used we made reference previously to that of Rudiman,[184] which was published in Philadelphia in 1776.[185] This was the first American edition. Another, Davy's *Adminiculum Puerile*,[186] or a help for school boys, containing fundamental exercises for beginners, syntax, cautions for mistakes, English for Latin verses, and so forth, which was made easily available by a Philadelphia reprint in 1758, may have been in use. We might expect to find that

Grammar used; others that were available

---

[177]P. C. S. M., I, 33.
[178]*Ibid.*, 14.
[179]Alexander Seaton, who came to the English School about 1754 (P. C. S. M. I, 117) had been teaching a school of the same nature in the upper part of the city, in which he taught mathematics. That school was also under the direction of the Board. (P. C. S. M., I, 90).
[180]*Ibid.*, 80.
[181]*Ibid.*, 104 f.
[182]*Ibid.*
[183]A list of the rules for the government of the schools, printed, in the P. C. S. depository.
[184]See page 189.
[185]Hildeburn, II, 266.
[186]*Ibid.*, 464.

some of the worthy masters, Pastorius, Willian, Thompson, Wilson, Proud, and others made some contribution in the way of Latin text-books; we are, in that respect, disappointed. Another grammar, but of the English tongue, was that prepared by James and John Gough, which, after being duly inspected by the Board, was adopted for use in the English School in 1761.[187] Since English grammar was also taught in the Latin School, it may have been used in that department also. Concerning the French book or grammar which Anthony Benezet may have used when he was engaged to teach that subject in 1742,[188] we cannot state definitely.

French grammars

However, there was a *French School Book* published in Philadelphia in 1730,[189] and it may safely be assumed to have been available for his use. The character of the book we do not know. Perrin's *Grammar of the French Tongue* was printed in Philadelphia, 1779,[190] and was no doubt the best book available for use of the schools at and subsequent to that time. It may be well to mention here some school books which were in the possession of Daniel Pastorius; their presence may indicate that they, or a part of them, were used in the school.

School books possessed by Daniel Pastorius

They were: *Education, The Young Clerk's Tutor, Elements of Geometry, A Short Introduction to Grammar, The English School Master*, G. Fox's *Primmer*, and *Teacher's Instruction for Children.*[191]

Some idea of the extent to which mathematics was taught may be gained from certain old exercise books. Some of those, which doubtless belong to the lower schools, dealt with

Mathematics

arithmetical exercises, with whole numbers, vulgar and decimal fractions, and commercial arithmetic.[192] Others, clearly more advanced, and doubtless belonging to the Latin school, though some were taught in the English, are chiefly filled with theorems and proven solutions in geometry, trigonometry, conic sections, and spherical trigonometry.[193] This

[187]P. C. S. M., I, 235.
[188]See page 57.
[189]*Pa. Gaz.*, Apr. 16, 1730.
[190]Hildeburn, II, 342.
[191]Pastorius, *Common Place Book* (*Mss.*) H. S. P.
[192]Books of Charles and Isaac Norris in *Norris Ms. Collection.*
[193]Books chiefly of Norris, I. Griffiths, and King, in the *Norris Ms. Collection.*

compares quite favorably with the courses suggested in the newspapers, as we have already mentioned.

METHOD

Concerning this topic little is to be added to what has already been suggested in connection with the discussion of the subject matter. Some points of method, of which we are reasonably certain, will be stated. In religious instruction, where the Bible, Penn's, Barclay's, Fox's, and other works were used as the material, a catechetical method was used by parents in the home, by the masters and mistresses in the schools, and in the youths' meetings, which were always among the first established. This method still prevails to some extent for the young children. Drill in spelling and handwriting has already been mentioned as urged by the overseers in their directions to the masters and mistresses in the Latin and English schools.[194] The chief elements of Latin and Greek instruction were: analysis, parsing, double translation, and the necessary memory drills. The pupils in Proud's school were also required to speak Latin so far as able to do so. We have also mentioned that in teaching writing the practise was to begin with simple lines, curves, etc., and proceed to the more complex performances.[195] In the majority of subjects "copybooks" were required to be kept. All of these the writer has been privileged to observe, being kept in a very neat and regular fashion.[196]

Methods

Catechetical method in religion

Drill in spelling and writing

Parsing, double translation in classics

OTHER LITERATURE USED IN THE MEETINGS

Besides the books already mentioned that are known to have been concerned directly with schools, there were innumerable others which were printed by Friends and circulated at their suggestion among all the meetings. They are largely religious and doctrinal treatises; many of them, though not found thus stated, may have been used in instruction. They were at least of educational importance to the

Books circulated regularly among meetings

[194]P. C. S. M., I, 104 f.
[195]See page 195.
[196]See *Norris Ms. Collection*, H. S. P.

communities that read them. They are mentioned in the minutes of every meeting. Though usually paid for by the meeting, the Board of Overseers in Philadelphia went on record to the effect that fines for absence from, or tardiness in coming to their meetings should be applied to the purchase of books for the school library.[197] Sometimes they were given by bequest, as in the case of the Philadelphia school, which received through the monthly meeting a large collection (for that day) from Thomas Chalkly.[198] The list, as given below, is made up from records of Sadsbury, Westland, Warrington and Fairfax, Uwchlan, Concord, Radnor, New Garden, London Yearly, Philadelphia Yearly, Gwynedd, Falls, Exeter, Wrightstown, Darby, Byberry, Horsham, Abington, and Buckingham meetings, and though perhaps it does not contain all, it does have those most commonly used. This list is as follows:

Usually purchased by the meetings; not always

A list of books most commonly found in the meeting

Banks, *Journal, Life and Travels.*
Barclay, *Anarchy of the Ranters.*
Bathurst, *Truth Vindicated.*
Benezet, *Account of the Friends* (in the German language).
     On the Keeping of Slaves.
Churchman, *Journal.*
Claridge, *Posthumous works.*
Crisp, *Epistles of Stephen Crisp.*
Davis, *Journal.*
Edmundson, *Journal.*
Elwood, *Works.*
Fothergill, *Journal.*
Fox, *Journal.*
Fuller, *Catechism.*
Hall, *A Mite into the Treasury.*
Holme, *A Serious Call in Christian Love to all People.*
Keith, *Way to the City of God.*
London Yearly Meeting's Epistles.
Penn, *No Cross No Crown.*
    Rise and Progress of the Quakers.
Travels in Germany.
Philadelphia Yearly Meeting's Epistles.
Richardson, *Life of John Richardson.*
Sewell, *History of Friends.*

---

[197]P. C. S. M., I, 239.
[198]*Ibid.*, 75.

Scott, *Journal.*
Spaulding, *Reason for leaving the National Mode of Worship.*
Stanton, *Journal.*
Treatises on Tythes.
Treatises on *Reasons for Silent Waiting.*
Turford, *Grounds of an Holy Life.*
Woolman, *Journal.*

SUMMARY

The first problem presented was how to establish some satisfactory means of school support, which should be permanent, and thus conducive to better schools in every way. Recommendations from the yearly meetings dwelt upon this point in the yearly advices, but being of a general and advisory character, could not compel the lower units to act at once. This lack of power in a control authority was the greatest weakness, and because of it, educational development was not so rapid as it might otherwise have been. The chief forms of school support were: (1) *subscription*, (2) *rates*, (3) *bonds*, and (4) *legacies*. In accordance with suggestions made by the yearly meeting, plans were adopted by most meetings (in the latter half of the century) for the establishment of permanent funds. These plans were based upon the subscription idea. The chief characteristics of the plans adopted were:

Support

Weakness in the organization

Forms of support

Subscription plans generally adopted

1. Voluntary subscriptions; interest-bearing notes given.
2. Trustees always named in the monthly meetings.
3. Reports to be made regularly to the trustees.
4. All money received was to be invested, real property preferred.
5. The monthly meeting to decide any disputes arising among trustees.
6. Funds were to pay salaries, and provide and repair buildings.

The organization was headed by the yearly meeting, whose advices were distributed among the lower units. The quarterly meeting was nothing more than a supervisory and directing group. The real work of organizing schools was performed by the monthly and preparative meetings. The other quarterly and monthly meetings worked through specially appointed committees.

Organization

Several schools, in Philadelphia and Abington, for example, very early acquired permanent lands for their foundation.

Others did not gain such foundations until the latter part of the eighteenth century. Even where land was possessed, the schools were quite often held for a time in the meeting houses. Sometimes the meeting house was used until late in the 19th century, as in the case of the Merion School. Other schools were held in the home of the teacher. The buildings were not large, and were often used for the masters' families, or parts of them let out to tenants. In one case in Philadelphia the schoolhouse was heated for a time with a brick stove.

There were always two classes recognized, the *pay pupil* and the *free pupil*. Every necessity was furnished the latter by the board or committee in charge of schools. Teachers (in Philadelphia, at least) had to keep a list of scholars and their expenditures and report to the board. The size of schools remained about the same, but the increase in number of schools indicated the growth of the system in Philadelphia.

Very explicit rules were laid down for the government of the pupils' behavior, both in school and out. By some masters they were enforced mildly; by others harshly. In spite of excellent rules and premiums offered, the masters were perplexed with the discipline and attendance problems. School was kept for five and one-half days per week and from seven to eight hours each day; however, some were kept only half days. Vacations were brief and seldom. The various student papers indicate the presence of a student organization. To promote the interest of the pupils and assist the master, visitations were performed at periods by the committee on schools.

The curriculum of the Latin School consisted of Latin, Greek, English grammar, writing and mathematics. There was some overlapping of the curricula of the English and Latin schools. Rudiman's *Grammar* was used, and Davy's *Adminiculum Puerile*, Gough's *English Mannor*, and Perrin's *Grammar of the French Tongue* were available for use. Whether classical authors were or were not included in the materials used in Greek and Latin classes is not shown by the records. It has been stated that parsing, analysis, double translation, and speaking Latin as much as possible in school, were the chief elements in the method of instruction. Mathe-

Margin notes:

The school lands

Houses

Two classes of pupils

Growth of schools

Length of school week and day

Vacations

Supervision

Curriculum of Latin School

Grammars used

Method

matics included anything as advanced as spherical trigonometry and conic sections.

The curriculum of the lower schools consisted of reading, writing, casting accounts and arithmetic. No mention is made that French was taught before Benezet's coming in 1742. Though no early explicit reference to spelling is made, we infer it must have been taught at an early date. Many schools were kept for poor children in which were taught reading, writing and sewing. The curriculum of the Negro School consisted of reading, writing and arithmetic. *Curriculum of lower schools*

In the Negro School

A large amount of literature of religious character was circulated through the meetings, and probably constituted a good part of the materials used in the schools. *Literature used in the meetings*

CHAPTER X

MASTERS AND MISTRESSES

Discussion
of individual
masters to
be brief

There is on this subject a considerable amount of available material, though much of it is difficult of access. Of a long list of Quaker masters, and mistresses too, for they employed women from the very earliest date, it will be impossible in the brief space of this chapter to say more than a word. Some will only be mentioned because of scarcity of material concerning them; others must be only mentioned, even though they are of such importance that the story of their lives have required and would require volumes to write.[1]

Before a discussion of the masters and mistresses employed in the Quaker schools, it should be ascertained, if possible,

Qualifica-
tions de-
manded of
teachers;
morality,
membership
and
competency

what were the ideals or standards which were consciously set up to guide in their selection. What sort of tutors did they desire? This has already been touched upon, in other chapters, so we may simply state the chief criteria without further discussion. These, as stated from time to time by the yearly meetings and reiterated by quarterly, monthly, and pre-paratives, were: (1) morality, (2) be a member of Friends, and (3) competent to teach the subjects for which employed.[2] The selection of teachers possessing such qualifications was usually entrusted to the care of committees as has already been sufficiently pointed out.

Serious
attempt
made to
meet the
standards
set

In a majority of cases there was a real concern on the part of the monthly meetings' committees to secure teachers possessing the above named qualities,[3] their success in so doing increasing towards the latter part of the 18th century.

---

[1]For instance, F. D. Pastorius, Anthony Benezet, Robert Proud, Christopher Taylor, and many others.

[2]Min. London Yr. Mtg., 4—9 to 11—1690, 52; 4—1 to 4—1691, 60; 3—13 to 17—1695, 89; also collected Advices of Philadelphia and Burlington Yr. Mtg., 250 ff.

[3]Min. Byberry Prep. Mtg., 2—22—1786.

(204)

The fact that they have been successful in securing Friends for teachers is usually mentioned in their reports.[4] In bequests of property for use of schools, it was quite customary to state that the masters or mistresses should be Friends, and to be otherwise conducted as directed by the yearly meeting.[5] There were of necessity some failures in the attempt to secure such qualified masters, the failures being sometimes recorded in the minutes.[6] The failures seem generally to have been caused by the scarcity of the masters rather than carelessness on the part of the meeting or its committees.[7]

The source whence teachers were secured was usually, in the case of the lower schools, home talent, no record having been found where a teacher was sent for or came from a great distance especially to take charge of schools. But innumerable instances, of which a few are cited later in this work, are at hand, where home talent was employed.[8] Enoch Flower, the first master employed, was "an inhabitant of the said town."[9]

Teachers in lower schools usually from the home locality

In the case of the classical school, the practice was quite different. The difference was doubtless the result of necessity, rather than of choice. The first master, Keith, of the school which was first established by the meeting, and his successors, Makin, Cadwalader, and Pastorius, were, of course, as much native to the place as were any of the early settlers in the city. Of later masters, however, quite a number were brought from England especially for the business of "keeping school" or sought in other of the colonies. Certain specific cases may be mentioned. In 1784 Robert Willian came from England "to undertake keeping Friends' school," producing a certificate from Scarborough Meeting in Yorkshire.[10] In 1746 the committee had been appointed to write

Many Latin School masters came from a distance

Willian

[4]Min. Goshen Mo. Mtg., 7—6—1792; Min. Kennett Mo. Mtg., 5—12—1785—814; Min. Radnor Mo. Mtg., 7—11—1786,4; Min. Uwchlan Mo. Mtg., 12—5—1782, 136; 11—7—1782, 132.
[5]Deed No. 88, New Garden, Tp. ,Chester Co. (In Fireproof of Orthodox Friends in West Grove, Pa.).
[6]Min. Goshen Mo. Mtg., 8-11-1797; Min. Ken. Mo. Mtg., 3—14—1793, 39.
[7]Min. Goshen Mtg., 8—5—1796.
[8]P. C. S. M., I, 3, 33, and 90; Min. Darby Mo. Mtg., 7—17—1692, 54; Min. Phila. Mo. Mtg., 1—29—1700, 254; 4—24—1720, 63.
[9]*Col. Rec.* I, 36.   [10]Min. Phila. Mo. Mtg., 6—26—1784, 64.

to England concerning a teacher for the Public School.[11] Previous to this time a similar attempt had been made to secure someone to take the place of William Robbins.[12]

Robert Proud

Similarly, Robert Proud was recommended by John Fothergill in 1758 to Israel Pemberton (of Philadelphia) as a very suitable master for the school.[13]   Their "teacher's agency" in England was constituted by two members, John Fothergill and John Hunt; at any rate, for some forty or fifty years they always informed them as soon as they had need of masters, and except in a few cases, masters were sent over.   At one time (1760) not being able to hear of a possible applicant in England, an attempt was made to induce Peter Warren, an inhabitant of Virginia, to come to the position, at a salary of £150, plus £20 to transport his family.[14]   In the ensuing correspondence it was stated by the said Warren that he chose to go to Pittsburg; to inhabitants of Philadelphia his choice must have seemed ridiculous.

Peter Warren

However, the overseers of the school were not daunted. Quite in keeping with the system of apprenticing the youth in various occupations to members of Friends, and also in keeping with the general custom of the day, they sought out the brightest and most capable poor lad in their limits, and if they found him interested at all in the "futures" of teaching, they made the offer of an apprenticeship in the school. Instances may be cited which will clarify their procedure.

To supply teachers, the apprenticeship system used

In 1756 it was proposed that Samuel Eldridge be apprenticed to the board to prepare him to become a teacher of Latin and Greek;[15] he was to study Latin, Greek, Arithmetic, Accounts, and Mathematics.[16]   He was to be furnished, besides the instruction, clothing and board, and was paid £30 annually. In return for this he studied and performed such duties in the capacity of usher as his progress in the various subjects would permit.   At the end of the period of his indenture (1760) the board manifested their approval of his services by a gift of £10.[17]   At another time shortly subsequent thereto there was

Samuel Eldridge apprenticed

and others

[11]P. C. S. M., I, 58.
[12]*Ibid.*, 5 f.
[13]*Ibid.*, 175.
[14]*Ibid.*, 208.
[15]*Ibid.*, 139.   [16]*Ibid.*, 141.   [17]*Ibid.*, 265.

mentioned the desirability of encouraging James Dickinson, Richard Dickinson, and Joseph Rice to continue their schooling in order to become school masters; members of the board were named to speak with them and to ascertain their desires and intentions.[18]   One of them, James Dickinson, was in 1762 indented to serve three years in the same manner as Eldridge.[19]   King also, in 1754, was taken in as usher at a very small salary, later to become a master in the school.[20]   The exact extent of the apprenticing of school masters is not determined, but it does not seem to have been widely practised in and around Philadelphia.   This appearance might, however, be corrected if greater sources of information were available.

The extent of the system not great

One would judge from the complaints of the yearly meetings, and their recommendations, that better and more permanent accommodations be afforded, so that teachers might be more easily kept,[21] that the tenure of the early Quaker schoolmaster was short.   The yearly meeting recognized the advantage accruing from longer tenure, and did seek to remove some of the causes which worked against it.   Just how much they were able to increase the tenure it is impossible to say.   We may, however, cite certain cases in which the duration of a master's service is known.   Benjamin Clift was apparently employed to teach in Darby for two years at least.[22]   Jacob Taylor, who was concerned with a school at Abington about 1701,[23] and became a land surveyor about 1706[24], may have continued to teach there between those two dates.   He seems to have been resident there in that period,[25] and the scarcity of teachers was everywhere evident, as has already been pointed out.   This is certainly not a proof of his incumbency; it indicates a probability.   Keith was employed from 1689[26] to 1691;[27]   Thomas Makin from the

The tenure of masters

Cases cited of B. Clift J. Taylor

G. Keith, Makin and others

---

[18]P. C. S. M., I, 237.
[19]*Ibid.*, 245.   [20]*Ibid.*, 116.
[21]See Yearly Meetings' Advices, 250.
[22]Min. Darby Mo. Mtg., 7—7—1692, 54; 9-20—1693, 56.
[23]*2 Pa. Arch.* XIX, 248.
[24]Bean, 680.
[25]There is found no record of his removal by letter, though he may have done so without, which, however, was not according to practice.
[26]Min. Phila. Mo. Mtg., 5—26—1689, 154.
[27]*Ibid.*, 3—29—1691, 146.

latter date, intermittently, until his death, 1733;[28] Pastorius from the latter part of 1697 or the first part of 1698[29] to 1700;[30] Robert Willian probably from 1748[31] to 1753;[32] Seaton from 1751[33] to 1763,[34] and Robert Proud, not continuously however, from 1759[35] to 1770[36] and again master in 1784.[37] These were taken at random. The longest period of service, doubtless, must be credited to Anthony Benezet who first taught in Philadelphia in 1742[38] and continued there with very brief intermissions until his death in 1784.[39]

These are only a few cases and the majority of them in the city where it was possible to employ the best, pay them better, and hence, keep them longer. Hence, too much weight must not be given to the facts above stated as proving a long term of service was common. If a study of a number of cases in country districts were possible, the results would probably be very different.

It is difficult to get information about the length of service of the mistresses. When first mentioned in Philadelphia records[40] they are spoken of as so many nonentities, their names not given. The term of service of Olive Songhurst, the first mistress whose name is mentioned,[41] we cannot determine. The women teachers seem quite frequently to have begun work under the overseers without much notice and to have left off with little more. There are, however, a few cases where we know that the term of service was of considerable length. Rebeckah Burchall seems to have taught continuously at one school from 1755[42] to 1761.[43]

Tenure of mistresses

Songhurst

Burchall

---

[28]*Weekly Mercury*, Nov. 29, 1733.
[29]Min. Phila. Mo. Mtg., 11—28—1697, 227.
[30]*Ibid.*, 1—29—1700, 254.
[31]P. C. S. M., I, 64.
[32]*Ibid.*, 101.
[33]*Ibid.*, 90.
[34]*Ibid.*, 266.
[35]*Ibid.*, 175.
[36]*Ibid.*, 334.
[37]Min. Phila. Mo. Mtg., 1—30—1784, 123.
[38]P. C. S. M., I, 33.
[39]Simpson's *Lives of Eminent Philadelphians*, 53. Min. Phila. Mo. Mtg., 1—30—1784, 128.
[40]*Ibid.*, 1—31—1699, 244.
[41]*Ibid.*, 1—27—1702, 326.
[42]P. C. S. M., I, 126.   [43]*Ibid.*, 221.

Whether she discontinued service on leaving that school is not known. Ann Thornton was probably not continued in service more than two years. She began in 1755 when she filled Anthony Benezet's[44] place and left in 1757.[45] In the meantime, it had been necessary for the board to draw up a set of special rules for the government of her school,[46] from the nature of which it is probable that she did not take another school under their direction.

Thornton

Her success questionable

From none of the sources of information does it appear that there was any license system whatsoever. The recommendation of well-known Friends was the best pass a teacher could have, as was instanced by those sent over by John Fothergill. In addition to the personal recommendation, the certificate of removal from his home meeting was an assurance to Friends in other parts that an individual was "clear" of all entangling alliances and might be received into full membership. In no case where a teacher came to teach, from a distance, did he fail to take and produce a certificate on his arrival. These, of course, did not certify the things which modern licenses do, but they, in conjunction with the personal recommendation as to ability, seem to have answered the purpose.

No system of license found

Recommendation and certificate of removal; their use

The term for which a teacher was hired was in most cases a year for trial, which was renewed again at the year's end, if satisfactory to both parties. Mention has been made of Benjamin Clift of Darby,[47] Keith, Makin, Cadwalader, Willian, Proud, and many others. Some were taken for a trial of six months,[48] and there were cases in which the board reserved the right to discharge the individual on three months' notice.[49] The board desired, and in some cases requested, that the employee should give six months' notice before his resignation should take place. Such notice was customary in 1755.[50] Two instances have come under the writer's attention, in which a contract was made for three

The term of employment usually a year

---

[44]P. C. S. M., I, 130.
[45]*Ibid.*, 161.
[46]*Ibid.*, 158.
[47]Min. Darby Mo. Mtg., 7—7—1692, 54.
[48]P. C. S. M., I, 133.
[49]*Ibid.*, 274.
[50]*Ibid.*, 131.

years. King (son of Joseph King) was employed in 1754 for the three years subsequent thereto at £40, £50 and £60 for the years respectively.[51] Mr. King resigned regardless of the contract, after six months' notice, because the school did not agree with his health or inclination.[52] The other case was that of Keith who was to be employed for one year at £50 and

No written contract found

for two years more at £120 each, if he should desire to stay.[53] In neither of the two cases does there appear to have been any instrument in writing.

The salaries and rates received by many of the teachers have been mentioned in several pages previous to this. For convenience for reference there is presented without discussion a table showing the pay received by various masters at

Teachers' salaries; tabulated

the times their respective services were rendered.* One case, neither so prosaic to us, nor so profitable to the master, defies tabulation, so it is given verbatim.

18th Day of X br 1735.

Reced of Richard Buffington, Junior 18 s per Hatt, 4s 6d by stockings, 17s 6d In money—In all forty Shillings; Being in full for a yeare Scholeing, I say Reced per

me JOH MORSE†.

Name	Year	per Q	per year	(Reference)
Flower, E.	1683	4/ 6/ or 8/ or	£ 10	*Col. Rec.*, I, 13.
Keith, G.	1689	(following)	50	Ph., 5—26—1689.
			120	
Makin	1697		40 }	Ph., 1—128—1697.
Pastorius	1697		40 }	
Cadwalader	1700	for a half year trial	20	Ph., 1—28—1700.
Cadwalader	1702		50	Ph., 1—27—1702.
Every, J.	1702	Usher	30	Ph., 4—26—1702.
Benezet, A.	1742		50	P. C. S. M., I, 33.
Willian, R.	1749		150	*Ibid.*, 73.
Wilson, J.	1750	Usher	60	*Ibid.*, 84.
Seaton, A.	1751	(allowed)	20	*Ibid.*, 90.
Wilson, J.	1753		70	*Ibid.*, 101.
Johnson, Wm.	1753	(allowed)	10	*Ibid.*, 106.
Benezet	1754		80	*Ibid.*, 117.

[51] P. C. S. M., I., 123.
[52] *Ibid.*, 131.
[53] Min. Phila. Mo. Mtg., 5—26—1689.
*In the references at the right hand margin of the table "Ph" refers to Minutes of Philadelphia Monthly Meeting for the date given; Darby refers to Minutes of Darby Monthly Meeting.
†Futhey and Cope, 308.

King	1754	(proposed in a contract)	40	*Ibid.*, 122.
			50	
			60	
Thornton, Ann	1755		20	*Ibid.*, 130.
Johnson, Wm.	1755	(assistant)	40	*Ibid.*, 131.
Thompson, Chas.	1755		150	*Ibid.*, 133.
Johnson, Wm.	1756	(raised 20 to keep him)	60	*Ibid.*, 141.
Fentham, Jos.	1756		85	*Ibid.*, 144.
Patterson, M.	1761		70	*Ibid.*, 235.
Thompson, J.	1770		200	*Ibid.*, 341.
Proud, Robert	1759		150	*Ibid.*, 175.
Proud, Robert	1784		250	Ph., 1—30—1784.
His usher			80	*Ibid.*
Todd, J.	1784	(for entrance 15/ and 20/)		*Ibid.*
		(for poor sent by Board 10/)		*Ibid.*
Weaver, I.	1784	30/	30	*Ibid.*
Brown, Wm.	1784	(whole days) 30/ half days) 15/		*Ibid.*
Lancaster, Sarah	1784	(children) 15/ (sent by board) 10/ (sent by board) half (sent by board half day) 7/6		*Ibid.*
Harry, Mary		(children) 15/		*Ibid.*
Clark, Joseph		(older girls 30/)		*Ibid.*
Mrs. Clarke		15/		*Ibid.*
Marsh, Ann		20/		*Ibid.*
McDonnell, Mary	1784	15/		*Ibid.*
Clift, B.	1693		£12	Darby, 9—20—1693
Underwood, Elihu	1773	(Credit for school keeping) 2/2/0/ by 2 raccoon skins 0/4/0/ By netting a pair of stockings 0/2/6/[54]		
Meccum, Eliza	1798	(Negro School)	50	Ph., 2—25—1798
Pickering, Elisha	1798	(Negro School)	150	*Ibid.*
Benezet, A.	1794	(Negro School)	120	*Ibid.*
Britt, Daniel	1793	(Negro School)	100	*Ibid.*, 1—25—1793
Dougherty, Sarah	1793	(Negro School)	50	*Ibid.*

---

[54]From an old account book in possession of Albert Cook Myers, Moylan, Pa.

As stated elsewhere in this work, the amounts received by masters and mistresses in the Friends' school measure about the same as those stated for other private masters in the city at the same time.   In the table above, the seeming increase from £50 per year in 1689 to £250 per year paid Robert Proud in 1784, and the slender salaries of the women as compared with those of the men, are worthy of attention.[55]   Though all of the teachers in the Negro School had had long experience, their salaries did not equal that of Classical School teachers; but they did keep pace with those in the English School.   The price paid for young children was usually low, about one-half that paid for older ones in the same subjects.   Children sent by the board were received at a less charge, or perhaps free of charge if that body had already made arrangement to that effect.   The contrast between the salary received by the country masters Clift (Darby) and Underwood (Warrington) is very interesting.   Such salaries were doubtless effective in causing unrest and a floating teacher population, against which the yearly meeting frequently remonstrated, and earnestly sought to correct.

In the pages following, brief attention will be given to several of the Quaker teachers who have come to the attention of the writer during the course of this study.   Many of them have been mentioned in other parts of it, reference to whom is to be found in the index.   Though the women were given more scanty attention in the records and seem to have filled a less prominent place in the schools, we may gallantly, yet illogically, give them first attention here.   In another light,

Pay of Friends' masters similar to that of other private masters

The charge for poor children less

Country masters ill paid

Mistresses to be first considered

---

[55]Dewey, D. R., *Financial History of the U. S.*, 39.

The reader is reminded of the fact that because of greatly depreciated currency the amounts paid, as shown in the above table, did not represent so much absolute increase.   That some exact idea of the extent of depreciation of the continental currency may be gained, there is given the following table for the year 1779, when the depreciation became most marked.

Jan. 14, 1779	8 to 1	June 4, 1779	20 to 1
Feb. 3	10 to 1	Sept. 17	24 to 1
Apr. 2	17 to 1	Oct. 14	30 to 1
May 5	24 to 1	No.v 17	38½ to 1

The fact of such depreciation was not officially recognized by Congress until March 18, 1780, it being then provided that paper be accepted for silver at a ratio of 40 to 1.

it may not seem illogical. Women were leaders in the Quaker meetings and were privileged to speak, a favor not granted elsewhere. In the early yearly meeting recommendations they urged good mistresses be chosen as well as good masters.[56] Women were also recognized by London Grove Monthly Meeting in 1795, when a committee of women Friends were appointed to meet with a like committee of men to consider the question of schools.[57]

As before stated, mistresses in Philadelphia were mentioned by the monthly meeting as early as 1699,[58] but we are not informed who they were. The first, Olive Songhurst, whose name is given, was employed for some time about 1702,[59] and if we may judge her service by a raise of salary granted in that year, it seems to have been acceptable to the meeting. After Olive Songhurst a long period of time passes in which the writer has found no mistress named in the minutes, though mistresses are frequently mentioned. It is not, therefore, to be assumed that this list is complete either in the case of masters or mistresses; those who are mentioned may prove of some interest or service to other students.

Olive Songhurst

Ann Thornton was mentioned as being employed by the board in 1755, when it was proposed that she might take Anthony Benezet's place in a Girls' School, which he had entered the year before. It is not very probable that she was an inexperienced teacher at the time, since the board was usually careful to place strong and proven teachers in its best schools. She was to receive no more than thirty scholars and had to promise to look after them in meeting, which seemingly unpleasant task she hesitated to take.[60] It is the writer's opinion, based on the fact that the board was forced to make a list of rules especially for her school,[61] and the tenor of her dismissal when Benezet was again available, and that she does not appear to have been employed again by the board,

Ann Thornton in Girls' School, 1755

---

[56]See page 20.
[57]Min. London Grove Mtg., 3—4—1795, 62.
[58]*Ibid.*, 31—1699, 244.
[58]*Ibid.*, 1—31—1699, 244.
[59]*Ibid.*, 1—27—1702, 326.
[60]P. C. S. M., I, 130.
[61]*Ibid.*, 158.

that her work in the school and agreement with the board were not satisfactory.

Rebeckah Burchall, employed near the same time as Ann Thornton, was engaged in teaching poor children.[62] It was also stipulated that she guard the girls in meetings, especially her pupils.[63] So in 1755, as we entered the quiet Friend's meeting we would have no doubt seen the two prim Quaker ladies just mentioned sitting in silent and upright watchfulness amid their youthful charges. Gentlemen were not immune from such duties.

Widow Mellor is mentioned in 1755 as keeping a small school,[64] which probably was quite similar to the one kept by Debby Godfrey, a poor woman to whom the board decided to send some poor children to learn to read and write.[65] The minute reads as though it was a condescension, and very likely it was a form of charity on their part.   Jane Loftu, likewise, (1761) taught thirty-two poor children, her charge made to the board for the service being £32.[66]   Ann Redman seems to have been a teacher of more than ordinary merit. She is first noted as a teacher at the Fairhill School, at which place she was visited by members of the Public School Board, who seem to have been so well impressed with her as a teacher that she was immediately asked to come into the school just vacated by Rebekah Burchall.   Her employment was teaching reading, writing, and plain sewing.[67] Mary Wily, a teacher employed by the board in 1762, received very little attention.   A question is raised concerning her, however, by an objection made by the board to her account presented for certain schooling.[68]   It was settled amicably it seems.   Ann Pattison, first mentioned as being employed in 1763,[69] is doubt-, less the same as the Patterson later employed in 1766.[70] She was employed in teaching poor children. Mary Gosnold, Rebecca Seaton, and Mary Moss are mentioned in 1764 as teachers of poor children.[71]   Rebecca Seaton does not appear in the ranks of teachers (at least on Friends' records) till after

Several
other mistresses
named,
many in
charge of
poor
children

---

[62]P. C. S. M., I., 126.
[63]*Ibid.*, 130.
[64]*Ibid.*, 128.
[65]*Ibid.*, 145.
[66]*Ibid.*, 216.

[67]*Ibid.*, 221.
[68]*Ibid.*, 239.
[69]*Ibid.*, 266.
[70]*Ibid.*, 288.
[71]*Ibid.*, 276, 277, 279.

the death of Alexander Seaton, her husband. It seems quite evident that the mistresses were assigned, more especially, to the keeping of school for the poor, though it was by no means limited to them. Sarah Mott was also a teacher for poor children.[72]

Hannah Cathall, we feel certain, must have been a teacher of considerable merit. She began her service at least as early as 1765[73] and in 1779 was still in that employment, being at that date engaged in a school with Rebecca Jones, for instructing girls in reading, writing, "and other branches suitable to them."[74] They also received poor girls sent by the overseers. Other mistresses employed by the board in 1779 were Sarah Lancaster, teaching the rudiments to young children of both sexes (sewing especially for girls), Essex Flower in a school similar to Lancaster's, and Ann Rakestraw who had charge of a reading and spelling school.[75] Sarah Lancaster still continued in the schools' service in 1784, having in attendance sixty-four scholars, part of whom attended only half days. The other mistresses mentioned at that time were Mary Harry, teaching a school for children, Mrs. Clarke, teaching boys and girls, reading and sewing for the girls; Ann Marsh in a school similar to that of Mrs. Clarke's, and Mary McDonnell, who taught fifteen young children, what studies we do not know.[76] The committee's report for that date shows that nearly one-half or perhaps more of the children attending the schools of the Friends' masters and mistresses were children of the members of other denominations. In almost every case the teachers were Friends, or, as they termed it, "people of friendly persuasions."

Mistresses devoted their abilities also to the instruction of the Negro children. Sarah Dougherty was for a time (about 1790) employed in the Negro School, but for some reason, unexplained, Elizabeth Meccum was employed in her stead.[77] Elizabeth Meccum remained in that capacity till the time of

Subjects of instruction; reading, writing, sewing, spelling, and other "suitable subjects for girls"

Other denominations in Friends schools

Mistresses in the Negro School

[72]P. C. S. M., I., 309.
[73]*Ibid.*, 288.
[74]Min. Phila. Mo. Mtg. 7—30—1779, 151.
[75]*Ibid.* (An extract of the report to the monthly meeting is given on page 71 ff., chapter on Philadelphia, showing the state of schools in 1784.)
[76]*Ibid.*, 1—30—1784, 123 ff.
[77]*Ibid.*, 1—25—1793, 184.

her death, which occurred between 1795 and 1798.[78] Joseph Foulke, in a letter concerning his schooling at Gwynedd Meeting, mentions Hannah Lukens who kept a "family school" and also Hannah Foulke,[79] both of whom were members of Gwynedd, but further information of them the writer does not have.

Teachers rated by the frequency with which they are mentioned by well recognized writers

If one were to measure American Quaker schoolmasters as some American men of science have been measured, by the amount of space they have gained in literature, they would not stand out very strikingly. Of fifty-five male teachers in and around Philadelphia, but twenty-one of them are mentioned in five standard works on local history and genealogy. None of the fifty-five teachers receive mention in all five of the works; three of them are chronicled in four; seven are mentioned in three of the five; ten are spoken of in two, twenty-one are given a place in one; and thirty-four receive no notice. If rated according to such a scheme, Partorius, Benezet, and Charles Thompson would head the list, while quite a number group themselves at the other end of it. The scheme, though it has not been carried out fully, for example no attempt has been made to measure the length of the notice, does seem to favor those who stood high at the time of their service.[80]

Individual notice to be very brief

In the brief notices following, concerning the male teachers, it is not intended to write biographies. Some of them have already been written, and to them the reader is directed, if he or she wishes a full account of the man's life. Others will not, cannot, ever be written for obvious reasons. In the space allotted to them here, there is set down only what has been found of interest concerning them as teachers.

Anthony Benezet

In 1842 Anthony Benezet came from Germantown where he had been engaged in a school,[81] to be employed by the Board of Overseers of Philadelphia. He was employed at a salary of £50 to teach arithmetic, writing, accounts, and

---

[78]Min. Phila. Mo. Mtg., 2—23—1798, 149.
[79]Quoted in Jenkins' *Hist. Collections of Gwynedd*, 396–7.
[80]The works from which the notices were taken: Watson, *Annals of Philadelphia;* Simpson, *Lives of Eminent Philadelphians;* Jordan, *Colonial Families of Philadelphia;* Oberholtzer, *Philadelphia City and Its People;* W. Thompson, *History of Philadelphia.*
[81]Vaux, *Memoirs*, p. 7; also Keyser, *Old Germantown*, I, 79.

French.[82]   He appears to have given very satisfactory service and to have remained in the same position until 1754 when he was placed in charge of the Girls School, under the Board's direction.[83]   Some students have been under the impression that the Girls School was entirely independent and a private venture;[84] but this could not have been true, for the Board named the subjects he should teach and specified that he receive at the school "no more than thirty scholars."[85]   The school was, however, the result of Benezet's proposal.

Given charge of Girls School

Not only was he kindly to the pupils as a teacher,[86] but he was a father to the poor lads whenever he could help them in any way.   In 1754 Samuel Boulds was bound to him, so that he might look after his schooling, and he further requested the Board to care for the same, if he should die or leave the school before the lad was grown up.[87]   His health not being good, he requested leave from his school during the summer of 1754.[88]   Apparently his health did not improve sufficiently and he did not return to the school till 1757, taking the place of Ann Thornton.[89]   Another instance of his philanthropy came to light in his request (1762) that certain of the children of the poor French neutrals be allowed to go to the Public School which was granted only upon his certification of those he felt sure would attend regularly.[90]   Shortly thereafter on account of ill health, he was again forced to leave the Girls School, which he did until 1767, when he returned to resume his work again.[91]   It was no difficulty for him to start a school.   The suggestion was made to the Board in one month, and in the following he was teaching the school, and made his regular report at their meeting.

Attitude as a teacher

Aids children of French neutrals

From the information the writer has assembled, it appears that he continued with the White school, after his return in 1767, until 1782, when at his request he was accepted by the

Enters the Negro School in 1782

[82]P. C. S. M., I, 33.
[83]*Ibid.*, 117.
[84]Oberholtzer, I, 233.
[85]P. C. S. M., I, 117.
[86]Vaux, *Memoirs*, p. 8
[87]P. C. S. M., I, 114.
[88]*Ibid.*, 115.
[89]*Ibid.*, 161.
[90]*Ibid.*, 244.
[91]*Ibid.*, 311.

committee to take charge of the Negro School.[92]   He had throughout his life written eloquently in defense of freedom's cause,[93] and the origin of the Negro School, in 1770, was perhaps due to him more than to any other man in the Friends' meeting.

Jonathan Binns was to have taken charge of the Public School in 1734, if his health improved, but no report being made by him it is inferred he did not perform such service.[94] Alexander Buller was employed in 1738 to teach writing, mathematics, and the Latin tongue.   Three years later he ran an advertisement in the *Pennsylvania Gazette*, as follows:

> Writing, Arithmetic, Merchants' Accounts, Navigation, Algebra, and other parts of the mathematics are taught by Alexander Buller, at the Public School in Strawberry Alley.   He proposes to keep a night school for the winter and begins on the 23d instant when constant attendance shall be given.   November 5, 1741.*

William Brown was teaching girls reading, writing, arithmetic and language in 1784.[95]   Daniel Britt interested himself in the instruction of Negroes in whose school he was employed from about 1790[96] to 1796 or 1797.[97]   He was succeeded by Elisha Pickering who probably taught till 1799, being followed by Benjamin Mears.[98]

John Cadwalader came to Philadelphia in 1699[99] and the year following was recommended by Griffith Owen as a man "fit for an assistant in the school."[100]   He was accordingly

Marginal notes: Jonathan Binns / Alexander Buller; one of few who advertised for pupils / William Brown, Daniel Britt, Pickering and Mears / John Cadwalader

[92]Min. Phila. Mo. Mtg., 5—31—1782, 28.
[93]For list of his works, see Hildeburn or Smith.
[94]P. C. S. M., I, 21.
*Pa. Gaz., No. 673, 1741.
(Advertising for pupils in newspapers was not the usual rule among Quaker masters in early Pennsylvania, though some cases occurred. 345 advertisements from 1730 to 1790 have been noted in various newspapers of the period.   Of a list of seventy Quakers who are known to have taught school, only 15 were found in the list of advertisers.   The papers examined were the *Weekly Mercury, Pennsylvania Gazette, Freeman's Journal, Evening Post, Pennsylvania Journal* and *Weekly Advertiser, Pa. Packet,* and the *Pa. Chronicle;* also the *Courrier Francais* (which is not mentioned in the bibliography).
[95]Min. Phila. Mo. Mtg., 1—30—1784, 123.
[96]*Ibid.*, 1—25—1793, 184.
[97]*Ibid.*, 2—23—1798, 149.
[98]*Ibid.*, 11—28—1800, 300.
[99]Oberholtzer, I, 181.
[100]Min. Phila. Mo. Mtg., 1—29—1700, 254.

employed, it being decided that he and Thomas Makin, who had entered the school as usher to Keith, should compete with each other to show the best results. From the records one cannot determine just when he left the school, though he stated, in 1702,[101] that he intended to do so. It seems likely, from a minute of 1703, that he must have taught longer than he intended when making the above statements.[102] Thomas Makin, with whom he was associated, was employed at various times until his death in 1733.[103] He is credited with being "a good Latinist,"[104] and was the author of a Latin poem in which he celebrated Pennsylvania. George Keith, Scotchman, kindly recommended him for the mastership in 1691, when he (Keith) decided to leave.[105] Keith had come to the school as first master when the school was set up in 1689. He is stated, by writers of history, to have been of disputatious disposition, and this probably accounted for the dissatisfaction which arose in the school. Soon after leaving the school he published in connection with Talbot a critical article, "Means of Quaker Stability,"[106] in which is evident the rancor toward the society, which he had previously concealed.

Concerning Benjamin Clift, schoolmaster at Darby, no additional information has been found, beyond that given in the minutes of the monthly meeting. Joseph Clarke was a teacher of a girls' school in 1784,[107] which was attended by about thirty girls. William Dickinson was first employed (1764) to take the place of Moses Patterson,* as usher to John Todd in the Latin School.[108] The Board seems to have taken exception to him, though nothing has been intimated elsewhere as to his character, for they reserved the right to discharge him on three months' notice, if they desired. Such reservations were not general.

Sidenotes: Thomas Makin — George Keith; dissatisfaction with him — Clift Clarke — Dickinson

---

[101]Min. Phila. Mo. Mtg., 2—24—1702, 329.
[102]*Ibid.*, 6—27—1703, 376.
[103]*Am. Wk. Mercury*, Nov. 29, 1733.
[104]Watson I, 287.
[105]Min. Phila. Mo. Mtg., 3—29—1691, 146.
[106]*Collections of the Protestant Episcopal Historical Soc.*, 1851, Vol. I, XIX to XX.
[107]Min. Phila. Mo. Mtg., 1—30—1784, 123 ff.
*Moses Patterson was the first teacher in the Negro School. Phila. Mo. Mtg. Min., 6—29—1799, 398.
[108]P. C. S. M., I, 274.

Moses Patterson, had begun his teaching career in 1760 when he undertook to teach a school at Fairhill Meeting.[109] He then was made usher to Alexander Seaton in which position he remained till 1764.[110] He desired then to quit as usher, and apparently did; he is next heard of in 1765 as teacher of "poor children."[111]

Robert Willian was employed in 1748, having been brought from England, to teach Latin, Greek and other learning.[112] His first term of employment was for one year, as was the Board's general custom in hiring teachers, but it seems that his contract was renewed until 1753, at which time his place was taken by John Wilson.[113] Wilson had entered the school's employ as usher in 1750, but was, in addition to that, granted permission to teach an evening school.[114] It is not known how long he remained as master, but in 1754 there was a proposition to allow J. King to go into the Latin School,[115] and it is likely he took Wilson's place. King, however, as stated elsewhere, did not remain there more than a year, because of ill health and inclination.[113] Wilson is later mentioned in connection with the Latin school (1769); how much of the time, between 1754 and 1769 he had spent in the Latin School it is impossible to say.

When King (1755) announced his intention to resign at the end of six months, the Board attempted to procure Paul Jackson, who at the time was instructor at the Academy.[117] Jackson was well qualified for the place and, besides his work at the Academy, had prepared lectures in "experimental philosophy" which he proposed to give for the "entertainment of the curious."[118] He did not find himself free at this time to remove from the employ of the trustees of that institution, but Charles Thompson, who had been employed there as usher was engaged for the Friends' School.[119] It seems that the logical man for the place would have been William

Margin notes:
Patterson

Masters in Latin School after 1748; Willian

Wilson and King

Latin School tries to obtain services of Jackson

Thompson engaged, however

---

[109]P. C. S. M., I, 208.
[110]*Ibid.*, 272.
[111]*Ibid.*, 288.
[112]Min. Phila. Mo. Mtg., 6–26–1748, 64.
[116]*Ibid.*, 131.
[117]*Ibid.*, 133.
[118]*Pa. Gaz.*, No. 1403, 1755.
[119]P. C. S. M., I, 133.

[113]P. C. S. M., I, 101.
[114]*Ibid.*, 84.
[115]*Ibid.*, 122.

Johnson, who first taught a school at Fairhill[120] (1753) and attended Latin School, free of charge, to prepare him to be an usher (1754).[121] The headship was not offered him, however, but a year later his salary for the assistantship was raised £20 to keep him from going to Burlington.[123] We find that Charles Thompson (from the Academy) remained in the Friends' School until 1760, when he decided to leave the business of school keeping for another.[124] His first training in Latin, Greek, and mathematics was gained in Alison's Seminary. After leaving the Friends' School he was interested in political life and became secretary of the Revolutionary Congress in 1775.[125]

His training and later interests

When Thompson indicated his desire to leave the Latin School, the Board took steps to secure a master from England. A letter was sent to J. Fothergill and John Hunt who recommended Robert Proud as a very likely candidate.[126] This recommendation was favorably considered and Proud accordingly came to Philadelphia. He immediately chose W. W. Fentham as his usher, whom, he stated, the Board might remove if they did not find him satisfactory.[127] It appears that Proud remained master from this time until 1770, when he announced his resignation.[128] He was again in the employ of the Latin School in 1784, having an usher to assist him in instructing the thirty boys who are stated to have been in attendance on that date.[129] How long this period of service continued the writer has not determined. The reader has already been introduced to Proud's school by means of the rules he constructed for it, which were presented on a previous page. His reverence for learning and his attempt to inculcate that respect for it in the minds of his pupils is perhaps best indicated by these lines:

Robert Proud recommended for master

Time of his service

> "To learning ever be inclined;
> With good instruction store thy mind,
> For without learning, living here
> Like Death and Darkness doth appear.[130]

---

[120]P. C. S. M., I, 106.   [121]*Ibid.*, 122.   [122]*Ibid.*, 131.
[123]*Ibid.*, 141.   [124]*Ibid.*, 188.
[125]Simpson, 912–13.   [126]P. C. S. M., I, 175.
[127]*Ibid.*, 234.   [128]*Ibid.*, 334.
[129]Min. Phila. Mo. Mtg., 1—30—1784, 123.
[130]Robert Proud *Ms. Col.*, No. 20, 27.

When Proud left the Latin school in 1770, Friends again had recourse to the English supply house, receiving from thence John Thompson, eldest son of Jonah Thompson, who had previously taught in Philadelphia.[131] John Thompson entered the school on twelfth month, fifth, 1770 and remained in that position at least until 1779. At that date he had twenty-four boys in charge, to whom he taught Latin and Greek, with occasionally some writing and arithmetic.[132]

John Thompson recommended

An interesting student's commentary on the "Hon. John Thompson" is furnished by the following extract from the publications of the *Public School Gazeteer*, 1777.

> On Thursday last in the afternoon the Hon. John Thompson, Esq., dismissed the school long before the usual time. This (we hope) is a prelude to the restoration of our rights.*

Masters of the English School: Seaton

One of the most worthy masters to be noted in the English School, near the middle of the century, was Alexander Seaton. In 1751 he desired to start a school in the upper part of the city, which was to be under the care of the Board. In this school, which was accordingly set up, were taught writing, arithmetic, and mathematics.[133] He was thus employed until 1754 when, as above stated, Benezet desiring to set up a girls' school, he was requested to take Benezet's place in the English School.[134] At various dates he was assisted by Moses Patterson, Phineas Jenkins,[135] and George Smith.[136] In 1763, when he died, his place was filled by John Todd.[137]

John Todd, a teacher for many years

Todd remained many years in Friends' School. In 1779 he is reported by the overseers as having 60 boys of various religious denominations, to whom was taught reading, English writing, arithmetic and some branches of mathematics.[138] A like condition prevailed in his school five years later, with the exception that the number of boys had increased to 88. The committee report states that the "master is careful to preserve good order in his school."[139] This agrees, but is a

---

[131]Watson, I, 282.
[132]Min. Phila. Mo. Mtg., 7—30—1779, 151.
*The Public School Gazeteer, 1777, in Norris *Ms. Collections*, H. S. P.
[133]P. C. S. M., I, 90.
[134]*Ibid.*, 117.
[135]*Ibid.*, 198.
[136]*Ibid.*, 199.
[137]*Ibid.*, 266.   [138]Min. Phila. Mo. Mtg., 7—30—1779, 151.
[139]*Ibid.*, 1—30—1784, 123 f.

much less picturesque statement of the case than is portrayed by Watson.[140] He is pictured as immoderately strict and as taking diabolic satisfaction in every opportunity to use the strap. Watson closes his description with the statement that "it was not that his love of learning was at fault, so much as the old British system of introducing learning and discipline into the brains of boys and soldiers by dint of punishment."[141]

Severity of his discipline

A number of other almost unknown masters who taught in and around Philadelphia may be briefly mentioned. William Waring is stated by Watson to have taught astronomy and mathematics in the Friends' School at the same time with Jeremiah Paul.[142] Associated with the school, at the same time with Paul, Todd, and Waring, was Jimmy McCue, who performed the services of usher.[143] Yerkes, mentioned as having been in a single school, is mentioned by the monthly meeting reports as though it were under the direction of Friends. When so reported (1779) he was teaching not more than 50 scholars (all Friends). The subjects of instruction were reading, writing, English, arithmetic, and some branches of mathematics.[144] No further information of Isaac Weaver has been obtained than is given on page 260.

Waring, J. Paul, and Yerkes mentioned

Leonard Snowdon was reported to have arrived from London about 1737 to take charge of a school, but no further particulars are found concerning him.[145] In 1757 William Thorne was reported as teaching poor children.[146] He is one of the very few masters who taught in the Friends' Schools, who advertised in the newspapers for pupils; such advertisement was possibly after he discontinued his services for the Board.[147] The advertisement does, however, serve to give us more information as to his qualifications, than we could otherwise obtain. He was engaged at the time (1766) in conducting a writing, arithmetic, mathematics and merchants' accounts school in Vidal's Alley.[148] At another time he

Snowdon

Thorne

Subjects taught by Thorne

[140]Watson, I, 290 f.
[141]*Ibid.*, 292.
[142]*Ibid.*, 290.
[143]*Ibid.*, 291.
[144]Min. Phila. Mo. Mtg., 7—30—1779, 151.
[148]*Ibid.*

[145]P. C. S. M., I, 24.
[146]*Ibid.*, 165.
[147]*Pa. Gaz.*, No. 1951, 1766.

advertised to teach writing, arithmetic, geometry, trigonometry, navigation, mensuration, surveying, guaging, and
accounts.[149]   John Sitch (1758) is mentioned as receiving
some of the scholars from William Johnson's school.[150]
Joseph Pemberton was encouraged by the Board to start a
school in 1758.   Its location, as everything else concerning
it, is very indefinite, being "in the upper part of town."[151]
Other masters mentioned by various authors, and to
whom reference has been made before, but whose history is
almost unknown, are Rowland Richards, John Every, Marmaduke Pardo, John Walby, William Coggins, Benjamin
Albertson, Hugh Foulke, John Chamberlain, Christian Dull,
Daniel Price, Samuel Jones, and Samuel Evans.[152]

Of Richard Brockden, who taught at Byberry about
1710 or 1711,[153] and later (about 1722)[154] for a short
time in Philadelphia, very little is known.   The minute just
referred to, however, leaves the impression that Friends were
very willing for him to leave the school, but, on his request,
allowed him to remain.   Walter Moor, a schoolmaster at
Byberry (about 1753) leaves no record as a master, but we are
certain his *character* was not satisfactory to Friends.   In 1753
they complained of his drinking to excess and removing from
place to place without giving notice of it.[155]   An instance of
this sort, though not entirely out of keeping with custom
in those days, was severely criticised at all times in the
meetings.   This is the only explicit case of drunkenness, on
the part of teachers who were employed by Friends, which has
come to the writer's attention.   The frequent mention of
reproof of members for that offense, in the early years of the
century, however, would lead one to believe that such great
success in eliminating it from those in the teaching profession
was scarcely possible.   However that may be, no case has
been found (in newspaper reports, where the names were

*Sitch,
Pemberton,
Richards,
Every and
others*

*Early school-
masters at
Byberry*

*Character of
Moor un-
satisfactory
to Friends*

---

[149]*Pa. Gaz.*, No. 1865, 1764.
[150]P. C. S. M., I, 164.
[151]*Ibid.*, 173.
[152]The last eight mentioned are named as teachers in Gwynedd neighborhood school, by Joseph Foulke. (Jenkins, 396-7.)
[153]Min. Abington Mo. Mtg., 4—25—1711, 73.
[154]Min. Phila. Mo. Mtg., 2—27—1722, 83.
[155]Min. Abington Mo. Mtg., 10—29—1753, 111.

mentioned) in which any Quaker master engaged in disreputable brawling was lodged in jail, which was noted on the part of several other private masters of Philadelphia.[156] This latter source of information is perhaps more reliable than the meeting records.

Among Quaker schoolmasters, who have been mentioned frequently, is Christopher Taylor. He was educated in Latin, Greek, and Hebrew, and, in 1695,[157] published a compendium of the three languages. He was a teacher at Waltham Abbey School,[158] and, coming to Philadelphia in 1682, established a school on Tinicum Island, of which very little authentic information is to be had. William Underwood was a teacher at Warington about 1740.[159] Elihu Underwood has already been mentioned on several occasions as the most extraordinary master of Warington, having executed an attractive copy of arithmetic exercises from an old English arithmetic.[160] Others, only to be mentioned, were: D. B. Ayres, Richland Meeting, 1793;[161] Christopher Smith, Byberry, 1784;[162] Bryan Fitzpatrick, Horsham, 1784;[163] Joseph Kirk, 1793,[164] and Isaac Carver, at or near Horsham, 1784;[165] Thomas Pearson at Maiden Creek (Exeter Monthly Meeting), 1784;[166] Benjamin Parks and wife, at Reading, 1784;[167] and Caleb Johnson at Reading, 1787.[168] An unknown master of Bucks County is mentioned by General John Lacey in his memoirs, as he comments on his early educational opportunities. He, himself, was a member of a family of Friends.

No extreme cases of lawlessness among Quaker masters

Taylor

Underwood

Teachers previously mentioned

---

[156]*Pa. Gaz.*, No. 2371, 1774.   *Ibid.*, No. 2147, 1770.   *Ibid.*, No. 2118, 1769.   *Ibid.*, No. 1821, 1763.
[157]Wickersham, 26.
[158]*Ibid.*, 27.
[159]Prowell, I, 539.
[160]*Ibid.*, 541
[161]Name found in the account book for the Jonathan Walton Fund used for that meeting, p. 1. (Deposited at Friends Meeting House in Quakertown, Pa.)
[162]Min. Horsham Mo. Mtg., 4—28—1784.
[163]*Ibid.*
[164]Min. Horsham Sch. Com., 1—11—1793.
[165]Min. Horsham Mo. Mtg., 4—28—1784.
[166]Min. Exeter Mo. Mtg., 4—28—1784, 510f.
[167]*Ibid.*
[168]*Ibid.*, 10—31—1787, 60 f.

I was early sent to school, such as it was. The master himself could neither read or write correctly, as he knew nothing of Grammar, it was not to be expected he could teach it to others. Grammar was never taught in any school I went to—no book of this kind, or the remote rudiments of it was—that I remember—talked of at any of the country schools I was acquainted with. None but Quaker families resided in the neighborhood where I was brought up, among whom the Bible and Testament and Dilworth's spelling-book were the only books suffered to be used in the Quaker schools from which circumstances no one will hesitate to acknowledge the extreme limited education and acquirements of literal knowledge by youth so circumscribed.[169]

Such were the country schools, if judged by his writing as a fair sample.

SUMMARY

Standards

The primary requirements for masters and mistresses, as determined by the yearly meeting, were (1) high morality, (2) membership with Friends, and (3) competency to teach the subjects for which employed. These standards were consciously striven for, as indicated by their reports on the subject.

Whence came teachers?

As a rule, the teachers selected for the lower schools were native to the place, though there were exceptions. A large number of the Latin masters, however, were secured through Friends in England. To supply the lack of teachers, in Philadelphia at any rate, recourse was occasionally had to the apprenticeship system, as instanced by the cases of Eldridge, and James Dickinson.

Tenure

The yearly assembly recommended better accommodations for teachers, that they might be more easily retained in the same position. The cases mentioned indicate a very good length of tenure; Clift, two years; Taylor, perhaps five; Keith, about two; Makin, intermittently for about forty; and many others, similarly. These figures are undoubtedly not representative, the majority being taken from the city.

No license system

Contracts

Personal recommendation and certificates of removal served some of the purposes of the teacher license system. The contract was verbal only, so far as evidence appears and the term of it usually for one year.

---

[169]*Pa. Mag. Hist.*, XXV, 3.

Attention is called to the seeming great increase in salaries during the century, and great variation in the amounts paid at any one time, especially between those of country and city masters. The salaries of women appear to have been very meager as compared with those of the men. No appreciable difference is found between the salaries or rates of Quaker masters and those of private masters in the city at the same time. Rates charged for poor children, schooled by the Board, were less than those fixed for others.

Salaries

A few mistresses in the schools are mentioned. For the most part, the length of their service is not known. A large proportion of them were engaged in teaching poor children, though not limited to that. A large proportion, over half of the poor children taught by them, were members of various denominations. Their service was not limited to the schools for Whites, some being employed in the Negro School, near the end of the century.

Women teachers considered

Brief attention is given individual masters. As rated by the frequency of their mention in five standard authorities, Pastorius, Benezet, and Thompson lead the list; it is not believed that this measure is adequate, however. Concerning the qualifications of the masters, we find that all degrees of ability and training were represented. Pastorius may be taken as a type of the classically trained master of the Latin School. The other extreme might be represented by several of the ill-paid country masters. John Lacey describes such a master and his school in his memoirs.

Masters Rank

One definite case of drunkenness on the part of a master has come to light. Though not probable that the record is so clear, it does appear that excessive outlawries were not committed. The chief sources studied on this point were the newspapers of the period and minutes of various Quaker meetings.

Character

CHAPTER XI

EDUCATION OF NEGROES AND INDIANS

EARLIEST TRACES OF THE NEGRO IN PENNSYLVANIA

Negroes
early in
Pennsyl-
vania

To the reader of the history of Pennsylvania, the statement that the colony was established in 1681 by William Penn seems sufficient reason for thinking that was the first settlement. But there were other people already established there and among them were to be found Negroes, as is very readily ascertained from the records. The people who occupied the territory along the Delaware, later to be called Pennsylvania, before its charter as a colony was granted, were chiefly Swedes, English, and Dutch, who had crossed over the river from the neighboring colonies.[1]

1639

Negroes were not numerous. There remains rather scant evidence of their presence in any considerable number, but authentic record of certain instances. It is found, for example, that as early as 1639 a convict was sentenced to South River, as the Delaware was then called, to serve out his time with the Negroes.[2] This is the earliest record found; though frequent mention is made of them after this date. In 1664, the West India Company agreed to furnish about fifty Negroes to work in the lowlands on the Delaware River.[3] This is the earliest explicit record that is found of trafficking in Negroes in Pennsylvania. The slave trade, thus begun by the Dutch Company, was continued, now rising, now falling, till the final abolition of slavery in 1780.[4] The law of 1780, which provided for a gradual abolition, was subjected to such frequent evasion that in 1788 it became necessary to

1664

Gradual
abolition by
law of 1780

[1]Proud, *Hist. of Pa.*, I, 233 and 109f. (see Ms. description of the province of Pennsylvania written by William Penn relating to the first settlement written 1682. A copy in Logan *Ms. Collections*, Vol. 1.
[2]*2Pa. Archives*, XVI, 234.
[3]Hazard, *Annals of Pa.*, 331. *N. Y. Col. Doc.* II, 213–14.
[4]*Col. Rec.*, XII, 99.

pass another for its clarification and enforcement.[5] By the middle of the seventeenth century, the importation of slaves had become a part of the regular work of the merchants of Philadelphia, with the exception of a few conscientious Quakers who refused to profit thereby. Records of the end of the century indicate that the number of Negroes had by that time become very considerable, though no exact figures are obtainable.[6]

But it is not to be assumed that because the slave trade began thus early and continued to grow, it did so without meeting any opposition. In fact it is probably due to a few years of opposition by various factors, which are here only mentioned briefly, that the slave trade did not become as prodigious in Pennsylvania as in other states, and that she was the first to pass an abolition law against it.[7] Chief among the factors which opposed the increase of Negro serfdom were these: (1) the conscientious scruples of Friends in reference to the traffic;[8] (2) the objection on the part of the German inhabitants (partially as Quakers, but not entirely);[9] and, (3) the dissatisfaction caused among White laborers by the enforced competition of the Negroes.[10]

Opposing factors

As a result of this opposition to the importation of slaves, there was enacted various legislation restricting it, although there was at the same time an urgent demand on the part of some for slave labor. One of the first attempts on the part of the Colonial Assembly to restrict slave traffic was the act of 1700, imposing the maximum duty of 20 shillings per head imported, which amount was in 1705 increased to 40 shillings.[11] Not entirely satisfied with this stroke, the Assembly attempted (1712) practically to prohibit importation by placing a levy of £20 per head, but this act was at once repealed by the crown.[12] However great may have been the

Restrictive legislation 1700, 1705, 1712

---

[5]*Laws of Pa.*, III, 269–272; *3 Pa. Archives*, XVIII, 303–430.
[6]*Ms. Ancient Rec. of Phila.*, July 28, 1702.
[7]Turner, *The Negro in Pa.*, 79.
[8]London Yr. Mtg., Epistles, 1772, 394.
[9]*3 Pa. Archives*, XVIII, 303–430.
[10]Turner, *The Negro in Pa.*
[11]*Stat. at Large of Pa.*, II, 107, 285.
[12]*Ms. Bd. of Trade Papers, Proprieties*, IX, Q, 39, 42; *Stat. at Large of Pa.* II, 543–4.

failure in legislation, it seems that the feeling against importation was quite marked and, for that reason, the number

Slack
demand for
slaves
indicated

imported fell considerably.   If the statement of a merchant,
Jonathan Dickinson, may be taken as indicative, we may
judge that it was the slack demand that brought about a
decrease in importation.   He says, writing to Jamaica, April,
1715,

> I must entreat you to send me no more Negroes for sale, for our people
> don't care to buy. They are generally against any coming into the
> country.[13]

However strongly the general public was opposed to the
slave importation, it was nevertheless possible for the interests of the few to dominate.   First, there was the desire on
the part of the trading company for the rich profits derived,
and the crown was loath to fail to safeguard the company in
its demands; this service it performed by regularly repealing
the obnoxious legislation, which was enacted and favored by

The trade
formed by
certain
classes: (1)
traders, (2)
manufac-
turers

the majority of the citizens represented in the Assembly.[14]
Second, certain influential classes of citizens, for example, the
iron masters, wished for the continuance of importation
because of the advantage accruing to them through the
competition between Whites and slave labor.   This is
instanced in 1727 by a petition on their part for the removal
of the duty because of the scarcity of available Whites.[15]

This conflict between the ideals of different classes, com-
plicated by the economic problem of labor, continued to be
fought out chiefly in words, and legislation, until by the
middle of the eighteenth century it is estimated, by some
historians of Pennsylvania, that importation had nearly
ceased.[16]   The period following 1750, however, saw importation again positively accelerated, due to the greater security

Trade
accelerated

in the possession of Negro slaves compared with that of the
White servants.   Passing over the crest of this wave of
increase, we find a rapid decline in importation and sale of
Negroes during the years immediately preceding the Ameri-

---

[13]Watson, *Annals of Phila.*, II, 264.
[14]*Ms. Bd. of Trade Papers, Proprieties*, IX, Q, 39, 42; *Stat. at Large
of Pa.* II, 543–4.
[15]*Votes and Proceedings*, 1726–1742, 31.
[16]Smith, *Hist. of Del. Co.*, 261; Kaln, *Travels*, I, 391.

can Revolution; but even after the Revolution, fought for the principles of freedom, independence and equality, there occur not infrequent instances of the traffic in human flesh and blood.[17] These cases form the exception rather than the rule, however, and in 1780 there was secured the law for gradual prohibition, to which reference has already been made.[18]

Decline in the trade about Revolution

The condition of the slaves in Pennsylvania was in many respects better than in other states; especially is this true if they are compared with those in the South, who were employed mostly in plantation work. Their clothing, if we may judge by the descriptions which usually accompanied the advertisement of runaways, was usually good and very striking in its variety, as witnesses the following description.*

Slaves: how circum-stanced in Pennsyl-vania

Three hundred dollars reward. Runaway from the subscriber on the evening of August 14, 1779. 20th of June, lost, a negro man named Dan about 24 or 25 years of age; 5 feet, 5 or 6 inches; something pitted with the smallpox; his dress when he went off is uncertain, as he took sundry clothes with him, amongst which are two coats, a light faggothy, and a brown jerkin with yellow buttons, three jackets, light blue, brown, and striped linen, a pair of new buckskin breeches, several pairs of old striped and two pairs of tow trousers, three pairs of stockings, three good shirts, and a round hat. Said negro is this country born, and talks the English and German languages; is fond of playing the fiddle, and is naturally left-handed, and what is very remarkable, he bows with the left hand when performing on the violin.[19]

Socially they were less restricted and did not suffer the sharp separation from the Whites that was characteristic of the South. They were not on an equality, that was not to be expected, but they enjoyed considerable freedom among themselves,[20] and the various religious societies were, at least to a considerable degree, interested in their spiritual welfare. We find, at any rate, no considerable opposition to their advancement as was present in Virginia, even at a much later date.[21] The Moravians, as before stated, were usually

Fewer social restrictions

[17]*Pa. Gaz. and Wk. Advt.*, 1779, No. 2580.
[18]*Col. Rec.*, XII, 99.
*The quality of the clothing on their backs does not necessarily mean they enjoyed a good location. It was in many cases stolen goods.
[19]*Pa. Gaz.*, No. 2568, 1779.
[20]Watson, *Annals*, I, 406.
[21]Heatwole, *Hist. of Ed. in Va.*, 299.

Care for
their religious
welfare

opposed to holding slaves, and where they were held, they
were on a basis of religious equality.[22] The Lutherans were
likewise tolerant, but it is to the credit of the Episcopalians
that most is due. Negroes were baptized in their church and
then instructed in religion by a minister provided for that
purpose.[23] Not only were the established congregations
favorable to the aid of the Negro, but many itinerant ministers were desirous of educating him.

There is one outstanding instance of the latter which
may serve as an illustration. It is that of Reverend
Whitefield, who took up five thousand acres of land on

Work of
Whitefield

the forks of the Delaware in Pennsylvania, where the
hoped to erect a Negro school. The movement was
given wide publicity and subscriptions were asked for
its support.[24] In the papers which advertise the beginning of the project, there is found no statement as to the
successful outcome of it; the whole scheme seems to have
melted away as easily as it had arisen. The scheme of
Whitefield, was equalled, and perhaps even excelled, by a
much earlier proposal, 1722, which was made anonymously
through the columns of the *Mercury*.[25] The service was to be
rendered to the servants of any religious denomination, and
without any expense to them whatsoever. It was chiefly
desired that the Negroes might be taught to read the Scriptures.[26]

If justice were to be done to the various attempts on the
part of itinerant ministers and the regularly established
churches to aid in bringing enlightenment to the Negroes in
Pennsylvania, it would require volumes. Such mention as has
been made is for the purpose of pointing out the universality
of the missionary spirit, so that it may not be understood that

Missionary
work for
Negroes not
limited to
Quakers

that the entire work was carried on under the direction of
Friends, to whose activities much more space must necessarily
be given in this work. In the pages following it will be
attempted to outline as definitely as possible, from the avail-

---

[22]*Pa. Mag. of Hist.*, XXIX, 363.
[23]Smith, H. W., *Life* of *W. Smith*, I, 238.
[24]*Pa. Gaz.*, 1740, 624; *Am. Wk. Mer.*, 1740, No. 1097.
[25]*Am. Wk. Mer.*, 1722–3, IV, 16.
[26]*Ibid.*

able records, what was actually accomplished by the organization of Friends towards Negro education.

QUAKER LEADERS AND THE NEGRO PROBLEM

However auspicious may have been the opportunity for attempts to plant slavery on the soil of Pennsylvania, it was neither destined to meet unqualified success nor to pass without rigorous opposition. The German population from the very outset, as we have already stated, was hostile to the idea of slavery.[27] Likewise, the Quakers were dominated by men who believed that slavery had no justification, and throughout their lives were actuated by this belief. Brief mention may be made of three of these leaders, sufficient at least to indicate their viewpoint and the remedy which they advocated.

Slavery's opponents

George Fox, their revered founder, was quite naturally referred to in matters of importance and far reaching consequence. Through the influence of his ministry, the doctrine of the freedom of all men and of inherent rights, which they possessed by virtue of being men, came to be accepted in the church organization, and was published in the discipline and various letters of that body.[28] These acts of the church organization will be dealt with presently. Fox defends his position mainly on the religious basis; it is quite likely that a religious training and education is uppermost in his mind throughout his plea for the Negro. He does not limit himself to their case, but insists, also, on the education of the Indian natives. The education (religious) which he specifically mentions, is for the purpose of their salvation, but the attention of Quakers was not limited to that alone. Religious education did, however, receive their first consideration. The essence of Fox's influential utterances on this subject is contained in the following extract.

George Fox

Pleads for education of Negro and Indian

And, also, you must instruct and teach your Indians and Negroes, and all others, how that Christ, by the grace of God, tasted death for every man and gave himself a ransom for all men to be testified in due time;

---

[27] *Pa. Archives*, XVIII, 303–430. *Ibid.*, XXI, 165–324. *Ibid.*, XVII, 489–685.
[28] Christian Doc. Prac. and Dis. Relig. Soc. of Friends, 1727, 122, (published 1861). *Ibid.*, extract of 1758.

and is the propitiation not only for the sins of Christians, but for the sins of the whole world; and that He doth enlighten every man that cometh into the world, with His true light, which is the life in Christ by Whom the world was made.[29]

John Woolman

From among the Quaker exponents of the freedom of all men, we can scarcely select one of greater influence than John Woolman. He was born in 1720,[30] and thus grew up to manhood in a period when the opposition to slavery on the part of Friends was on the increase, and lived through its zenith, after which slavery among Pennsylvania Friends scarcely existed.[31] He was well educated. The greater part of his life was spent travelling as a minister from place to place, now working among the Indians[32] and again visiting meetings in the interest of the freedom of the Negro.[33] His journeys throughout the colonies served to keep the individual meetings awake to the problem before them, and the firm conviction of the man won no less number of supporters than the eloquence of his appeal. The influence of Woolman did not,

His sermons, tracts, etc.

however, limit itself to the channels of his sermons; in 1754 appeared one of his best expressions on the traffic, entitled *Some Considerations on the Keeping of Negroes*. Nothing was permitted to stand in the light of his conviction as to the right; he refused to continue his practice of writing wills in all cases where the disposition of slaves was involved.[34]

But it is impossible to give in this limited space an adequate resumé of the work of this great spokesman of freedom. A brief representative statement from his works, added to what has already been said, is perhaps the most satisfactory treatment that can be given.

Woolman on slave holding

Many slaves on this continent are oppressed, and their cries have reached the ears of the most High. Such are the purity and certainty of His judgments, that He can not be partial in our favor. In infinite love and goodness He hath opened our understandings from one time to another concerning our duty to this people; and it is not a time for delay. Should we now be sensible of what He requires of us, and through respect to the interest of some persons, or through a regard to some friendships which do not stand on an immutable foundation, neglect to do our duty in firmness and constancy, still waiting for some

[29]*Friends' Lib.*, I, 79.
[30]Woolman's *Works*, 15.
[31]Turner, *Negro in Pa.*, 67.
[32]Woolman's *Works*, 156–7.
[33]*Ibid.*, 78.
[34]*Ibid.*, 44.

extraordinary means to bring about their deliverance, it may be by terrible things in righteousness, God may answer us in this matter.[35]

Man is born to labor, and experience abundantly sheweth that it is for our good; but where the powerful lay the burden on the inferior, without affording a Christian education, and suitable opportunity for improving the mind, and a treatment that we in their case should approve, that themselves may live at ease and fare sumptuously, and lay up riches for their posterity, this seems to contradict the design of Providence and, I doubt not, is sometimes the effect of a perverted mind; for while the life of one is made grievous by the rigor of another, it entails misery to both.[36]

While speaking of the life and work of the two above mentioned Quaker reformers, one other person seems to call imperatively for attention. His work was equally widespread and the public was kept open to his influence through several of his books and pamphlets published on the subject of slaves and slaveholding.[37] A French Hugenot by birth, Anthony Benezet came early to America, where he was a staunch member of Friends, and in whose society he performed a continuous service for the freedom and education of the Negroes, until the time of his death in 1784.[38] His immediate connection with the Negro School, established by Friends in 1770[39] will be considered more fully elsewhere. The arguments advanced by him against slavery are based on the grounds of practicality and justice. The system is injurious to the slave and the master, and inconsistent with the ideals of a free community. We, ourselves, must agree with him in his position as set forth in the following selection.

Anthony Benezet; his influence through books, pamphlets, etc.

The bondage we have imposed on the Africans is absolutely repugnant to Justice. It is highly inconsistent with civil policy: *First,* as it tends to suppress all improvements in arts and sciences, without which it is morally impossible that any nation should be happy or powerful. *Secondly,* as it may deprave the minds of the free men, steeling their hearts against the laudable feelings of virtue and humanity. And *lastly,* as it endangers the community by the destructive effects of civil commotions; need I to add to these what every heart, which is not callous to all tender feelings) will readily suggest—that it is shocking to humanity, violative of generous sentiment, abhorrent utterly

Extract from Benezet

---

[35]Woolman's *Works*, 96–7.
[36]*Ibid.*, 244.
[37]Most significant works are given in the bibliography.
[38]Min. Phila. Mo. Mtg., 1—30—1784, 128.
[39]*Ibid.*, 6—29—1770, 398.

from the Christian religion; for as Montesquieu very justly observes, "We must suppose them not to be men, or a suspicion would follow that we ourselves are not Christians." There can not be a more dangerous maxim than that necessity is a plea for injustice. For who shall fix the degree of this necessity? What villian so atrocious who may not urge this excuse; or, as Milton has happily expressed it,—"and with necessity, the tyrants plea, excuse his devilish deed"?[40]

Besides the three representatives mentioned, there were a host of others, many of them still earlier but perhaps none who exercised so great an influence. Among those worthy of mention were George Keith, a dissenter among Quakers, but one of the earliest teachers in Philadelphia, and a very ardent antagonist of slavery. Others, whose zeal outran their discretion, such as Ralph Sandiford, Benjamin Lay,* and William Southeby, might be profitably discussed here, but lack of space eliminates their consideration. Still other itinerant ministers, Banks, Pennington, and Chalkley, though not so precipitous in their actions as the three above named, were none the less worthy spokesmen of the cause.

(margin note) George Keith and other antagonists of slavery

THE CHURCH ORGANIZATION AND THE NEGRO QUESTION

Under this head it is intended to present, (1) the activity of the society as an organization, and (2) the establishment of Negro education in the various meetings where any record of it remains. In doing so, let the reader keep in mind the principles set forth previously by the three representatives who have been mentioned as leaders in the cause of Negro education and liberation.

(margin note) Study of the meeting records referring to Negro education

As is quite naturally expected, after this brief introduction to the belief of the Quaker leaders, we find that the society placed itself as a unit opposed to the perpetuation of bondage among the Blacks. Friends were astonished to find, when they arrived, that slavery existed in Penn's colony, and as early as 1688 those settled at Germantown entered a memorable protest against it.[41] Five years later George Keith, a

(margin note) The meeting organization against slave traffic

---

[40]Benezet, *A Short Account of the People Called Quakers*, 81–2.
*Vaux, *Memoirs of Lay and Sandiford*.
[41]*Pa. Mag. of Hist.*, XIII, 265; Old Germantown, *Lippincott's Mag.*, Feb., 1884, 118 ff., containing an account of the protest; Phila. Quarterly Meeting would not take action, it being considered too weighty a question (Min. Phila. Q. Mtg., 4—4—1688, 136.)

Quaker who a few years later came into disfavor with the society, entered a vigorous denunciation of the practice of holding slaves.[42] The general tenor of these protests is against *perpetual bondage*, their idea being that since it already existed, there should be a time limit set at the expiration of which all those held should become free.

Germantown memorial against it

It would have been possible for individual protests and those of smaller meetings to have gone on indefinitely and still have accomplished but little in the way of influencing others. Similar expressions from a central organization, speaking with some semblance of authority, could have accomplished much more, and did so, though not till some years later. The advices issued by the yearly meeting were usually in the nature of reproof, scarcely or never mandatory. One of the earliest was drawn up at the yearly meeting in 1727 and sent to the meetings subject thereto.

It is the sense of this meeting that the importation of negroes from their native country and relations by Friends, is not a commendable or allowable practice, and is therefore censured by this meeting.[43]

Yearly Meeting regarding slave trade

It is difficult to understand how any communication of this nature could have force in a situation that seemed to demand something in the way of command. But when it is recalled with what persistence such advices were given, and again repeated in the appropriate meetings, and that they were received by the monthly and preparative meetings very much as dutiful children would listen to the advice of father or mother, then the influence exerted by them does not seem so strange.

Moreover, there is ample evidence in the reports of various meetings at all times that the advices of the yearly meeting were being followed with considerable success. Philadelphia reported (1756) that they knew of no Friends who had been concerned in importing Negroes or other slaves.[44] By 1772 the yearly meeting reported by way of letter that, due to the discouragement of the practice of slaveholding on the part of Friends in the colonies, it had greatly diminished in some

Reports made to yearly meeting concerning slaves

---

[42]*Pa. Mag. of Hist.*, 266, 268.
[43]Christian Doc. Prac. and Discipline, 1727, pub. 1861, 122.
[44]Min. Phila. Mo. Mtg., 4—30—1756, 215.

parts, and in others disappeared almost altogether, as was true in the case of Pennsylvania.[45] For the sake of more complete illustration of the type of expression issued, the following is quoted more at length.

We fervently warn all in profession with us that they be careful to avoid being in any way concerned in reaping the unrighteous profits arising from the iniquitous practice of dealing in Negroes and other slaves; whereby in the original purchase one man selleth another, as he doth the beast that perisheth, without any better pretension to a property in him than that of superior force; in direct violation of the gospel rule, which teaches all to do as they would be done by and to do good to all; being the reverse of that covetous disposition, which furnishes encouragement to those poor ignorant people to perpetuate their savage wars, in order to supply the demands of this unnatural traffic, whereby great numbers of mankind, free by nature, are subjected to inextricable bondage; and which hath often been observed to fill their possessors with haughtiness, tyranny, luxury, and barbarity, corrupting the minds and debasing the morals of their children, to the unspeakable prejudice of religion and virtue, and the exclusion of that holy spirit of universal love, meekness, and charity, which is the unchangeable nature, and the glory of true Christianity. 1758.[46]

Warning of 1758 against being concerned with slaves

The reader will have noticed that the chief emphasis is placed upon the wrongfulness of bartering slaves; this may be explained by saying that that was the first problem they had to face. Not until they were able to secure the Negroes' freedom could an education be of much value to him, for all that he made of his life belonged to his master. But as soon as he became free, there arose other needs, other desires. New prospects opened before him, and there was a possibility that he might accomplish something for himself and his posterity. This was realized by the church organization and it followed the move for freedom by emphatic requests that the meetings take care of the spiritual and intellectual education of the negroes. The following will illustrate very clearly the insistence with which the local church investigated the activity of its members, and the penalty levied on the disobedient one. In 1759, it was reported that . . . . had purchased several Negroes; this being a breach of discipline, two members were appointed to speak with him on the subject, according to their custom. The final report on his case

Freedom had to come before their education

Local meetings persistent in their investigation of slave conditions

---

[45]Epistles London Yr. Mtg., 1772, 394.
[46]Christian Doc. Prac. and Discipline, 1758, pub. 1861, 122.

was made in 1762. They may be praised for longsuffering and condemned for inefficiency.

. . . . appeared at this meeting and after much weighty advice given him in that affair, it is left for him weightily to consider whether he can not find freedom to bring up such of his negroes as are young in useful learning, endeavoring to instruct them in the principles of Christianity, and at a proper age, if they desire it, to set them free, and if otherwise, that he can not have the unity of Friends.[47]

Instances similar to this one are almost without number; reference is made to a few of them only.[48] The work of each of the particular meetings is more completely brought out in the following pages.

Of all meetings in the Philadelphia Yearly Meeting, there were none which accomplished more for the education of the Negro than did Philadelphia Monthly. As has already been noted elsewhere in this work, there was quite early a considerable interest manifested by the meeting in regard to the question of servitude, and also the masters' care in giving them Christian instruction.[49] There is no record to show that at these early dates there was any permanent school; all care was, without question, left to those who had Negroes in their employ, education being tutorial entirely. The master's care was well guarded by the meeting's committee on Negroes, however, and in this way a central responsible party was provided. In addition, there was also established a meeting which was held once each three months in the interest of Negroes.[50]

No early school recorded

Meetings for Negroes

In 1770 there came to the front a definite movement for the establishment of a systematic means of educating Negro children. The proposal for its consideration, made first month, 26th, was referred to the meeting in second month for action.[51]

---

[47]Extracts Buckingham Mo. Mtg., 12—6—1762, 107.
[48]Min. Phila. Mo. Mtg.,4—30—1756,215; Concord Mo. Mtg., 6—9—1779, 86; Horsham Sch. Com,8—17—1792; ChesterMo. Mtg., 10—25—1779, 31; Uwchlan Mo. Mtg.,9—9—1779, 65f.; Sadsbury, 7—17—1782, 340.
[49]Min. Phila. Mo. Mtg., 4—30—1756, 215 and 1—25—1765, 7.
[50]*Ibid.*, 7.
[51]*Ibid.*, 1—26—1770, 371; (Proud in his Ms. *History of Philadelphia* gives Benezet the whole credit of establishing the Negro school. There were two branches, one for boys and one for girls, taught by different tutors. He says the successful outcome of this school of Benezet's was the incentive which caused the Abolition Society to establish others.) See Proud's Ms. *History*, p. 64. H. S. P.

On that occasion, there being expressed a definite sentiment in favor of action, a committee was appointed consisting of twenty-two members with permission for any other Friends to attend its deliberations who cared to do so.[52]   The date for the committee meeting was set by the monthly meeting. At the subsequent monthly meeting, the committee made its first report, which being acceptable to all was approved, and further steps were taken to secure immediate action. A digest of the report and proposals of the committee is here presented.[53]

Committee appointed on Negroes

1.   The instruction of Negro and mulatto children in reading, writing, arithmetic, and other useful learning—sewing and knitting, according to their capacity, is to be provided.

Digest of committee's report

2.   The instruction is to be under the care of Friends.

3.   The monthly meeting to nominate a committee of Friends, whose duties are:

a.   To employ a suitable master or mistress for not more than thirty children at once.

b.   To have the charge of admitting pupils to the school.

c.   A subscription of £100 a year for three years to be promoted.

d.   To employ another master or mistress if necessary and funds adequate.

e.   To visit the school at least once a month, and to observe the improvement and conduct of the pupils.

f.   Rules to be prepared for teachers and pupils; provision for attendance at religious services at least on Sunday.

g.   The committee to appoint a treasurer from its number who is to make payments upon an order signed by at least four of them.

h.   Four members are sufficient number to transact business; in difficulties, they are advised to consult the monthly meeting.

---

[52]Min. Phila. Mo. Mtg., 2—23—1770, 376.
[53]*Ibid.*, 3—30—1770, 379.

i. To keep a record of proceedings, receipts, and
     expenditures, and make a report to the meeting
     once a year or more.

4. The children of free Negroes and mulattoes are to be
given preferment.

5. Tuition to be free of any expense to the parents.

6. If enrollment of such children is not large enough, the
committee may admit others according to their judgment.

Acting upon the recommendations incorporated in the
report, a subscription paper was at once prepared, and the
campaign for funds began.[54] A committee of the following
named Friends was appointed to assume the direction of the
school agreeable to the articles of the report, viz.; Israel
Pemberton, Samuel Emlen, James Pemberton, Richard
Blackham, John Drinker, Hugh Forbes, and Edward Jones.[55]
Their term of service was stated as "until a new nomination
be made by this meeting" and any vacancy occurring in the
meantime was to be filled in the same way.[56]   Only three
months later (sixth month) the committee of seven reported
they had agreed with Moses Patterson as teacher, hired a
house, and that a number of children were already admitted
for instruction.[57] In first month of the following year the committee requested permission to erect a school for the use of
the Blacks, on the same lot occupied by the almshouse.
The request was at once granted.[58]

Though it was originally stated that the committee should
report once a year to the monthly meeting, there was by no
means a full report recorded in the minutes each year.   They
are adequate enough, however, to furnish some idea of the
progress made with the school.

The details of a few reports will be presented.   It appears
from the records that the committee's reports were always
made the basis of judgment as to whether the meeting would
continue the school or abandon it.[59]   Fortunately, the reports
were usually favorable, excepting in matters of financial
consideration; in this respect there was quite often a short-

Marginal notes:

Subscriptions for school solicited

Moses Patterson in the Negro school

Full yearly reports not made

Reports taken as a measure of the school's success

---

[54]Min. Phila. Mo. Mtg., 3—30—1770, 379.
[55]*Ibid.*   [56]*Ibid.*, 1–25–1771, 430.
[57]*Ibid.*, 6–29–1770, 398.   [58]*Ibid.*, 1–25–1771, 430.
[59]*Ibid.*, 2–28–1777, 438.

age.[60]   In the report of the first twelve years there is little that deserves repetition. The school continued regularly, according to statements made at intervals, and all things seemed to convince Friends that it was worthy of their support. Let us note the condition of the school at the end of twelve years, 1782.

For the five years preceding the instruction had been under the care of John Houghton, who, unfortunately, had to retire because of failing health.[61]   His place was taken two months later by Anthony Benezet, a teacher of great merit, and one who perhaps had the welfare of the Negro more at heart than any other man in the colony.[62]   At his suggestion, the school was removed from the house erected for that purpose and established in his own home.   Great tribute was paid to the character of the work done by Houghton, with special reference to his painstaking visiting of families, seeking thus to increase the interest of parents, and ultimately the school attendance.   It is stated that during the five years he was employed, two hundred and fifty children and grown persons had entered the school.[63]   The chief value derived, according to the committee's view, was the increased appreciation aroused among the Whites for the Blacks.   They were forced to realize that the Negro had talents which might be developed as their own, giving him an insight into greater possibilities which were not beyond his reach.

The report on the financial status was not so hopeful.   The fees for the master, for the years 1779, 1780, and 1781 were eighty, ninety, and one hundred pounds respectively; in addition, there was the expense of odd jobs of work, wood for winter use, and also the item of books.[64]   To increase the difficulties arising from mere items of expense, there was introduced another factor, the payment to the treasurer of paper money which had greatly depreciated in value since it was subscribed.*   The result of the experiment, up to date, financially, was a deficit of £74/7/10.   A part of this amount was covered by outstanding subscriptions, a considerable

John Houghton and Anthony Benezet

Financially the school was no success

Payments in depreciated money

[60]Min. Phila. Mo. Mtg. 5—31—1782, 28; 1—25—1793, 184; 3—30—1770, 379.
[61]*Ibid.*   [62]*Ibid.*   [63]*Ibid.*   [64]*Ibid.*
*Dewey, p. 39.

number of which could not be collected.[65] The meeting was appealed to, to make up the deficit as usual by subscription. This method, though commonly resorted to, was in most places supplemented by special legacies left to trustees for any purpose the donor might designate.[66] Legacies for schools were particularly urged by the quarterly and yearly meetings.

Legacies and subscriptions used for support

In 1784 there seems to have been but one school for the Blacks, the one taught by Benezet. The report stated that there was a decided need for another one in the near future; in 1786 it appears by answers to the queries that the school has been added and that both are supported by the voluntary contributions of Friends.[67] The attendance problem was evidently not yet solved satisfactorily; it would perplex a teacher to-day. About one hundred were under the instruction of Benezet in 1784, but only fifteen to thirty-five generally attended.[68] The progress of this number in reading, writing, and arithmetic was deemed satisfactory, though it was admitted it might be improved with more regular attendance.

Irregular attendance

The salary paid Benezet at this time was £100 plus the £20 which was allowed as the rent for his dwelling, which he continued to use as a school house.

Salary paid Benezet

From 1786 two schools continued. In 1790 the incumbent of the master's position was Daniel Britt; the mistress of the other was Sarah Dougherty. The latter served only to sixth month, 1790, at which time she was replaced by Elizabeth Meccum who later became the wife of Daniel Britt.[69] Though there was a very large enrollment at this time, the actual attendance was between eighteen and thirty in each of the schools.[70] The instruction continued as above stated and was recognized on the whole as satisfactory, its only failure being due to irregular attendance, occasioned by illiberal masters, who detained the Negroes in their service. The master's salary for the year, £100, was double that paid to the

Two Negro schools under Daniel Britt, Sarah Dougherty, and Elizabeth Meccum

[65]Min. Phila. Mo. Mtg., 3—30—1770, 379.
[66]*Ibid.*, 4—26—1771, 444, and 21—25—1772, 145.
[67]*Ibid.*, 7—28—1786, 271.
[68]*Ibid.*, 1—30—1784, 128.
[69]*Ibid.*, 1—25—1793, 184.
[70]*Ibid.*

mistress. Finances were generally in a bad state, though
they had been considerably augmented by a generous gift of

School receives gift from England

£175 from England, and a special donation by William
Craig.[71]   In spite of this, the committee was still indebted to
the estate of Anthony Benezet to the extent of about £100.*
These difficulties do not seem to have been insuperable, however; the regular annual income (about 1784) was fairly well
established, being derived from the rental of property and
grounds.[72]

Under the direction of Daniel Britt and his wife the school
continued to progress; most gratifying was the increase of

Regular attendance about eighty

the regular attendance to about eighty, which was as large as
could be conveniently accommodated in the two schools.[73]
The services of Britt and his wife ceased in the period from
1795 to 1798, the latter having died and the former being aged

Elisha Pickering, master

and infirm.   The master's place was taken by Elisha Pickering, at a salary now grown to £150 per year.   That of the
mistress still remained at the mark of former years, £50.
The amount of annual rents had increased to £190/9/11 and
besides this there was an interest from £146/7 which was a
part of the bequest of Anthony Benezet.[74]   The annual
expenditures were estimated at £230, which considerably
exceeded the income.   It was customary to require tuition
for the children whose masters were "bound by indenture to
give them school learning," and from this source was eked out
the sum necessary to defray expenses.[75]   There is found no
statement in the committee's reports to indicate the amount
of tuition usually demanded.   The following bill may be of
interest, however, since it shows various items of expenditures
of the school committee.**

---

[71]Min. Phila. Mo. Mtg., 1—25—1793, 184.
[72]*Ibid.*
*For an insight to the real value of the money see note p. 212 of this
work; also Dewey, p. 39.
[73]*Ibid.*, 2–23,1798, 149.
[74]*Ibid.*
[75]*Ibid.*
**Ms. *Minutes of the Committee on Negro Education*, I, 19; other
expenditures mentioned are for copy books, ciphering books, child's
spelling books, lessons for youth, writing paper, red blotting paper,
slates, quills, ink, tutors' assistants, Cheap Repository, 4 volumes, and
one set Murray's *Introduction*, I, 138.

Committee of education, to Othneil Alsop, Dr.

1797 9–23. Cash advance to Bustill . . . . $ 10.00
       9–30. Paid J. Schæffer for 4 benches for North Liberties
           School 3.50
               24 printed alphabets 27
               6 spelling books 1.50
    10–2. Paid A. Williams quarter's salary 25.00
  10–28. Advanced Cyrus Bustill 10.00
  11–6. Two cords of wood, hauling, etc 12.35

               Total $62.62

From available records it is impossible to give more than an elementary knowledge of how the school was run. Nothing is found concerning the inner organization. We can know its purposes, its means at command for attaining them, and approximately the number of children it was able to reach. The length of school term is not quite clear; it seems evident that there were summer and winter sessions, how long we do not know, and that there was scarecely any interruption of their continuity. Occurrences which caused an interruption of the session usually were commented on in the committee's reports.[76] A summary of the report showing the status of the schools in 1800 is given below.[77] At that time they were under the direction of committees of the northern, central, and southern districts.

Summer and winter sessions

    1. Benjamin Mears, master at $500 a year; Elizabeth Meccum, mistress at £50 per year.

    2. Schools have been kept open throughout the year 1798–99 with the exception of twelve weeks on account of sickness.

Status of Negro schools in 1800

    3. The attendance, from seventy to eighty day scholars, winter and autumn.

    4. Some applicants for admission have been refused because of a lack of room; room enough for all in summer.

    5. Finance:

        a. Total bequest of Anthony Benezet, plus that which was owing to him at the time of his death, makes an income of £193/4

[76]Min. Phila. Mo. Mtg., 11—28—1800, 300; *Ibid.*, 2—23—1798, 149.
[77]*Ibid.*

b. Annual amount of donations from other
sources £117/5/11

Total £220/9/11

In hands of treasurer................£ 8/12/6

For two reasons it has been thought advisable to present as fully as possible the situation in regard to the Negro's education in Philadelphia. *First*, they were present in Philadelphia in so considerable numbers that it necessitated a complete organization on the part of the society if any aid was to be offered; *second*, the method of dealing with them was closely followed in other localities, in case there were sufficient numbers to warrant it. The activity of other monthly meetings in this question of oversight and education of the Negro will be touched upon briefly.

As was above suggested, and will be shown more explicitly hereinafter, there were many of the country districts where the Negro problem scarcely existed.[78] In many others the number of the race was so small that a separate school was entirely out of the question; but more was needed than the mere presence of a White school, to make certain that they received even the rudiments of an education. A constant readjustment of the general ideal of attitude toward them was necessary for each individual community. The details of information concerning the work of each meeting was interesting enough, but perhaps it will be more instructive to point out and illustrate the general characteristics which applied to most, or at least a large number of them.

As a general rule, if Negro inhabitants were numerous, a committee was delegated to the service of their care and education.[79] In some places this was made a standing committee having specified duties; in others, the committees were appointed only to investigate conditions and make a report, so that further action might be taken by the meeting. It may be well to note the type of this service which the commit-

Marginal notes:
Not enough Negroes for a separate school

Negro education usually delegated to a committee

---

[78]Min. Exeter Mo. Mtg., 7—26—1764, 519.
[79]Min. Uwchlan Mo. Mtg., 9—9—1779, 65; Min. Sadsbury Mo., Mtg., 7—17—1782, 340.

tees were required to perform. The duties, performed by the
two kinds of committees, were but slightly differentiated; the
chief difference lay in the length of the term of service.

The *first* task for them was to actually visit the Negro
families within the compass of the particular meeting;[80] the
second, to determine as exactly as possible the economic status
of the home;[81] the *third*, to ascertain the number of children
capable of receiving schooling; [82]*fourth*, to inform themselves
as to the attitude of the parents towards their children's education;[83] *fifth*, to deal with members of Friends who possessed
slaves or paid servants, endeavoring to point out to them the
obligation for their education, and also for their freedom;[84]
sixth, to inform themselves as to the occupation pursued by the
Negroes, if any;[85] and *finally*, to make a report of conditions,
in such shape that it might be transmitted to the quarterly
meeting, and outline the plan of procedure, according to the
demands of the situation.[86] From such a range of information, considering the characteristic thoroughness of the
people, it must be inferred that they were able to understand
the needs, which is always a first requisite for their satisfaction. Moreover, the knowledge that the quarterly meetings
demanded written statements of what they had done always
worked to facilitate prompt action as soon as the situation
was defined. Rather late in the century,, 1779, the yearly
meeting became insistent as to the treatment of those who
held slaves, though the punishment for failure to educate
them was not so drastic. Extracts sent to the meetings in
that year required that all members holding slaves should be
disowned.[87] Instances where this punishment was used are
not wanting.[88]

The financial burden of Negro education usually fell on the
local meeting. Those owning slaves were required to pay for

Seven duties for the committees to perform

---

[80]Min. Uwchlan Mo. Mtg., 9—9—1779, 65f.
[81]*Ibid.*
[82]Min. Deercreek Mo. Mtg., 7—24—1779, 304.
[83]*Ibid.*, 11—23—1776, 274.
[84]*Ibid.*
[85]Min. Sadsbury Mo. Mtg., 7—17—1782, 340.
[86]Min. Chester Mo. Mtg., 10—25—1779, 31.
[87]Extracts, Buckingham Mo.Mtg.,12—6—1779, 202; (this was a part
of the discipline).
[88]*Ibid.*, 12—6—1762, 107.

their education, but when they became free, as most of them did by the time of the Revolution, it was impossible for them to pay for themselves. This burden, which the society assumed, was usually met: (1) by subscription,[89] (2) by special legacies, and (3) by income from investments in property. In the smaller localities, the first was the predominate means; in the larger, such as Philadelphia, a larger proportion was derived from the second and third,[90] though the first was common to all.

The situation at Exeter Monthly Meeting seems to have been well disposed of, if one may judge by the brevity of their annals. Writing, 1764, in answer to an inquiry on the part of Philadelphia Quarterly Meeting, to which they belonged, they report:

> But one negro amongst us, who has sufficient food and raiment, but his religious education is still neglected, which is now under notice.[91]

In 1758 they had reported two Negroes only, and with substantially the same comments.[92]   The report may either mean they had no problem at the outset, or that they were remarkably successful in their attempt to solve it.

Radnor Monthly Meeting reported in 1756 that they were clear with respect to buying, importing, disposing of, or holding slaves,[93] and continued substantially the same report until 1768.[94]   They were all, according to reports, well fed and clothed and many attended meetings,[95] but no statement is made at that early date concerning any attempt to educate them.   From sundry reports after 1768 it seems necessary to assume that the earlier reports were not entirely accurate in stating that the meeting was "clear" of slaves. Without this assumption, it is difficult to understand the great increase in the cases of discipline for that offense.   This increase was doubtless due to a closer scrutiny of the Negro question than had been formerly customary.

Marginal notes:

Support similar to that of other schools

Negro education at Exeter

Radnor

No early mention of their schooling at Radnor

---

[89]Min. Uwchlan Mo. Mtg., 9—9—1779, 65f.
[80]Cf. Report on Philadelphia, pp. 68f.
[91]Min. Exeter Mo. Mtg., 7—26—1764, 519.
[92]*Ibid.*, 10—26—1758, 301.
[93]Min. Radnor Mo. Mtg., 10—12—1756, 287.
[94]*Ibid.*, 1—11—1757, 300; 4—10—1759, 28; 6—8—1764, 54; 7—8—1766, 139.
[95]*Ibid.*, 7—8—1766, 139.

Beginning with 1768, there were several cases reported of dealing in slaves, either buying, selling, or holding. First, there was "one slave sold,"[96] and two years later the records state "none imported but some purchased and some sold since last account."[97] It was further admitted (1770) that "nothing has yet been done by us in visiting those who hold slaves,"[98] but a few years later (1776) there is ample evidence cited that they attended to each individual case; there are several instances where expulsion from the society was threatened,[99] and actually carried into execution.[100] In 1778 the committee on slaves reported: (1) they had visited all members holding slaves, (2) obtained manumissions from David Harvard for two slaves, (3) Anthony Tunnis also released a slave, and (4) mentioned two other cases for consideration—(a) that of John Harvard, holding one slave though he admits it to be wrong, and (b) that of Samuel Harvard who refuses to set free a Negro man aged forty, though he condemns the slaveholding practice.[101] In 1780 the meeting reported *none imported, sold,* or *purchased,* and almost none *held,*[102] and by 1790 even the latter had disappeared.[103]

Report of committee on slaves

There was at this time constant oversight of the freed Negroes and some of the children were given the opportunity of schooling without charge to the parents.[104]

Some schooled without charge

Negro slavery flourished early in Bucks County,[105] and still continued to persist until after the abolition in 1780,[106] which resulted in a gradual diminution of slavery throughout the state. A little later we shall notice the distribution of slaves as indicated by the registration which was required by the law in 1782.[107]

Slavery in Bucks County

The presence of Negroes in the compass of Middletown is first made known through the record of 1703 which stated

---

[96]Min. Radnor Mo. Mtg., 7—12—1768, 209.
[97]*Ibid.,* 7—10—1770, 286.
[98]*Ibid.*
[99]*Ibid.,* 10—8—1776, 102; 8—13—1779, 171; 11—12—1779, 179.
[100]*Ibid.,* 12—10—1778, 145.
[101]*Ibid.,* 11—13—1778, 140.
[102]*Ibid.,* 7—1—1780, 198.
[103]*Ibid.,* 7—13—1790, 7.
[104]*Ibid.*
[105]See p. 228ff.; also Davis, *Hist. Bucks Co.,* II, 294.
[106]*Col. Rec.* XII, 99.   [107]Davis, *Hist.,* II, 297.

Slaves
mentioned at
Middletown
1703

that Robert Heaton and Thomas Stackpole were appointed to fence off a portion of the ground to bury Negroes in.[108]   The first reference to their liberation (other than by death) is the case of Jeremiah Langhorne, who in 1742 freed all of his Negroes, the entire number being about thirty or forty.[109] Just how frequently such liberations occurred and how generally they were participated in by Friends is not accurately ascertainable from the records, but by the year 1782 just following the stringent abolition act we have the following report:

No slaves
held; the
children
schooled

We have none to charge with buying or holding slaves, and care is taken to give the young ones learning and some care has been taken to encourage them in a religious and virtuous life.[110]

In 1783 a similar report issued from the monthly meeting, stating that a noteworthy care was evident among them for the Negroes, both old and young, but that a more considerable care was necessary to be taken in regard to their education.[111]

Buckingham

In 1759 Buckingham Meeting appointed John Ely and Isaac Pickering to speak with one of their members who had purchased slaves.[112]   This was done because it was a conflict with the discipline.   The burden of their advice is that he

Negro to be
educated
and given
religious in-
struction

should bring up the young Negroes in useful learning and Christianity, and later set them free if they desired it.   There is nothing further to indicate the nature of the education, and since there is no evidence of a school for them, it was probably in their homes or in connection with the White schools.   No

No evidence
of separate
Negro school

other references are found which point to any progress until 1778 when the meeting appointed Thomas Watson and Oliver Paxson to advise and assist the free Negroes in their religious duties and also in regard to their school education.[113]   This appointment was made in accordance with the more stringent regulations which were given out by the quarterly and yearly meetings in 1777.[114]   These regulations requested only that

[108]Davis, *Hist.*, II, 295.
[109]*Ibid.*
[110]Min. Middletown Mo. Mtg., 8—1—1782, 535.
[111]*Ibid.*, 8—7—1783, 557.
[112]Extracts, Min. Buckingham Mo. Mtg., 12—6—1762, p. 107.
[113]*Ibid.*, 11—2—1778, 181.
[114]Min. Bucks Q. Mtg., 8—28—1777, 29.

committee be appointed to look into the status of the Negroes and seek to better their conditions, but the one next following, 1779, required those holding slaves to be disowned.[115]

The records of Bucks Quarterly Meeting are in very substantial agreement with those of the individual meetings, Falls, Wrightstown, Middletown and Buckingham, which constituted it.[116] The question of the rightfulness of buying or owning slaves seems to have come first to a conscious consideration about 1730, when it was debated in the meeting.[117] They were unable to come to a decision in the matter and accordingly referred it back to the yearly meeting.[118] Though unsuccessful in debating the question satisfactorily, their practical success seems to have been very commendable, for in 1766 there is reported only one Negro purchased lately throughout the quarter.[119] This does not mean that no Negroes were held, for as will be shown later there were many in that region; it does mean, however, that their control of any increase in slaves was very satisfactory to the yearly meeting's demands. By 1772 the record has still been greatly improved, as they report:

Slave holding debated in meeting

clear of importing or buying negroes as far as appears, but their religious education is not so strictly attended to as the import of the query seems to require.[120]

Though all indications are to the effect that slave purchasing was near the minimum, the meetings were clearly not satisfied. Committees were at all times kept by both the quarterly and monthly meetings,[121] to visit with those who held slaves to persuade them to give them their freedom. The committee for this service in the quarterly meeting reported in 1777:

We of the committee appointed by the quarterly meeting in order to treat with our members who hold their fellowmen in bondage, in connection with the several meetings committees, now report that there has been considerable time spent in laboring with them in order to convince

Report of committee on slaves

---

[115]Min. Buckingham Mo. Mtg., 12—6—1779, 202.
[116]Min. Bucks Q. Mtg., 2 vols., 1684-1804. Newtown First Nat'l Bank.
[117]*Ibid.*, 6—27—1730.
[118]*Ibid.*
[119]*Ibid.*, 8—28—1766.
[120]*Ibid.*, 8—27—1772.   [121]*Ibid.*, 8—28—1777, 29.

them of the evil of the practice, which labors of love have been by some kindly received, and they have complied so far as to give those they had in bondage their liberty by instruments of writing . . . . but there are others who still persist in holding them as slaves, notwithstanding the repeated care and labor of Friends extended towards them.[122]

The next report made in the eleventh month of the year is substantially the same, several slaves having been "manumitted or set free," and, also, the defiant attitude being still present among some members.[123] The similarity of these reports continues till the very last years of the century, with however a few additions. At some time prior to 1795, not more than three years, there were established meetings for Negroes which were held at stated times, always under the direction of Friends.[124] In 1799 the quarterly meeting was able to report "no slaves among us" and that "some care" is extended to those set free.[125]

Very early, the meetings were urged to give their attention to the religious and school education of the negroes that were in their possession,[126] but a majority of the reports from meetings are to the effect that this did not receive satisfactory attention.[127] No evidence remains in any records to show that there was a separate school ever established for Negroes, and it is quite possible that there never was during the 18th century. The demands transmitted through Bucks Quarterly were not so strictly enforced in regard to education as in regard to liberation, and it is more than probable that it was in most cases determined by the individual conscience than by the group. In regard to forcing liberation by public opinion, there are many examples where individuals were singled out and threatened with ejection from the society if they refused their slaves freedom,[128] but there are few references to such action taken for failure to educate them; there are, however, occasional ones mentioned. Most references to their education were in the nature of advice, which doubtless was followed in many cases,[129] and disregarded in many more.

Sidenotes:
Meetings set up for Negroes

No mention made of separate school

Social approval given those who freed slaves

---

[122]Min. Bucks Q. Mtg., 8—28—1777, 29.   [123]*Ibid.*, 11—27—1777, 33.
[124]*Ibid.*, 8—27—1795.   [125]*Ibid.*, 2—28—1799, 289.
[126]Min. Falls Mo. Mtg., 2—2—1757.   *Ibid.*, 2—7—1758.
[127]*Ibid.*, 8-7-1771, 86; 8—5—1772, 105; 9—6—1780, 275; 8—6—1783, 350.
[128]*Ibid.*, 8—1—1781, 301; 3—2—1763; 2—4—1767; 7—2—1769.
[129]Min Buckingham Mo. Mtg., 11—2—1778; 181; 8—1762, 107.

In spite of the continuous exertions of the Friends' meetings to keep down the number of slaves purchased, and to increase the number of liberations among those already possessed by their members, it appears from an investigation of the matter made by Davis, that almost one-third of the total number of slaves in 1782 (Bucks County) were to be found in the townships Falls, Middletown, Lower and Upper Makefield, Bristol and Wrightstown, where the Quakers were most numerous.[130] The entire number of slaves registered in 1782 was five hundred and twenty, and this may be regarded as fairly accurate since failure to register them meant the loss of the slave.[131] The number registered in the townships where Baptists and Presbyterians were settled, Warwick, Warrington, New Britain, Newtown and Bedminster, was very small, while the German districts registered but thirty-two.[132]

Registration of 1782 showed large proportion of slaves in Quaker townships

The meetings constituting Western Quarterly Meeting (Chester County), Kennett, London Grove, and New Garden have very meagre references to slaves or slave holding up to about 1770. One of the monthly meetings, London Grove, was not established until 1792,[133] and between that date and 1800 made no reports of any consequence.

Early records of slave holding meagre

In 1770 Kennett Meeting's committee performed a general visit to all possessed of slaves and found there was not the desired willingness to manumit them which they had expected.[134] From the report made seven years later, we must judge the situation had not changed very considerably since we find one member signified to them that he did not incline to release his Negroes from bondage, nor did he know that ever he should.[135]

Visit performed to all salve holders

It does not, however, seem that the occasional stubborn brother had a discouraging effect on the rest of the meeting. In 1779 the records stated,

It is desired that Friends attend to the circumstances and the situation of such negroes as have been set free, that we may fully discharge our duty to them, by endeavoring to instruct them, both for their spiritual and temporal good. . . .[136]

---

[130]Davis, *Hist. Bucks Co.*, II, 297.
[131]*Ibid.*, 296.   [132]*Ibid.*, 297.
[133]Min. London Mo. Mtg. 1792, I (deposited at L. G. Mtg.).
[134]Min. Kennett Mo. Mtg., 8—16—1770—439.
[135]*Ibid.*, 10—16—1777, 619.   [136]*Ibid.*, 1—14—1779, 658.

A committee of three men was immediately appointed to perform the service. This work with committees continued constantly, with the result that nine years later (1889) the meeting reported "none held as slaves amongst us" and that attention was given to education.[137]   The registration of 1780 showed only three held as slaves in the whole township.[138]

New Garden

In New Garden attention was early called to the Negroes,[139] and a committee appointed then, reported in 1781 that most of them were living among Friends and were generally well provided for.[140]   That committee was released,[141] and a new one reported in 1785 the following state of affairs:

Most Negroes reported able to read and write

> We have paid some attention to the case of free negroes, and find there are but few amongst us, most of whom we have visited where they reside. . . .   They are generally well provided for with the necessaries of life and some care ta'en of their religious education, in which we believe there may be an improvement.   We also inspected their school education and find most of them can read and some write.[142]

In 1789 one case of holding a slave came before the meeting, but at its direction a writ of manumission was immediately secured for the same.[143]   The registration in 1780 for New Garden township returned one slave only, held by a Scotchman.[144]

Uwchlan

Uwchlan Monthly Meeting (Caln Quarterly), as early as 1765, received a report from a delegation sent from the quarterly meeting stating it as their opinion that Friends ought to inspect into the care which Friends who had Negroes, extended toward them with regard to their education.[145]   A committee was accordingly appointed by the monthly meeting to serve in that capacity.   How considerable was their activity in the interval elapsing between their appointment and their first formal report of conditions which was returned to the meeting in 1779, one cannot judge accurately.   We may judge from the report above mentioned that there was no

---

[137]Min. Kennett Mo. Mtg., 8—14—1788, 887.
[138]Futhey and Cope, 424.
[139]Min. New Garden Mo. Mtg., 12—5—1778, 419 (committee had been appointed in 1774).
[140]*Ibid.*, 5—5—1781, 108.
[141]*Ibid.*, 9—1—1781, 119.
[142]*Ibid.*, 8—6—1785, 256.   [143]*Ibid.*, 9—5—1789, 419.
[144]Futhey and Cope, *Hist. of Chester Co.*, 424.
[145]Min. Uwchlan Mo. Mtg., 3—1—1765, 66.

Negro school, for that race alone; it was perhaps not demanded by the numbers who would have been eligible.[146] It
appears the committee had visited all (Wilmington excepted)
who had been freed, and found all generally in a very satisfactory state. Some are reported not able to give their children
schooling, and for them aid is solicited;[147] for others advice is
requested to guide them in their outward affairs. The direction of the Negroes' education, as nearly as can be made out,
was of the most practical nature, laying emphasis on the
industrial side, at that time an apprentice type of education.[148]
The interest in the apprentice did not stop as soon as he was
placed, but continued, for it was customary to place him
with Friends, if possible, and the member of Friends was
responsible to his meeting for the fulfilment of his contract
with the apprenticed. The following extract from the Middletown records will serve to show the general regulation by
which the apprenticing was carried on among members of
the society.

> . . . . and his sonnes giving security to the orphans court, and to
> pay interest for the money that belongs to the said . . . . ever
> since the time it became due, and also the said Thomas do abide at
> Robert Heaton's house for his table and to be kept to school for a year,
> or so long as the Meeting may think fit.[149]

Sadsbury, 1782, reported they had visited the free Negroes,
who were situated nearly as before.[150] No statement was
given of the entire number within this locality, but five were
listed as having no trade.[151] It appears, however, in spite of
that fact, they were not dependent on the community for
support. One woman owned a house and lot, "her own purchase"; a man with family rented a small tenement; and the
other three worked as common laborers.[152]

The Bradford minutes (also of Caln Quarterly) devote
almost no space to the status of the Negro in their vicinity.

Marginal notes: No Negro school. Aid solicited to school poor Negroes. Sadsbury report on situation of Negroes.

---

[146]Min. Uwchlan Mo. Mtg., 9—9—1779, 65f.
[147]*Ibid.*
[148]*Ibid.*
[149]Min. Middletown Mo. Mtg., 1—7—1699, 113.
[150]Min. Sadsbury Mo. Mtg., 7—17—1782, 340.
[151]*Ibid.*
[152]*Ibid.*

Bradford
reported few
slaves

This may have been because there were few slaves there.   At the registration of slaves, compelled by law in 1780,[153] the townships of East and West Bradford returned none whatever.[154]

Concord
Quarterly

In the discussion of Concord Quarterly there will be material presented from Chester, Concord and Goshen.   In 1779 Chester Monthly Meeting reported they had made a visit to all freed Negroes, of whom it was said, some were quite poor and unable to school their children.[155]   The visiting committee recommended that the poor should be put out to trades and given schooling, and suggested

Poor
Negroes to
be put to
trades

that a subscription should be raised for that purpose.   The meeting was heartily in favor of this and at once appointed a committee to look after the subscriptions and their application.[156]   Two years later (1781) after a similar visitation by committee, it was reported that they had been advised of their temporal and religious duties, many

Negroes
sent to
books sent
among them

sent to school and books distributed among them.[157]   At these dates no special schools for Negroes were mentioned, and the date of their establishment is not found, but in 1785 the report of the committee on Negroes, requesting a new subscription for supporting Negro schools, indicated that there were special schools established for them.[158]

Concord

The situation at Concord Meeting was very similar to that of Chester, as appears by their report of 1779.   Following the customary visitation, it was stated that the visit was satisfactory in many places, but in some families were found small

8 children
reported of
school age
but not in
school

children, eight of whom were of school age, but whose parents were unable to school them.[159]   The meeting was asked to give its attention to the matter, but nothing was found in the minutes to indicate what they did further to remedy the matter.

Goshen

The Goshen Meeting seems from its answers to the queries in 1756 to be in a very satisfactory state with regard to slave-

---

[153]*Col. Rec.*, XII, 99; *Laws of Pa.*, III, 268–272.
[154]Futhey and Cope, 424.
[155]Min. Chester Mo. Mtg., 10—25—1779, 31.
[156]*Ibid.*
[157]*Ibid.*, 7—30—1781, 73f.
[158]*Ibid.*, 9—23—1785, 177.
[159]Min. Concord Mo. Mtg., 6—9—1779, 86.

holding, "none having been purchased of late years," though
they consider they are not careful enough in educating them
in Christian principles.[160] They were, however, careful to
deal individually with those few who were engaged in any
manner in holding slaves in bondage.[161] In 1758 the record
stated:

> Those few negroes amongst us we believe are provided with a suffi-
> ciency of food and clothing, but doubt some are too careless in affording
> them religious instruction.[162]

Four years later conditions were somewhat improved, and
their report stated:

> No purchase since our last account that we know of. Those amongst
> us who keep negro slaves, we believe afford them a sufficiency of food
> and clothing and endeavors are used with some to learn them to read.[163]

Endeavors
to teach
negroes to
read, re-
ported

If we read a little further the records for the same year, we
are informed that some were sent to school, supposedly to a
"White school" due to the small number of Negroes among
Friends.[164] From the above references, then, taken in connection with one of the second month, 1764, we are led to
infer that the education of the Negroes under Friends' care was
carried on in a school and not in the home, under individual
instructors, whoever might be able to do it. The reference
of 1764 stated "some are sent to school to learn to read."[165]

Negroes
sent to
school

Simultaneously with this care in their education, the meeting was working on each individual case, among the members,
to convince them of the propriety of the manumission practice. In 1776 Randel Mailin manumitted his Negro man
Peter Cuff, and produced his record of the same to the meeting to have it recorded on their books.[166] The next year
(1777) Nathan Hoop manumitted a Negro woman, 18 years
old, and her two mulatto boys as soon as they should become
21 years of age.[167] The following brief extract is illustrative
of the many cases where pressure was brought to bear in a
kindly way, to the end that this or that person might set
Negroes free.

Manumis-
sion con-
tinually
urged

---

[160]Min. Goshen Mo. Mtg., 10—18—1756.
[161]*Ibid.*, 7—18—1757.
[162]*Ibid.*, 7—17—1758.   [165]*Ibid.*, 2—10—1764.
[163]*Ibid.*, 2—5—1762.   [166]*Ibid.*, 4—5—1776.
[164]*Ibid.*, 8—6—1762.   [167]*Ibid.*, 3—7—1777.

Discipline
of members
guilty of
slave
dealing

Complaint is brought against Thomas Pennington for buying and selling a negro woman. Joseph Thomas and Randle Mailin are appointed to deal with him as our discipline directs.[168]

In 1778 the Goshen Meeting appointed a committee, Randle Mailin and Caleb Maris, to join with a committee appointed by the Quarterly Meeting (Concord) to advise together concerning the education of the Negroes.[169]   This is a very good indication that organized action was taken, educationally, and that it was not left to individual choice. In 1780 the monthly meeting reported to the yearly meeting

Schooling of
Negroes
under care

that its committee (the one formerly appointed) had been "advising Negroes" on their religious education and had their "schooling under care."[170]   The registry of slaves in 1780 showed thirteen as the full quota for Goshen township.[171]

Low return
in Quaker
townships
in 1780
registra-
tions

As a general rule very few were returned from the Quaker townships while the vast majority came from those of the Welsh (Charlestown, Tredyffrin and East Nantmeal) and the Scotch-Irish (Newtown, Londonderry, Oxford and East Nottingham.)[172]

Abington
Quarter

From the meeting records in the Abington Quarter there will be presented some of the material relating to Horsham, Byberry (not established a monthly meeting till 1810),[173] and Gwynedd, which may be taken as representative of that quarterly meeting.

Horsham
Monthly

Though there is scant evidence in the Horsham Monthly Meeting minutes to indicate what they did in reference to the Negroes' education, we are not left entirely in the dark.   The Horsham School Committee, which made a report of its own

Negroes
schooled at
expense of
school com-
mittee

after 1783, made occasional reference thereto, and it must be understood from these reports that the Negroes were schooled at the expense of the school committee.   The only proof of this statement, given in the records, is found in statements like the following:

---

[168]Min. Goshen Mo. Mtg., 7—10—1778.
[169]*Ibid.*, 12—11—1778.
[170]*Ibid.*, 8—11—1780.
[171]Futhey and Cope, 424.
[172]This statement is based on the results of G. Cope's study of local history.
[173]Bunting, *Recs.*, Mtg. Phila. Yr. Mtg., 24.

An account of Thomas Hallowell for schooling Griffith Camel's and negro Caesar's children was produced and considered, and the treasurer ordered to pay him grant given. That of Caesar's lies for inspection,[174]

This makes clear that cases of Negro schooling were taken before the same committee as cases of poor Whites and were investigated and disposed of in the same manner.

Byberry Preparative Meeting makes no reference during the early years to the status of the Negro in its limits. Martindale, in a *History of Byberry and Moreland*, states that slavery came into Byberry about 1721,[175] the slaves being employed by the more opulent class to do the roughest work. The inventory of a Friends' property (1727) showed that he possessed "one negro girl, £20, and one negro boy, £30."[176] Of their intervening history little is recorded, though the Negroes were set free by many members of Friends, and in 1779 the meeting authorized Silas Walmsley and William Walmsley to provide a suitable burying ground for the use of Negroes who had been freed.[177] What was done for their education is not known.

It is noticeable that in the earliest answers to the query concerning Negroes (about 1756) the majority of the monthly meetings usually answered in an offhand manner that they were "clear" or there were "none to be charged with that breech," or something to that effect. The writer believes these reports first sent in were perhaps made from only a general knowledge of the situation, and not the result of an exact knowledge of their members' practices. This statement is not capable of an exact proof, but the remarkable similarity in all the meeting records for the first few reports, certainly indicate that such was the case. Quite frequently, yes, in most cases, the "clear" reports are followed after a few months or years by statements that some are imported, a few held as slaves, or one Negro sold and similar reports. This was true in the case of Gwynedd. In 1756 the meeting reported "we have not to charge any,"[178] and three months following,

Marginal notes:
Byberry

Slaves in 1721

1727

Records not always to be relied upon

---

[174]Rec. Horsham School Com., 11—15—1793.
[175]Martindale, *Hist. of Byberry and Moreland*, 49.
[176]*Ibid.*, 50. (The sources used by Martindale are not found.)
[177]Min. Byberry Prep. Mtg., 9—15—1779.
[178]Min. Gwynedd Mo. Mtg., 4—25—1756, 215.

"Friends think themselves clear in this respect";[179] the nature of the wording in the last would imply it was based more on implicit faith than explicit judgment. Eleven years thereafter we have more definite reports, such as:

> . . . . clear of importing negroes; the few possessed by Friends are well used, their slavery excepted,[180] and none bought or sold that we know of; those that have them use them well as to the necessities of life and some are brought to meetings at times.[181]

From that time forward the reports made to the monthly meeting were very definite. In 1775 a report was brought in which purported to cover the entire compass of the meeting. It stated the number held, their status, and what was done for their benefit. It is interesting to note that a few enjoyed some educational opportunities, limited to be sure, the details of which are presented here, as they appeared in the minutes of the meeting.

Report on Negroes in 1775

We of the committee appointed by the Monthly Meeting to visit such of our members as are possessed of slaves, and detaining them in bondage, contrary . . . . visited all such of our members that are under that circumstance as we know of, which are eight in number, who are possessed of sixteen negroes and one mulatto, viz.: 1st possesses one negro girl about 17 years of age and appeared in a disposition rather to justify the practice of detaining her in bondage during life than otherwise. 2d, possesses five negroes one of which is a man about 35 years of age, who he said he intended to set free at the next quarter sessions. The other four—three boys and a girl, are young, whom he said he intended to set free as they came of age, the boys at 21 and the girl at 18, giving them learning to fit them for business. 3rd, two negroes, a man and a woman, the man about 30 years of age, who was in the possession of a Friend, lately deceased, now in his executors, who said he intended they should soon enjoy their liberty. 4th, possessor of three negroes, one a woman 20 years old, who he said he expected should have her liberty in a short time—the other two, a man and a woman about 20 years of age, both as we thought, incapable of freedom. 5th, possessor of 2 negroes, a woman about 32 years old, who he said should have her liberty, when she earned him thirty pounds. The girl about ten years old who he said is to be set free by his last will when she arrives at the age of 30 years. 6th. Possessor of two negroes, both women, one about 34, the other about 19 years old; the said Friend not in a capacity of giving any account of what might be done for them. 7th. Possessor of

---

[179]Min. Gwynedd Mo. Mtg., 7—27—1756, 164.

[180]*Ibid.*, 7—28—1767, 13.

[181]*Ibid.*, 7—26—1768, 40.

a mulatto girl about 11 years old, bound to him till she is 31, who he said he intended to set at liberty at the age of 21, with endeavors to learn her to read. 8th. Possessor of a negro girl about 17 years old, who her mistress said she intended to do the best she could by.[182]

In 1779 it is reported that the affairs of Negroes are still in the hands of the committee for that purpose, but that not much more has been accomplished than was last reported.[183] It would seem though that the committee was decidedly active in dealing with individual cases of discipline both at that time and in the years following. Especially did they urge first the freedom of the slave, and when this was refused, as it occasionally was, they did not hesitate to eject the recalcitrant member.[184] So effective was their service that by 1790 there were none held as slaves by Friends and in regard to their education they reported: "Some care and labor is extended towards the instruction and education of such Negroes as are under Friends' care."[185]

Members disciplined for failure to manumit slaves

It would be interesting to compare the Friends' own account of their activity with that of an outsider who merely looked on, but the writer has been unable to find any opinion on the subject by any contemporary, either through this investigation or from those made by others. Many, it is true, comment on their social and economic status but little mention is ever made of their education.[186]

The Warrington and Fairfax Quarterly Meeting (Baltimore Yearly Meeting) reported in 1776 that their Negroes were well taken care of, but their education was "much neglected."[187] Three years later they reported:

Warrington and Fairfax Quarterly

By the accounts now received it appears that the religious education of such negroes and their children as have been restored to freedom has been attended to and a visit performed to most of them to good satisfaction, and there appears to be a hopeful prospect that those who have been under their immediate care will comply with Friends' advice with respect to the school education. Some care has been taken therein.[188]

Some care taken in their education

[182]Min. Gwynedd Mo. Mtg., 8—27—1775, 202.
[183]*Ibid.*, 5—25—1779, 306.
[184]*Ibid.*, 8—26—1783, 172.
[185]*Ibid.*, 7—27—1790, 112.
[186]Kaln, P., *Travels into North America*, I, 390, 394.
[187]Min. Warrington and Fairfax Q. Mtg., 9-16-1776, 11.
[188]*Ibid.*, 9—20—1779, 73. (Warrington Meeting, in the County of York.)

ATTITUDE TOWARD THE INDIANS

The uncommon relation existing from the time of the first settlement of Penn's colony throughout the entire colonial history, is well known to every schoolboy; such relations, between any possibly antagonistic groups, have been without parallel in the history of this country. Applegarth, speaking of this happy relationship, states that the results of his study revealed but two instances in which Friends had been massacred by Indians, and these cases were entirely the results of misunderstanding.[189]

Friendly relation of Quakers and Indians

It is aside from the point to relate at length the means employed by Penn and the Quakers to cultivate the friendship of these people. Nothing was more forceful than his immediate association with, and travels among them, and the messages in which he explained that he and his people were one with them and that they were all the "Friends of Onas."

Indian affairs were considered in a rational manner and occupied much of the time of the Governor and Council. Instances of a solicitous interest in the Indians* are seen in the laws of 1701, forbidding the sale of rum to any but the chiefs, who should distribute it as they thought best,[190] and a still more restrictive law in 1722, which prohibited the sale of liquor to Indians. Of still more importance was the establishment of the principle that an abuse committed by an Indian towards the Whites must be adjusted by the Indian chief, not revenged by the Whites, which was given out in the instructions to colonists; and the converse stated later (1728) by the Governor, that if a White injured an Indian he should make complaint to the Whites, who would then punish the offense under their own laws.[191]

No rum to any but chieftain by law, 1701

Friends' ministers were also active in the missionary work among the Indians, which was first urged and practiced by

---

[189]Applegarth, *Quakers in Pa.*, Johns Hopkins Univ. Studies, VIII–IX, 56.
[190]*Col. Rec.* II, 16.
[191]*Ibid.*, III, 356.
*Mention should also be made of the Friendly Ass'n for Preserving Peace with the Indians. For reference see Vol. 3, Penn's MS., relating to Indian Affairs, pp. 17–18, an address to Governor Dewey, 1757; also p. 89, an address to Proprietaries Thomas Penn and Richard Penn on same subject.

George Fox. Not only the numerous excursions of Penn, but also those of Thomas Story, Thomas Turner, Chalkley and others, evidence the ready spirit with which the commands of Fox were received.[192]   Besides the general missionary work and relief for the Indians, that from time to time is mentioned in the several meetings, there is no evidence that anything considerable towards a school education was attempted till the latter part of the century.   In a letter of the yearly meeting in 1796, it is stated that Friends are,

Work of missionaries

engaged in an undertaking to furnish them with some of the comforts of civilized life.   A fund is raising to supply the expense of instructing them in Agriculture, in mechanic arts, and in some useful branches of learning.[193]

Specific educational work

An excellent illustration of this movement towards the education of the Indian, and the naive friendly manner with which they made known their needs is found in the following communications, which are self-explanatory.

To the children of the friends of Onas, who first settled in Pennsylvania: Brothers, The request of Cornplanter, a chief of the Seneca Nation.

The Seneca Nation sees that the Great Spirit intends that they shall not continue to live by hunting, and they look around on every side, and inquire who it is that shall teach them what is best for them to do. Your fathers have dealt fairly and honestly with our fathers, and they have charged us to remember it; and we think it right to tell you that we wish our children to be taught the same principles by which your fathers were guided in their councils.

The Indians request aid

Brothers, we have too little wisdom among us, we cannot teach our children what we perceive their situation requires them to know, and we therefore ask you to instruct some of them; we wish them to be instructed to read and write, and such other things as you teach your own children; and especially teach them to love peace.

Brothers, we desire of you to take under your care two Seneca boys, and teach them as your own; and in order that they may be satisfied to remain with you, and be easy in their minds, that you will take with them the son of our interpreter, and teach him according to his desire.

Brothers, you know it is not in our power to pay you for the education of these three boys; and therefore you must, if you do this thing, look up to God for your reward.

Brothers, You will consider of this request, and let us know what you determine to do.   If your hearts are inclined toward us, and you will

---

[192]Bowden, II, 70.
[193]London Yr. Mtg. Epistles, 1795, 487.

afford our nation this great advantage, I will send my son as one of the boys to receive your instruction, at the time which you shall appoint.[194]

	Cornplanter	his
Signed 2–10–1791	X	
In presence of Joseph Nichols.		mark

To Cornplanter, The Seneca Chief:

His request granted

The written message of Cornplanter, dated at Philadelphia, on the 10th of February last, was not received by us until some weeks after. His request that we would take under our care two Seneca boys, one of them his own son, accompanied with the son of Joseph Nicholson, we have considered, and do agree to receive them when they can conveniently be sent to us; intending they shall be treated with care and kindness and instructed in reading, writing and husbandry as the other children of our Friends are taught; the Governor of Pennsylvania, when informed of this proposal, having expressed his approbation thereof, as did General Knox.[195]

Signed on behalf, and by appointment of a meeting of the representatives, of the said people, on the second day of the sixth month, called June, 1791. By several Friends.

Committee appointed by yearly meeting in 1795

Oneidas and Tuscaroras willing to accept assistance

School established

In 1795 a committee was appointed by the Yearly Meeting of Pennsylvania and New Jersey for the promotion and improvement of the Indian natives.[196] Their first act was to attempt to learn the Indian's attitude towards such an activity on the part of Friends.[197] Accordingly a circular letter was sent out to the various neighboring tribes, and also accompanied by a letter from the secretary of state, signifying the government's coöperation and sanction.[198] From the responses it appeared that only the Oneidas and part of the Tuscaroras were willing to accept any assistance, so the following summer of 1796, three Friends, approved by the committee, were sent and settled among the Oneidas.   In the winter of 1796 they established a school, continued for several years, and taught by an Indian who had been educated in New England.[199]   The Indians were found, at first, to be quite averse to any continuous labor, and it was necessary fo the Friends to establish themselves, and to improve a piece of land, in the hope that the Indians would see the results and

---

[194]Conduct of the Society of Friends towards Indians, 98–99.
[195]*Ibid.*
[196]A brief account of the Committee's proceedings (pub. in Phila.), 7.
[197]*Ibid.*
[198]*Ibid.*
[199]*Ibid.*

become interested in the process. This seems to have worked quite satisfactorily, for in 1799 they report that the Indians have improved some lands and "sowed them with wheat."[200] The various occupations mentioned as being taught the boys were: smith work, tilling soil, sewing, the preparation of lumber in sawmills, and the details included therein. The girls were frequently instructed in spinning, knitting, sewing, school learning, etc.[201]

Occupations taught

At this time (1799) the Oneidas became distrustful of the motives of those in charge of the settlement, thinking that such an investment in implements and the permanent nature of the farms laid out, indicated an intention to seek after a time to take their territory from them. The settlers became aware of this feeling and to prove their good faith, decided to leave the settlement with all implements and improvements in sole charge of the natives. The preparations to leave were accomplished in a friendly conference, held in September, 1799.[202] The success of this work, for the Oneidas, had been watched by the Seneca tribes, and resulted in an interest in the same thing, culminating in the letters requesting the Friends' assistance, which have already been presented.[203]

Indians distrustful

SUMMARY

Though slavery had fixed itself, very early, as an institution in Pennsylvania, it was not destined to continue its growth unmolested. Some of the chief factors working against it were: (1) The scruples of Friends, and other sects, (2) the Germans and (3) the opposition of White labor. Restrictive legislation was passed in 1700, 1705 and 1712, placing an ever increasing duty upon those imported. Gradual abolition was provided for by statutes of 1780 and 1788. Socially and economically the condition of the Negro in Pennsylvania was more desirable than in states of her latitude and further south.

Slavery in Pennsylvania

To three Quakers, opposed to Negro slavery, some brief attention is given. Their expressions also indicate a solici-

---

[200]Conduct of the Society of Friends towards Indians, 10.
[201]*Ibid.*, 8, 9, 10.
[202]*Ibid.*, 11. [203]See page 263.

tous interest in the education of the Indian. Their influence

Quaker Antagonists of Slavery

was extended by missionary journeys, speaking in public, and numerous pamphlets published on that subject. This work was by no means limited to the Quakers. Slavery was denounced as impracticable, unjust and inconsistent with the ideals of a free nation.

The Quaker organization against slavery

(1) Not only individual leaders, but also the organized meetings arrayed themselves to fight against slavery. The first memorial to that effect was on the part of Germantown Meeting in 1688. This was sent to the Quarterly Meeting of Philadelphia, but at that date they took no action in regard to it. In 1727 the Philadelphia Yearly Meeting's advisers censured the practice of trading in slaves. A more extensive warning and reproof was administered in 1758. Throughout the early half of the century efforts were made to secure favor for the slaves' freedom; it was necessary that in some measure that should come first.

Schools for Negroes

(2) After the active campaign for freedom, the interest in education increased, and, in the last half of the century, there are frequent statements of that nature in records of meetings. Separate schools were established for them where possible. One in Philadelphia was set up by the meeting, though in large measure due to the active personal influence of Benezet, who, after 1782, taught in the school till his death. Moses Patterson was the first teacher; after 1786 two schools are always mentioned in reports. In the five years preceding 1782 it is estimated that two hundred and fifty Negroes attended the school.

In country and small towns

Some attention is given to the Negroes and their education, or lack of it, in each of the meetings. The care of this subject in those meetings was in the charge of a committee, the general character of whose duties was indicated on page 247. The support of the Negro schools and the education of the poor children was similar to that of other schools.[204] Reports on the progress in freeing, supporting, and educating the Negro, were required by their superior meetings.

---

[204]No summary is given of conditions in each of the meetings; if desired, see in index, "negro education."

The relations between Friends and Indians were most cordial from the beginning. Though their education was preached early by missionaries and practised in a smaller way, little organized effort was made until 1795. In that year the yearly assembly took the necessary steps to establish schools among neighboring tribes, the first mentioned being for the Oneidas. The desire of the Indian for aid in these matters is indicated by the quoted letter of Cornplanter, the Seneca chief.

Education of
Indians

CHAPTER XII

CONCLUSION

The society, established by George Fox, near the middle of the seventeenth century, increased rapidly in numbers, due very largely to the efforts of its founder and the services of the men whom he associated with him in his work. This influence was extended by means of (1) journeys made to foreign parts; (2) letters; and (3) preaching out of doors to all who would listen. Fox, from the first, was interested in education, particularly moral and practical, and recommended the establishment of several schools. He was primarily interested in (1) moral training; (2) religious instruction; and (3) in education of a practical sort which would fit every individual to earn a livelihood. These ends which he strove for were likewise accepted as worthy to be achieved, and consciously striven for by the society in its organized meetings. This organization of meetings itself was devised by Fox and regularly constituted in various parts before the time of his death. It consisted of yearly, quarterly, monthly, and particular meetings, whose relations were well defined. The functions of the first were general and directive; those of the last were particular and effective. The chief weakness, already pointed out in previous chapters, was the lack of compulsory power in the yearly meeting. Its recommendations gained results, but might be neglected in communities desiring to do so.

An organization, of itself, performs nothing. Its accomplishments depend on men who have purposes, and the determination and ability to execute them. A considerable number of such men were members of Friends, and expressed themselves definitely on education. Such leaders as Penn, Fothergill, Fox, Banks, Chalkley, Crisp, Crouch, Pastorius, Benezet and others as important, were responsible for its

(268)

educational guidance and in the end, accomplishments. From a study of their expressions it appears that the criticisms, concerning the Quakers' antipathy to education, are without foundation, and arose ,for the most part, from their statement that a *classical education* was *not essential for a minister*. The life and the education of most of them attest the fact that they sought a higher education for themselves and promoted it for others. Not only for their own society, but for the rich and poor of others, were efforts made to establish schools. The education of Indians and Negroes was similarly urged both on the part of individuals and the organization. The tangible results of their efforts in this regard were seen in the various local meetings.

Quaker antipathy to education appears unfounded

Education of Negroes and Indians urged and effected

In the establishment of schools, the direction lay in the hands of the yearly meeting. Philadelphia Yearly Meeting's advices on that subject, for the first half century, were very general in nature and seemingly of little import to the various lower meetings. A development is noticed, however, toward a definite plan for schools to be established. The advices of 1746 and continuing thereafter, 1750, 1751, 1753, 1755, 1778, and following, are definite in their ideas as to what should be done, and the persistency with which they were urged in the meetings, where all school affairs came to be attended to by committees, seems to have effected tangible results. Committee reports on educational conditions increased greatly in definiteness after 1777, which allows a better estimate to be made of what was done. From such reports it is estimated that by the end of the century there were sixty or seventy schools established "according to direction" given by the yearly meeting. Many others are reported in various meetings, which did not measure up in any great degree to the standards set.

Schools established

School affairs in care of committees

Number of schools in Pennsylvania

These standards[1] (stated elsewhere in this work) demanded a high moral quality in masters and mistresses, as well as training in the subjects to be taught. From a study of the manuscript records and newspapers it appears that the moral standards, met by Quaker masters, were as high, and, in Philadelphia, perhaps higher than those of the other private

The Master

---

[1]The digest of the standards to be attained may be seen on pages 172f.

school masters.   The cases of open lawlessness are at least
more numerous in the latter case.   The degree of preparation
for teaching ranged from the highest, the best college trained
men of the day, to the lowest, those who possessed a most
elementary education.

Curriculum
similar to
that in
private
schools

The opportunities offered for study, both in the lower and
in the Classical School, were at all times equal at least to those
of the other schools of the day.

The Quakers established no system of *public schools*,
though they were called such quite frequently.   As public
school sentiment grew, and the Quaker schools correspondingly
declined in many places, they often were taken over as public
schools.   In that sense they were, truly enough, the foundation of public schools.   Education was free to the poor; in a
few cases the funds might be applied to lower the rates paid
by the regular pay scholars, but such were exceptional.

No free
public
schools

Number of
schools
about 1750

In 1750 there were about fifty particular meetings in the
territory covered by this study; those were under the direction of seventeen monthly meetings.[2]   With the exception of
nine of them we know from their reports that they had
schools then, or established them in the period following 1750,
in which the increased activity and interest of the yearly
meeting brought the subject more fully to their notice.   From
the nature of the reports, it is often impossible to determine
the date of establishing such a school, and because of the
irregularity of reports it is not known how long a school may
have been in operation before reported.   For these reasons
any estimate such as made above is very unsatisfactory.

It is not to be understood that at the time above mentioned
the schools were in all cases "according to the plan" of the
yearly meeting.   Many reports have been quoted wherein
schools were mentioned which did not measure up to the
standards.[3]   Some lacked buildings, grounds, Friends as masters, masters' accommodations, and so forth.

Assuming the nine meetings, for which no schools were
reported in the minutes, did not have them, there were

[2]Bowden, II, 247 ff. (tables showing the particular monthly, and
quarterly meetings, etc.).
[3]See in index: Merion and Valley, for example.

about forty schools under control of the Quakers, who at that date constituted one-third of the entire population.[4] The population estimated by Oldmixon was about 100,000 in 1741.[5] Though the colony increased rapidly by immigration,[6] the Quaker increase was not proportionate to their numbers stated above.[7] In 1795 it is stated that the Episcopalians and Quakers together constituted but one-third of the whole population, which then numbered about 434,373.[8] The number of regularly established Quaker schools at that date was between sixty and seventy.

Quaker population one-third of total

Proportionate number of Quakers decreases

If in 1741 we estimate the number of school age children of Quaker parentage between six and seven thousand, which is probably a less number than there actually were, it is apparent that the schools *regularly established* were in no way adequate to the school population. The remainder were doubtless cared for in the frequently mentioned *mixed schools* and *neighborhood schools*, which are known to have been common. These were sometimes under partial control of the Quaker meetings. What proportion the number of Quaker schools bears to those established by other agencies is not known. No studies made up to the present time have attempted to estimate the number of schools established by all or particular agencies. Any comparison is impossible until such a study is made.

Number of regularly established schools inadequate for their population

---

[4]Bowden, II, 157.
[5]*Ibid.*, 156; quoted from Oldmixon, I, 304.
[6]6,200 new settlers came in 1729 (Bowden, II, 156).
[7]*Ibid.*, 157.
[8]Winterbotham, II, 438–439; also, census report, 1790.

BIBLIOGRAPHY

MANUSCRIPT SOURCES

Abington Monthly Meeting Minutes, 1682–1893, 10 vols. Abington Friends' Meeting House, Jenkintown,Pa.

Abington Monthly Meeting Minutes (Extracts from) 2 vols. H. S. P.

Abington Quarterly Meeting Minutes, 1786–1800, 1 vol. 15th & Race Streets, Phila., Pa.

A Collection of Christian and Brotherly Advices . . . . by the Yearly Meeting of Philadelphia and Burlington, 1 vol. Swarthmore Friends' Library.

Ancient Records of Philadelphia, collected by Wallace. H. S. P.

Bradford Monthly Meeting Minutes, 1737–1827, 8 vols. 142 North 16th Street, Phila., Pa.

Board of Trade Papers Proprieties, 1697–1776, vols. 2–24, transcribed 1901–1902.

Buckingham Monthly Meeting Minutes, 1720–1792, 3 vols. First National Bank, Newtown, Pa.

Buckingham Monthly Meeting Minutes (Extracts from), 1720–1803. H. S. P.

Bucks Quarterly Meeting Minutes, 1684–1804, 2 vols. First National Bank, Newtown, Pa.

Byberry Preparative Meeting Minutes, 1721–1824, 3 vols. 15th & Race Streets, Phila., Pa.

Chester Monthly Meeting Minutes, 1681–1802. (Minutes, 1721–1760 missing). Meeting House, Media, Pa.

Concord Monthly Meeting Minutes, 1684–1877, 7 vols. Meeting House, Concordville, Pa.

Concord Quarterly Meeting Minutes, 1683–1813, 1 vol. Meeting House, Media, Pa.

Darby Monthly Meeting Minutes, 1684–1807, 3 vols. Meeting House, Darby, Pa.

Exeter Monthly Meeting Minutes, 1737–1808, 3 vols. 15th & Race Streets, Phila., Pa.

Extracts, London Yearly Meeting, 1 vol. Property Bucks Quarterly Meeting, First National Bank, Newtown, Pa.

Falls Monthly Meeting Minutes, 1683–1718, 4 vols. First National Bank, Newtown, Pa.

Falls Monthly Meeting Minutes, 1683–1788, 3 vols. 142 North 16th Street, Phila., Pa.

Falls Preparative Meeting Minutes, irregular for years 1765–1800. First National Bank, Newtown, Pa.

Goshen Monthly Meeting Minutes, 1722–1807, 4 vols. 142 North 16th Street, Phila., Pa.

Gwynedd Monthly Meeting Minutes, 1714–1802, 5 vols. 142 North 16th Street, Phila., Pa.

Haverford Meeting Minutes, 1684–1686, 1 vol. 15th & Race Streets, Phila., Pa.

Horsham Monthly Meeting Minutes, 1782–1879, 5 vols. 15th & Race Streets, Phila., Pa.

Horsham Preparative Meeting Minutes, 1757–1881, 4 vols. 15th & Race Streets, Phila., Pa.

Horsham School Committee Minutes, 1792–1816, 1 vol. 15th & Race Streets, Phila., Pa.

Kennett Monthly Meeting Minutes, 1686–1808, 3 vols. Meeting House, London Grove, Pa.

Logan Papers and Letters, 45 vols. H. S. P.

London Grove Monthly Meeting Minutes, 1792–1807, 1 vol. Meeting House, London Grove, Pa.

Merion Monthly Meeting Minutes, 1693–1699, 1 vol. 15th & Race Streets, Phila., Pa.

Merion Preparative Meeting Minutes, 1702–1705, 1 vol. 15th & Race Streets, Phila., Pa.

Middletown Monthly Meeting Minutes, 1683–1861, 6 vols. 15th & Race Streets, Phila., Pa.

Middletown Monthly Meeting Minutes, 1683–1800, 2 vols. H. S. P. Collections.

Minutes of the Committee on Negro Education, 1797–1803, 1 vol. H. S. P.

New Garden Monthly Meeting Minutes, 1718–1790, 4 vols. (2d vol. missing). Orthodox Meeting House, West Grove, Pa.

Norris Family. *Letters, Papers, and Schoolbooks.* H. S. P.

Pastorius, F. D. *Letters and Papers,* 4 vols. H. S. P.

Pemberton. *Ms. Collections,* 70 vols. H. S. P.

Penn. *Letters and Papers, Private and Official and Indian Affairs,* 21 vols. H. S. P.

Penn Charter School: *Overseer's Minute Books,* 1712–1813, 3 vols., also additional loose papers, rules, advices, etc. Provident Life and Trust Building, Phila., Pa.

Philadelphia Monthly Meeting Minutes, 12 vols. 304 Arch Street, Phila., Pa.

Philadelphia Quarterly Meeting Minutes, 1682–1826, 5 vols. 304 Arch Street, Phila., Pa.

Philadelphia (and Burlington) Yearly Meeting Minutes, 2 vols. 304 Arch Street, Phila., Pa.

Proud, Robert. *Papers and Letters,* 3 boxes, also vol. of Mss. H. S. P.

Radnor Monthly Meeting Minutes, 1699–1803, 14 vols. (1704–1712 not found). 15th & Race Streets, Phila., Pa.

Richland Monthly Meeting Minutes, 1742–1806. 4 vols. Meeting House, Quakertown, Pa.
Richland School Committee Minutes, 1 vol. Meeting House, Quakertown, Pa.
Richland: Accounts of Jonathan Walton Fund, 1 vol. Meeting House, Quakertown, Pa.
Sadsbury Monthly Meeting Minutes, 1737–1824, 2 vols. 15th & Race Streets, Phila., Pa.
Uwchlan Monthly Meeting Minutes, 1763–1809, 3 vols. 142 North 16th Street, Phila., Pa.
Warrington Monthly Meeting Minutes (Extracts from), 1747–1856, 1 vol. H. S. P.
Warrington and Fairfax Quarterly Meeting Minutes, 1776–1787, 1 vol. H. S. P.
Western Quarterly Meeting Minutes, 1758–1818, 2 vols. Orthodox Meeting House, West Grove, Pa.
Westland Monthly Meeting Minutes, 1785–1865, 1 vol. H. S. P.
Wrightstown Monthly Meeting Minutes, 1734–1800, 2 vols. (first vol. not found). First National Bank, Newtown, Pa.

PRINTED SOURCES

A Brief Account of the Concern of the Yearly Meeting of Philadelphia in relation to the guarded religious education of their youth. . . . Phila., 1835.
Abolition, The Constitution of the Pennsylvania Society for the—of Slavery. . . . Phila., 1787.
Acts of Parliament relative to those Protestant Dissenters called Quakers from 1688. London, 1757.
Africans, The case of our fellow creatures, the oppressed Africans, respectfully recommended to the serious consideration of the Legislature of Great Britain by the people called Quakers (by A. Benezet), London, 1784.
BALL, GAWEN. Premonitory Extracts, selected from various authors of the Religious Society of Friends. N. P., 1819.
BANKS, JOHN A. A Journal of his Life, Labors and Travels. London, 1712.
BARCLAY, ROBERT. A Catechism and Confession of his Faith, N. P., 1673.
    Apology for the true Christian Divinity. London, 1678.
BELLERS, J. Proposals for raising a college of industry of all useful trades and husbandry . . . . London, 1818.
BENEZET, ANTHONY. Short Account of the People called Quakers. Phila., 1780.
    The Pennsylvania Spelling Book or Youth's Friendly Instructor. Dublin, 1800.
    Some observations on the situation, disposition and character of the Indian natives. Phila., 1784.

Notes on the Slave Trade, 1780, H. S. P.

Observations on the enslaving, importing, and purchasing of
negroes . . Germantown, 1760.

Brief Considerations on Slavery, and the Expediency of its Abolition. Burlington, N. J., 1773.

BESSE, JOSEPH. Edition of a collection of the works of William Penn.
London, 1726.

Collections of the Sufferings of Quakers. London, 1753.

BIDDLE, OWEN. A pamphlet of 52 pages on a plan for a boarding
school. Phila., 1790.

BUDD, THOMAS. Good Order established in Pennsylvania and New
Jersey in America. Phila., 1685.

BUGG, FRANCIS. The Quakers detected, their errors confuted. London,
1685.

CHALKLEY, THOMAS. A Collection of the works of . . . . in two
parts. Phila., 1749.

CHARTERS. William Penn's Charters of the Public Schools founded by
Charter in the town and county of Philadelphia 1701,
1708, 1711. Phila., No date.

CHESTERFIELD, LORD. Advice to his Son. Phila., 1781.

CHURCHMAN, JOHN. An Account of the Gosepl Labors and Christian
Experiences of. London, 1829.

CLARIDGE, R. Life and Posthumous Works of, collected by J. Besse.
London, 1726.

COLONIAL RECORDS OF PENNSYLVANIA, published by the State, 16
vols. Harrisburg and Phila., 1852–1853.

COLLECTIONS OF THE PROTESTANT HISTORICAL ASSOCIATION.

COMLY, JOHN and ISAAC. Friends' Miscellaney, 12 vols. Phila.,
1831–1839.

Cox, S. H. Quakerism not Christianity . . . Boston, 1833.

CRAWFORD, CHARLES. Observations on Negro Slavery. Phila., 1784.

CROUCH, WILLIAM. Posthuma Christiana or a collection of his works.
London, 1712.

DARUSMONT, F. W. Views of Society and Manners in the United
States, 1818–1820. London, 1821.

EARLY CHRISTIAN INSTRUCTION in form of a dialogue between mother
and a child. London, 1807.

EPISTLES FROM THE YEARLY MEETING IN LONDON, 1681–1817. London,
1818.

EXTRACTS FROM THE MINUTES AND ADVICES OF THE YEARLY MEETING
IN LONDON. London, 1802.

FISHER, SAMUEL. Testimony of Truth Exalted by the collected labors
of . . . N. P., 1679.

FOTHERGILL, SAMUEL. Discourses, Epistles and Letters. London, 1803.

FOX, GEORGE. Journal. 2 vols. London, 1852.

To all Magistrates, Teachers, Schoolmasters and People . . .
who teach your children the way of the heathen . . .
London, 1660.

A Primmer for the Doctors and Scholars of Europe. . . London, 1659.

A Warning to all Teachers of Children who are called Schoolmasters and Mistresses to Parents. London, 1657.

Fox, George and Hookes, Ellis. Instruction for Right Spelling, Reading and Writing . . . London, 1697.

Friend, The. A religious and Literary Journal published weekly at Philadelphia since 1827.

Friends' Library, The. 10 vols. Phila., 1837.

Friends' Year Book, 1917. Published by the Representative Committee of the Philadelphia Yearly Meeting. 15th & Race Streets.

Friends' Christian Doctrine and Practice and Discipline. London, 1861.

Fry, John. Alphabetical Extracts of all Annual Printed Epistles sent to the Quarterly Meeting in London. London, 1762.

Furly, Benjamin, Fox, George, and Stubbs, John. Battledore for Teachers and Professors to learn Singular and Plural. London, 1660.

Genealogical Society of Pennsylvania, Publications. Vols. 1–5, 1895–1910; other numbers to date. Phila.

Germantown, Extracts from Records of the Court held in 1691–1701. Phila., 1853.

Gough, John and James. A Practical Grammar of the English Tongue. Dublin, 1792.

Gough, John. Treatise of Arithmetic in Theory and Practice. Phila., 1788.

Grammar, Practical Syntax in English and French . . . . and intended chiefly for the use of the Society called Quakers. London, 1795.

Griffith, John. Journal of Life and Travels . . . London, 1779; Some Brief Remarks upon Sundry Important Subjects. London, 1768.

Hazard, Samuel. Editor, Register of Pennsylvania, 16 vols. Phila., 1828–1835.

Hicks, Elias. Journal of the Life and Religious Labors of Elias Hicks. New York, 1832.

Holme, Benjamin. Collection of Epistles and works of . . . . London, 1754.

Indians, A Brief Account of the Committee appointed in 1795 . . . . for promoting . . . . civilization of Indian Natives. Reprint, London, 1806.

Intelligencer, Friends. Published weekly at Philadelphia since 1844.

Kaln, Peter. Travels into North America, 3 vols., first vol., Warrington, 1770; second and third vols. London, 1771.

Keith, George. Journal of his Travels . . . . London, 1706. Standards of Quakers Examined; An Answer to the Apology of Robert Barclay. London, 1702.

LANCASTER, JOSEPH. Improvements in Education . . . . School at Borough Road. London, 1805.

LAWS OF THE COMMONWEALTH OF PENNSYLVANIA OF 1700–1802, 6 vols. Republished under the authority of the Legislature of Philadelphia. Phila., 1803.

LAWS OF DUKE OF YORK. Charters of William Penn and Laws of Pennsylvania, 1682–1700. London, 1805.

LESSONS FOR YOUTH, Selected for the use of schools. Phila., 1799.,

LONDON YEARLY MEETING EPISTLE. . . . Advice to Parents. . . . Care for the Education of their Children. . . . London, 1723.

MINUTES OF THE PROVINCIAL COUNCIL OF PENNSYLVANIA. 10 vols., published by the State, Philadelphia.

MISCELLANIES, Moral and Instructive in Verse and Prose for the Use of Schools. Phila., 1787.

MORE, HANNAH. Strictures on the Modern System of Female Education (in pamphlets published 1823, 2 vols.). London, 1823.

MURRAY, LINDLEY. An Abridgment of Murray's English Grammar . . . London, 1798.

OLDMIXON, JOHN. British Empire in America, 2 vols. London, 1708.

PARRISH, EDWARD. An Essay on Education in the Society of Friends. Phila., 1866.

PASTORIUS, F. D. Geographical Description of Pennsylvania, 1770. Translated by L. H. Weiss, Memoirs of H. S. P. Phila., 1850.

PENN, WILLIAM. Extract from the Advice to his Children. London, 1819.
A Brief Account of the Rise and Progress of the People called Quakers. London, 1748.

PENNINGTON, ISAAC. Works, 4 vols. London, 1784.

PENN'S LETTER TO HIS WIFE AND CHILDREN. London, 1822.

PENNSYLVANIA ARCHIVES. First Series, 12 vols. Edited by Samuel Hazard. Phila., 1852–1856.

PENNSYLVANIA ARCHIVES. Second Series, 19 vols. Edited by J. B. Linn and W. A. Egle. Harrisburg, 1878–1896.

PENNSYLVANIA ARCHIVES. Third Series, 30 vols. Edited by W. H. Egle. Harrisburg, 1894–1899.

PENNSYLVANIA GERMAN SOCIETY PROCEEDINGS. Published by the Society, 20 vols. Lancaster, 1891–1911.

PENNSYLVANIA HISTORICAL SOCIETY MEMOIRS, 14 vols. Phila., 1826–1895.

PENNSYLVANIA MAGAZINE OF HISTORY, 39 vols. Published by the H. S. P., Phila., 1877–1915

PENNY, NORMAN. The Journal of George Fox. University Press. Cambridge, 1911.

PHIPPS, JOSEPH. Original and Present State of Man . . . Trenton, 1793.

PIONEER, DER DEUTSCHE. Erinnerungen aus dem Pioneer-Leben der Deutschen in Amerika. 18 vols. Cincinnati, 1869–1887.

PRITTLE, PRATTLE, or a familiar discourse on the I, thou, he or she, we, ye, or you etc. . . by a Lover of the Truth. London, 1752.

PROTESTANT EPISCOPAL HISTORICAL SOCIETY PUBLICATIONS, Vols. 1 and 2. 1915.

PROUD, ROBERT. History of Pennsylvania, 2 vols. Phila., 1877.

PURVER, ANTHONY. Counsel to Friends' Children on Education, by J. Freame, with . . . . poems. London, 1799.

RELIGIOUS INSTRUCTION IN OUR SCHOOLS. A letter issued by an executive of the Friends' Guild of Teachers, No. 9, in a volume of pamphlets. York, No date.

RUTTY, JOHN and WIGHT, THOMAS. History of Quakers in Ireland. London, 1811.

SCOTT, JOB. Journal of the Life, Travels and Gospel Labors . . . . New York, 1797.

SOME ADVICE IN THE YEARLY MEETING'S EPISTLE, 1709, concerning the education of children . . . . London, 1710.

STANTON, DANIEL. Journal of his Life, Travels and Gospel Labors. Phila., 1772.

STATUTES AT LARGE OF PENNSYLVANIA. Compiled by J. T. Mitchell and Henry Flanders. Harrisburg, 1896–1909.

TRACTS ON MORAL AND RELIGIOUS SUBJECTS. London, 1823.

TUKE, HENRY. Works. York, 1813.

TUKE, SAMUEL. Principles of Religion as professed by the Society of Quakers. London, 1852.

VAUX, ROBERT. Memoirs of Anthony Benezet. Phila. 1817.

VOTES AND PROCEEDINGS OF THE HOUSE OF REPRESENTATIVES OF THE PROVINCE OF PENNSYLVANIA, 1682–1776. Phila., 1752–1776.

WESCOTT, THOMPSON. History of Philadelphia, 1609–1829 (made up of cuttings from the Sunday Dispatch). Phila., 1867–1884.

WIGHAM, JOHN. Christian Instruction in a discourse between a mother and her daughter. Phila., No date.

WINTERBOTHAM, W. An historical and geographical, commercial and philosophical view of the American United States, 4 vols. London, 1795.

WOOLMAN, JOHN. Serious Considerations on Subjects of Importance, London, 1773; Works. Phila., 1806; The Journal of . . . . Introduction by J. S. Whittier. London, 1903.

NEWSPAPERS

Pennsylvania Gazaette. Published by B. Franklin, beginning 1729; incomplete files.

The American Weekly Mercury. Published by William Bradford, beginning 1719; incomplete files.

The Freeman's Journal or North American Intelligencer. Incomplete files from 1781–1787.

The Pennsylvania Evening Post. Incomplete files from 1775–1781.

The Pennsylvania Journal and Weekly Advertiser. Incomplete files between 1742 and 1788.

The Pennsylvania Packet or General Advertiser. Incomplete files from 1771–1800.

The Pennsylvania Chronicle. Incomplete files from 1767–1774.

NOTE: The newspapers above mentioned were examined in so far as the rather incomplete files at the New York Public Library and the library of the Pennsylvania Historical Society permitted. Though the files of neither were complete, the seven taken together cover the period studied very well. School advertisements and occasional anonymous articles on education are the chief items they offer, which are of value.

SECONDARY MATERIALS

A Brief Sketch of Schools for Blacks and their descendants established by the Religious Society of Friends in 1770. Phila., 1867.

APPLEGARTH, A. C. Quakers in Pennsylvania. Johns Hopkins University Studies. Baltimore, 1892.

ASHMEAD, H. G. History of Delaware County, Pennsylvania. Phila., 1884.

ASHMEAD, H. G., and JOHNSON, W. S. Historical Sketch of Chester on Delaware. Chester, 1883.

AYTON. History of Great Ayton School, published for the Jubilee Committee. Middlebrough, 1891.

BEAN, THEODORE W. History of Montgomery County. Phila., 1884.

BALDERSTON, G. W. Historical Sketch of Falls, Bucks County, Pennsylvania. Phila., 1882.

BOWDEN, JAMES. History of Friends in America, 2 vols. London, 1884.

BOWEN, DANIEL. A History of Philadelphia to 1837. Phila., 1839.

BRAILSFORD, M. R. Quaker Women, 1650–1690. London, 1915.

BUCK, WM. J. History of Bucks County. Doylestown, 1855; History of Montgomery County within the Schuylkill Valley. Norristown, 1859.

BUNTING, MORGAN. A List of Records of the Meetings constituting the Philadelphia Yearly Meeting. Phila., 1906.

CLARKSON, THOMAS. Memoirs of the Private and Public Life of William Penn. London, 1813.

CLARKSON, THOMAS. Portraiture of Quakerism, 3 vols. N. Y., 1806.

COMLY, ISAAC. Sketches of the History of Byberry, in the Memoirs of the Pennsylvania Historical Society, vol. 2. Phila., 1827.

COPE, G. and FUTHEY, JOHN. History of Chester County. Phila., 1881.

DARBY. Proceedings Centennial Anniversary Friends Meeting House. Darby, Pennsylvania, 1905.

DAVIS, W. W. H. History of Bucks County, Pennsylvania. Doylestown, 1876.

DEWEY, D. R. Financial History of the United States. New York, 1912.

DEWEES, W. W. A Centennial History of Westtown Boarding School from 1799 to 1899. Phila., 1899.

ELLIS, FRANKLIN and EVANS, S.   History of Lancaster County, Pennsylvania.   Phila., 1883.

FISHER, GEORGE S.   The Making of Pennsylvania.   Phila., 1898.

FISKE, JOHN.   The Dutch and Quaker Colonies in America, 2 vols. Boston, 1899.

GERMANTOWN, History consisting of papers read before the Site and Relic Society of Germantown.   Germantown, 1915.

GERMANTOWN, Old and New, *Lippincott's Magazine*, Feb., 1884.

GLENN, THOMAS ALLEN.   Merion in the Welsh Tract.   Norristown, 1896.

GOUGH, JOHN and SEWELL, WILLIAM.   A History of the People called Quakers . . . from Works of Sewell, 2 vols. London, 1799.

GOUGH, JOHN.   History of the Quakers, 4 vols.   Dublin, 1789.

GREEN, JOHN R.   A Short History of the English People. 4 vols. New York, 1898.

GUMMERE, A. M.   The Quaker in the Forum.   Phila., 1910.

HAVERFORD.   A History of Haverford College.   Phila., 1892.

HAZARD, SAMUEL.   Annals of Pennsylvania, 1609–1682.   Phila., 1850.

HEATWOLE, C. J.   History of Education in Virginia.   New York, 1916.

HILDEBURN, CHAS. R.   A Century of Printing, The Issues of the Press of Pennsylvania, 1685–1784, 2 vols.   Phila., 1885.

HISTORICAL SKETCHES—A Collection of Papers prepared for the Historical Society of Montgomery County.   Norristown, 1900.

HISTORY OF THE ASSOCIATIONS OF FRIENDS FOR THE FREE INSTRUCTION OF THE ADULT COLORED PERSONS IN PHILADELPHIA.   Published by direction of the Association.   Phila., 1890.

HOBSON, F. G.   Addresses on Local History, Early Schools and School Teachers.   1898.

HOLDER, CHAS. F.   The Quakers in Great Britain and America. New York, 1913.

INDIANS—Some Account of the Conduct . . . . of Friends towards the Indian Tribes, to 1843.   London, 1844.

JANNEY, SAMUEL M.   The Life of William Penn, with selections from his correspondence and autobiography.   Phila., 1852.
History of the Society of Friends from its rise to 1828, 4 vols. Phila., 1859–61.
Life of George Fox.   Phila., 1856.

JENKINS, HOWARD M.   Historical Collections of Gwynedd.   Phila., 1884; Memorial of the City of Philadelphia from its first settlement to the year 1895, 2 vols., edited by Young.   New York, 1895.

JONES, R. M., assisted by ISAAC SHARPLESS, and GUMMERE, A. M. Quakers in American Colonies.   London, 1911.

JORDON, JOHN W.   Colonial Families of Philadelphia, 2 vols.   New York and London, 1911.

JORDAN, JOHN W.   A History of Delaware County, Pennsylvania. 3 vols.   New York, 1914.

KEYSER, NAAMAN H. Old Historic Germantown (an address before the Pennsylvania German Society, 14th Annual Meeting). Lancaster, 1906.

Old Germantown. Germantown, 1907.

KNIGHT, FRANCIS A. History of Sidcot School. London, 1908.

LEARNED, MARION D. The Life of Francis Daniel Pastorius. Phila., 1908.

LEVICK, J. J. Early Friends and their Services in America. Phila., 1883.

MAGILL, EDWARD H., Educational Institutions in the Society of Friends. Chicago, 1893.

MARTINDALE, J. C. A History of the Townships of Byberry and Moreland. Phila., 1867

MERION. Bicentennial Anniversary of the Friends Meetinghouse at Merion, Pa. Phila., 1895.

MICHENER, EZRA. A Retrospect of Early Quakerism. Phila., 1860.

MOMBERT, J. I. Authentic History of Lancaster County. Lancaster, 1869.

MONTGOMERY, M. L. History of Berks County. Phila., 1886.

MOON, ALPHEUS WILBERFORCE. Early Quaker Education in New Jersey (Master's Ms. dissertation in Columbia University), 1905.

MYERS, ALBERT COOK. Immigration of the Irish Quakers into Pennsylvania, 1682–1751. Swarthmore, 1902.

Sally Wister's Journal. Phila., 1902.

Hannah Logan's Courtship. Phila., 1904.

Quaker Arrivals at Philadelphia. Phila., 1902.

NODAL, JOHN H. Bibliography . . . of Ackworth School. Manchester, 1899.

OBERHOLTZER, ELLIS P. The Literary History of Philadelphia. Phila., 1906; Philadelphia, A History of the City and its People, 4 vols. Phila., 1911.

PENNYPACKER, HON. S. W. The Settlement of Germantown. Phila., 1899.

PROWELL, GEORGE R. History of York County, Pa., 2 vols. Chicago, 1907.

SEIDENSTICKER, OSWALD. Die erste deutsche Einwanderung in Amerika und die Gründung von Germantown im Jahre 1683. Phila., 1883.

SEWELL, WILLIAM. History of Friends, 2 vols. London, 1811.

SHARPLESS, ISAAC. Two Centuries of Pennsylvania History. Phila., 1900.

SHEPHERD, W. R. History of Proprietary Government in Pennsylvania. New York, 1896.

SHORE, W. T. John Woolman, His Life and Our Times. London, 1913.

SIMPSON, HENRY. Lives of Eminent Philadelphians now Deceased. Phila., 1859.

SMITH, C. H. Mennonites of America. Scottsdale, Pa., 1909.

SMITH, H. W. Life of W. Smith. Phila., 1877.

SMITH, GEORGE.   History of Delaware County.   Phila., 1862.

SUMMARY OF THE HISTORY, DOCTRINES, AND DISCIPLINE OF FRIENDS. London, 1790.

TAYLOR, CHRISTOPHER.   Account of Waltham Abbey School.   Phila., 1797.

THOMAS, A. C. and THOMAS, R. H.   A History of the Friends in America. Phila., 1905.

THOMAS, GABRIEL.   Historical and Geographical Account of the Province and Country of Pennsylvania and of West Jersey. London, 1698.

THOMPSON, HENRY.   A History of Ackworth School.   London, 1879.

TOTAH, K. A.   The Friends Secondary Schools in the United States (Master's Ms. dissertation at Teachers College), 1912.

TRAILL, HENRY D., editor.   Social England, 6 vols.   London and New York, 1909.

TURNER, E. R.   Negro in Pennsylvania, American Historical Association Publications.   Washington, 1911.

VAUX, ROBERT.   Memoirs of Benjamin Lay and Ralph Sandiford. Phila., 1815.

WATSON, J.   Account of the First Settlement of the Townships of Buckingham and Solebury.   H. S. P. Memoirs, Vol. I, pp. 285–319.

WATSON, J. F.   Annals of Philadelphia and Pennsylvania, 3 vols. Phila., 1887.

WICK, B. L.   The Amish Mennonites.   Iowa City, 1894.

WICKERSHAM, JAMES PYLE.   A History of Education in Pennsylvania, Private, Public, Elementary and Higher.   Lancaster, 1886.

WOODSON, C. G.   Education of the Negro before 1861.   New York and London, 1915.

WRIGHT, RICHARD R.   The Negro in Pennsylvania.   Phila., 1912.

WRIGHT, PAUL W.   Educational Work in New York Yearly Meeting of Friends prior to 1860.   (Master's Ms. dissertation at Teachers College, Columbia University) N. P., 1913.

ABBREVIATIONS

Am. Wk. Mer.—*American Weekly Mercury.*
Col. Rec.—*Colonial Records of Pennsylvania.*
G. S. P. P.—*Genealogical Society Publications of Pennsylvania.*
H. S. P.—*Historical Society of Pennsylvania.*
Min. Mo. Mtg.—*Minutes of the monthly meeting.*
Min. Prep. Mtg.—*Minutes of the preparative meeting.*
Pa. Gaz.—*Pennsylvania Gazette.*
Pa. Ger. Soc.—*Pennsylvania German Society.*
Pa. Mag. of Hist.—*Pennsylvania Magazine of History.*
P. C. S. M.—*Penn Charter School Minutes.*
Q. Mtg.—*Quarterly meeting.*
Yr. Mtg.—*Yearly meeting.*
Wk. Advt.—*Weekly Advertiser.*

INDEX

Abington, school land, 106; school, 106f.
Ackworth School, 22.
Aims of educ., 7ff., 36ff., 161, 268.
Apprenticeship educ., recommended, 9; 85, 86, 159, 206.
Attendance, 180, 185; in Negro School, 243f.

Baptists, 5.
Barclay, on educ., 31.
Benezet, on educ., 31ff.; employed in Phila., 57–58; 216ff.; on keeping slaves, 235f.
Biddle, 73.
Birmingham, 131, 134, 163.
Blue Hill, 151.
Books, distributed, 24; used in schools, 109, 142, 193ff.
Bradford, 123f.; 134, 136ff.
Birstol, school, 88.
Buckingham, school, 95ff.
Budd, educ. scheme of, 36ff.
Buildings and grounds, 65ff.; interior of, 67ff.
Byberry, school, 74ff.; report, 76f.; schoolmasters at, 224f.

Chester, 148ff., 151.
Chichester, 163.
Children, apprenticeship of, 159; cared for by meetings, 122f., 141.
Classic languages, 11, 59, 71; not *necessary* for ministers, 31, 35.
Clerkenwell, school at, 22.
Committees, on schools, functions, 80, 168, 141, 143; school coms. appointed, 111, 116, 118.
Concord, 162ff.
Cox, criticism by, 26ff.
Crouch, on educ., 34f.
Curriculum, 190ff., 215, 270; Classical School, 196; English School, 197; Negro School, 192; Latin and Greek, 59, 71; letter writing, 191; mathematics, 30, 71f.; spelling, 192; subjects recommended, 29ff.

Darby, 23f., 154ff.
Discipline, 186, 223.

East Bradford, 131.
East Caln, 137f.
Education, before the Quakers, 147; moral, 86; for Negro and Indian, 233ff., 269; practical, by apprenticeship, 9, 10; provided in Frame of Government, 42; public, recommended, 30; recommended by yr. mtg., 20ff., 109, 123, 174.
English School, masters of, 222ff.
Evening Schools, 187.
Exeter, 79ff.

Falls, 86ff.
Fox, sketch of life, 2ff.; conclusions of, 4; educ'l creed, 7ff.; recommended schs., 10; educ. of ministers, 11f.; mo. mtgs. recommended, 16.
Free Schools, 180.

Germantown, 77ff.
Girls' School, 70, 213, 217.
Goshen, 130ff.
Gwynedd, 110, 113.

Haverford, 162.
Horsham, 114ff.

Indians, educ. recommended, 8, 12, 37, 269; friendly relation with, 262; issue of rum to, 262; missionaries among, 263; aid requested by, 263; educ'l. work among, 263f.; occupations taught, 265.
Inner light, 2, 4, 7, 13.

Kennett, 122f.; discontinued, 124; 137, 169f.

Lampeter, 142.
Land, for school use, 81, 87ff., 106, 125, 131f., 148f., 176f.
Latin School, masters of, 220ff.
Legacies: Carter, 74, 107f.; Wade, Lineham and Richards, 63; Bryner and Baldwin, 90; Harker, 93, 95; Holcomb, 95; Abbitt, Buckman and Twining, 101; Roberts and Walton, 103; Keen and Hoskins,

148; Taylor and Hall, 149; Turner 151f.; Evans, 152; Meed, 153; Blunston, 154; Lobb, 157; Yarnall, 165; Barnes, 106f.; under care of trustees, 75, 107f.
Literature, used in meetings, 199ff.
London, yearly mtg. established, 17; advices on educ., 172f.
London Grove, 140.

Maiden Creek, 80f.
Makefield, 88.
Meetings, established, 15f., 79, 85, 105, 122, 147.
Mennonites, 4f.
Merion and Valley, 114.
Methods, 197, 199.
Middletown, 92ff., 149f., 151.
Montgomery Township, 112.
Monthly meeting, function, 19, 169, 175.
Morristown, 111.

Nantmeal, 139f.
Negro, educ. recommended, 8, 12, 37, 269; manumission, 252, 257, 261; educ. of —— in Phila., 239–246; Exeter, 248; Radnor, 248f.; Middletown, 249f.; Buckingham, 250ff.; Kennett, 253; New Garden and Uwchlan, 138, 254; Sadsbury and Bradford, 255; Concord and Goshen, 256; Abington and Horsham, 258; Byberry and Gwynedd 259ff.; Warrington and Fairfax, 261; attitude of sects toward ——, 231ff.; meetings for ——, 239; com. on —— affairs, 240f.; duties of com. on ——, 246–7; —— in Pa. 228ff.
Negro School, established, 241f.; support, 64; housed, 70, 71; 215, 217 status in 1800, 245; support of, 243f., 247f.; attendance, 243f.; teachers in, Patterson, 241; Houghton, 242; Benezet, 242; Britt, Dougherty, Meccum, 243; Pickering, 244; Mears, 245.
New Garden, 123f., 128ff., 137.

Organization, of meetings, purpose, 15; explained, 18; with regard to schools, 172–190; weakness of, 268.

Pastorius, 47, 53, 77ff.
Pay scholars, 180.

Penn, on educ., 28ff.; coming to Phila., 41.
Penn Charter School, 45; petition to incorporate, 47ff.; first charter, 49ff.; rechartered, 52; self perpetuating corporation of, 53, 106.
Philadelphia, reports on schs. in, 58ff., 71ff.
Plymouth, 112.
Poor, educ. of, 32, 38, 59, 74, 91, 112f., 117, 149, 159.
Preachers, journeys of, 5f.
Preparative meeting, functions, 19.
Printing, encouraged, 152.

Quakers, origin of, 1ff.; growth of, 6.
Quarterly meeting, functions, 19, 168, 174.

Radnor, 158ff.
Rates, 71ff.
Reading, 81f.
Regulations, adopted for schools, 115f., 125f., 182ff.
Rewards, 186.
Richland, 102f.
Robeson, 80f.

Sadsbury, 141ff.
Salary, 43, 45, 47, 54f., 62, 210f., 154; compared, 212.
School control, 80, 186, 141, 143; coms. appointed on, 111, 116, 118.
Schoolday, length of, 186ff.
Schoolhouses, 177ff.; school property, urged necessary, 176f.
Schoolmistresses, 54, 58ff., 130, 208, 212f.
Schools, modern tendency, 39; number established estimated, 121, 270.
School support, 39, 45f., 60–65, 71ff., 89f., 92f., 98f.; 127f., 133, 139ff., 143f., 148, 150f., 157f., 160, 164 167–172; distribution of funds, 108; of Negro School, 64.
Schwenkfeld, Caspar, 4.
Schacklewell, school, 10, 22.
Slavery, beginning of in Pa., 228; opponents of, 233ff.; classes interested, 230; attitude of Quakers, 236ff.; laws regarding, 228f.; increase of, 230; condition of slaves, 231; attitude of Fox, 233; Woolman, 234; Benezet, 235f.; Keith, 236.
Spelling, 192.
Springfield, 151.
Student papers, 188f.
Supervision of schools, 96f., 189.

Teachers, selection of, 100, 110; scarcity, 150; source, 205f., 209; qualifications, 204; tenure, 207f., 209; duties, 214; rated, 216; no contract for, 210; morality, 225; 269.

Teachers named: Albertson, 113; Ayres, 225; Brockden, 56, 74; Brientnall, 58; Brown, 59, 72, 218; Britt, 218; Buichell, 208, 214; Binns, 218; Buller, 218; Benezet, 31ff., 57, 58, 216ff., 235f.; Cadwalader, 54, 55, 209, 218; Cathrall, 59, 215; Clarke, 60, 72, 219; Carver, 225, 116; Clift, 207, 209, 219, 154; Coggins and Chamberlain, 114; Dickinson, 207, 219; Dougherty, 215; Dull, 114; Every, 55, 224; Eldridge, 206, Evans, 113; Flower, 42f., 45, 59; Fitzpatrick, 225, 116; Foulke, 114; Hartshorne, 60, 74; Harry, 60, 72; Houghton, 57; Josai, 58; Jones, 59, 114; Jackson, 220; Johnson, 225; Keith, 45, 207, 209, 219; Kirk, 225; King, 207, 220; Lancaster, 59, 72; Makin, 46, 53, 54, 56, 57, 207, 209, 219; Marsh, 60, 73; McDonnell, 60, 73; Mears, 218; Moor, 224; Meccum, 215; Naylor, 55; Pardo, 110, 114; Parks, 225; Patterson, 220; Pastorious, 47, 53, 77ff.; Proud, 59- 71, 183ff., 206, 209, 221ff. Pickering, 218; Pemberton, 224; Pearson, 225; Price, 114; Rakestraw, 59; Robbins, 56; Richards, 224; Smith, 58, 116, 225; Songhurst, 54, 208, 213; Snowden, 223; Sitch, 224; Taylor, 107, 207, 225; Thompson, 58, 220f., 222; Thorne, 223; Thornton, 209, 213; Todd, 58, 59, 72, 222; Underwood, 225; Walby, 55; Warden, 56; Weaver, 59, 72; Willian, 57, 205, 209, 220; Wilson, 220; Waring, 223; Warren, 206; Yerkes, 58, 223.

Tuke, on educ., 34f.

Uwchlan, 138ff.

Waltham, school at, 10, 22.

Warrington, 117.

Westtown Boarding School, 60, 73, 89, 145, 151.

Whitehead, on educ., 34f.

Willistown, 132.

Women, as teachers, 54, 58f., 130; on school com., 118, 140.

Woolman, on educ., 33f.; on slave holding, 234.

Writing school, 195.

Yearly meeting, recommends education, 20ff., 109; functions, 18.

York, 119.

Youths' meetings, 105f., 117.

LA355 .W66 1969   SUNY GENESEO

Early Quaker education in Pennsylvania.   YGMM

3 0260 00156372 9